Documents in Modern History

The making of German democracy

D0140936

MANCHESTER
1824

Manchester University Press

DOCUMENTS IN MODERN HISTORY

Series editor:
Dr G. H. Bennett (University of Plymouth)

Series advisor:
Dr Kevin Jefferys (University of Plymouth)

The *Documents in Modern History* series offers collections of documents on the most widely debated and studied topics in modern British and international history. The volumes place fresh primary material alongside more familiar texts, and provide thought-provoking introductions to place the documents in their wider historical context.

All volumes in the series are comprehensive and broad-ranging. They provide the ideal course textbook for sixth-form students, first-year undergraduates and beyond.

Also available:

Anglo-American relations since 1939
John Baylis

Roosevelt's peacetime administrations, 1933–41:
a documentary history of the New Deal years
Harry Bennett

The Labour party: 'socialism' and society since 1951
Steven Fielding

The American Civil Rights Movement
Robert P. Green, Jr. and Harold E. Cheatham

From Beveridge to Blair: the first fifty years of Britain's welfare state
1948–98
Margaret Jones and Rodney Lowe

Women, politics and society in Britain, c.1770–1970:
a documentary history
Fiona A. Montgomery

Television and the press since 1945
Ralph Negrine

The impact of immigration in post-war Britain
Panikos Panayi

The Vietnam wars
Kevin Ruane

Britain in the Second World War: a social history
Harold L. Smith

British trade unions 1945–95
Chris Wrigley

Documents in Modern History

The making of German democracy

West Germany during the Adenauer era, 1945–65

Armin Grünbacher

Manchester University Press

Manchester and New York

distributed in the United States exclusively by Palgrave Macmillan

Published by Manchester University Press
Oxford Road, Manchester M13 9NR, UK
and Room 400, 175 Fifth Avenue, New York, NY 10010, USA
www.manchesteruniversitypress.co.uk

Distributed in the United States exclusively by
Palgrave, 175 Fifth Avenue, New York,
NY 10010, USA

Distributed in Canada exclusively by
UBC Press, University of British Columbia, 2029 West Mall,
Vancouver, BC, Canada V6T 1Z2

British Library Cataloguing-in-Publication Data
A catalogue record for this book is available from the British Library

Library of Congress Cataloging-in-Publication Data applied for

ISBN 978 0 7190 8076 0 *hardback*
ISBN 978 0 7190 8077 7 *paperback*

First published 2010

19 18 17 16 15 14 13 12 11 10   10 9 8 7 6 5 4 3 2 1

Typeset in Sabon by
Koinonia, Manchester
Printed in Great Britain by
CPI Antony Rowe, Chippenham, Wiltshire

Dedicated to my father Hermann
and
in memory of my mother-in-law Maria Schwarz,
who both made the 1950s so much more interesting for
me by sharing some of their personal experiences
of the time with me.

Contents

Contents

List of plates

Preface

'German history did not end on 8 May 1945.' Sometimes it seems difficult to bring this message across to a generation of students whose only interest appears to be the history of the Nazis. However, during several years of teaching twentieth-century German history, both on the Nazis and on the post-war period, I encountered an increasing student interest in 'what happened after Hitler'. Satisfying this interest, in particular in form of a source-based teaching module, proved to be difficult. Although most aspects of post-war German history up to the 1970s have been explored by now in countless books and articles, no comprehensive collection of sources were available in English which made teaching such a module to non-German-speaking students quite difficult. It is hoped that with this source reader a tool is provided for teachers, lecturers and students that will allow them to take a closer look at developments in post-war Germany during the period from 1945 to the mid-1960s.

Overall, less than 20 per cent of all documents used in this reader have ever been published in English before. Most of those were taken from two sources: either from Beate Ruhm von Oppen's *Documents on Germany under Occupation, 1945-1954*, an edition of laws, ordinances and directives issued by the Allies during 1945-1954, including treaties the Western Allies concluded with West Germany; or, in a larger part, from publications by the US State Department. The latter include the *Foreign Relations of the United States (FRUS)* and the Cold War-driven publication series *Documents on Germany*. The scope of these documents is limited to diplomatic issues and some political topics as well as military- strategic considerations.

Some 80 per cent of all documents used in the book are available in English for the first time, with about one-fifth of the total previously unpublished primary sources. A wide variety of source readers on the topic is available in German. They contain sources on the everyday life of ordinary people and social, political and economic matters during the Adenauer era. I would like to express my thanks – not only, but in particular – to Professor Annette Kuhn, Professor Werner Abelshauser, Professor Werner Bührer and Professor Christoph Kleßman for their kind permission to use some of their sources. Special thanks has to go to Robert Kreis of the Bundespresseamt, the German Federal Press office, for his efficient service and selection of photographs. It is hoped that the sources and images will help contemporary students to understand the events of the 'long 1950s' and the transformation that occurred in West Germany during those years.

In (West) Germany, the period 1945–63 is called the Adenauer era, after the first Chancellor of the Federal Republic of Germany. While having his fair share of flaws and, of course, not being the only one who contributed to 'the making of German Democracy', Adenauer remains the central figure in this process, and therefore a certain number of sources deal specifically with his person and his policies.

It is my hope that this source reader will shed some more light on particular events and developments in post-war West German history; it is even more my hope that it will encourage more students to develop a real interest in 'what happened in Germany after Hitler' and why the Cold War was so important in shaping the country's development after 1945. Specific German words in the sources which are difficult to translate as well as some key phrases of the time have been italicised in the text to stress their original meaning or significance. Here I am happy to acknowledge the help of Phil Hotchkiss who proofread my translations and came up with better English alternatives – any remaining mistakes and 'Germanisms' are, of course, mine.

I also wish to thank my colleagues Corey Ross and John Grenville who read and commented on an earlier draft and gave inspirational advice respectively. I am particularly grateful to Sabine Lee. Her feedback and the comments she gave and the suggestion she made were, as usual, well beyond what could be expected from a colleague. Finally I want to say thanks to my wife Juliane Schwarz. I am immensely grateful for all the interest she showed in, and all her encouragement she gave to me during, the compilation of this book. It made my work so much easier.

Acknowledgments

The author and publishers wish to thank the following for permission to use copyright material.

All plates courtesy of Presse- und Informationsamt der Bundesregierung (Bundesbildstelle), except no. 9, © Schindler Foto-Report, Oberursel and *Bild* front page, 16 August 1961, © Axel Springer AG.

Anna Merritt for the use of the OMGUS Report No. 182, reprinted in: Anna and Richard Merritt (eds) *Public Opinion in Occupied Germany: The OMGUS Surveys 1945–49*, University of Illinois Press 1970.

Annette Kuhn for the use of sources from Annette Kuhn (ed.), *Frauen in der deutschen Nachkriegszeit Bd. 1 Frauenarbeit 1945–1949: Quellen und Materialien*, Düsseldorf 1984.

Archiv für Christlich-Demokratische Politik (ACDP) der Konrad-Adenauer-Stiftung for the *Ahlener Programm* and the *Düsseldorfer Leitsätze*.

Arnulf Baring for the use of Heinrich v. Brentano's letter to Adenauer, September 1961, reprinted in: *Sehr verehrter Herr Bundeskanzler: Heinrich von Brentano im Briefwechsel mit Konrad Adenauer, 1949–1964*, Hoffmann und Campe 1996.

Atrium Verlag Zürich, for Erich Kästner, 'Wert und Unwert des Menschen', in: Erich Kästner, *Gesammelte Schriften, Bd. 5, Vermischte Beiträge*, Kiepenheuer & Witsch 1959.

Auswärtiges Amt for the use of: The Treaty of Rome; letter by the

German Ambassador in Havana to the AA; Elysée Treaty, from: Auswärtiges Amt (ed.), *Aussenpolitik der Bundesrepublik Deutschland: Dokumente 1949–1994*, Bonn 1995 and Adenauer's Directive on European Policy from: Auswärtiges Amt (ed.), *Die Auswärtige Politik der Bundesrepublik Deutschland*, Köln 1972.

Axel Springer AG for the article by Peter Boenish on the Spiegel Affair in *Bild*, 12.11.1962 (Doc 150).

Christoph Kleßmann for the use of sources reprinted in his book *Das gespaltene Land: Leben in Deutschland 1945–1990*, C.H. Beck Verlag 1993.

Dietz Verlag for the use of 'The SPD's seven preconditions for ECSC membership', in: *Kurt Schumacher, Reden – Schriften – Korrespondenzen 1945–1952*, Hg. Willi Albrecht, Verlag J.H.W. Dietz Nachf., Bonn 1985.

Die Zeit for the use of Ernst Friedlaender 'There is no escape from the refugees' and Gerd Buccerius, 'Rechnung für Hitlers Krieg', in *Die Zeit*, 22.9.1949 and 13.4.1979 respectively.

Frauenmuseum Bonn for 'Family Reunion' and 'Divorce Rates' from: A. Kuhn, M. Pitzen and M. Hochgeschurz (eds), *Politeia: Szenarien aus der deutschen Geschichte nach 1945 aus Frauensicht*, Frauenmuseum Bonn, 1999.

Fred Ritzel for the translation of 'Wir sind die Eingeborenen von Trizonesien', printed in: 'Was ist aus uns geworden? Ein Häufchen Sand am Meer', in: *Popular Music*, vol. 17, no. 3 (1998).

Kurt Tudyka for the use of Michael Mansfeld's article 'The Hypocrisy of West German Foreign Policy', in: *Das geteilte Deutschland: Eine Dokumentation der Meinungen*, Verlag Kohlhammer, 1965.

Le Monde for the use of the Monnet Memorandum, *Le Monde*, 9 May 1970.

Neue Gesellschaft/Frankfurter Hefte, for the Introduction of *Frankfurter Hefte*, No 1.

Acknowledgments

Oldenbourg Wissenschaftsverlag for the excerpt from *Heinrich Troeger, Interregnum: Tagebuch des Generalsekretärs des Länderrats der Bizone 1947–1949*, hrsg. von Wolfgang Benz und Constantin Goschler (Biographische Quellen zur deutschen Geschichte nach 1945, Bd. 3) München: R. Oldenbourg Verlag 1985. Eine Publikation des Instituts für Zeitgeschichte München-Berlin.

Piper Verlag GmbH for an excerpt from Alexander und Margarete Mitscherlich, *Die Unfähigkeit zu trauern: Grundlagen kollektiven Verhaltens*, © 1977 Piper Verlag München.

Spiegel Verlag Rudolf Augstein GmbH, for the excerpt of 'Bedingt abwehrbereit' in: *Der Spiegel* no. 41, 1962.

Stiftung Bundeskanzler-Adenauer-Haus for excerpts from *Adenauer, Briefe, 1945–1947*, Berlin 1983, and *Heuss-Adenauer: Unserem Vaterland zugute. Der Briefwechsel 1948-1963*, Siedler 1989.

Thames & Hudson Ltd for an excerpt of *Prosperity through Competition*, by Ludwig Erhard, translated and edited by Edith Temple Roberts and John B. Wood, © 1959 London.

Verlag Duncker & Humblot for the table 'Die Beteiligung der Wirtschaftsbereiche an den in der Bundesrepublik von 1949 bis 1956 vergebenen ERP Krediten und der Anteil an den Brutto-Anlage-Investitionen', in: Egon Baumgart, *Investitionen und ERP Finanzierung*, Berlin 1961.

Verlag Kiepenheuer & Witsch for Heinrich Böll on Group 47 in Heinrich Böll, *Werke: Essayistische Schriften und Reden 2. 1964–1972*, Hrsg. von Bernd Balzer, © 1979 Verlag Kiepenheuer & Witsch, Köln.

Weidenfeld & Nicolson, an imprint of the Orion Publishing Group, for Adenauer's Reaction on the Schuman Plan Proposal, in: K. Adenauer, *Memoirs*, trans. Beate Ruhm von Oppen, London 1966.

Werner Abelshauser for the use of sources reprinted in his book *Die langen fünfziger Jahre: Wirtschaft und Gesellschaft der Bundesrepublik Deutschland, 1949–1966*, Schwann Verlag 1987 and for the tables from *Wirtschaftsgeschichte der Bundesrepublik Deutschland 1945-1980*, Suhrkamp 1983.

Werner Bührer for the use of Otto Vogel's speech on culture and civilisation; excerpts from the BDI Annual Report 1956/7; Karl Kuehne's essay on hire purchase in *Gewerkschaftlichen Monatshefte*; and Ulrike Meinhof on the Adenauer era, all from his book *Die Adenauer Ära: Die Bundesrepublik Deutschland 1949–1963*, München 1993.

Every effort has been made to trace copyright holders, but if any have inadvertently been overlooked, the author and publishers will be pleased to make the necessary arrangements at the first opportunity.

List of abbreviations

ACDP	Archiv für Christlich-Demokratische Politik
BDA	Bundesverband deutscher Arbeitgeberverbände (Federation of German Employer Associations)
BDI	Bundesverband der deutschen Industrie
BHE/GB	Block der Heimatvertriebenen und Entrechteten/Gesamtdeutscher Block
CDU	Christlich Demokratische Union
CEEC	Conference for European Economic Co-operation
CFM	Conference of Foreign Ministers
CSU	Christlich Soziale Union
DGB	Deutscher Gewerkschaftsbund
DM	Deutsche Mark
ECA	Economic Co-operation Administration
ECSC	European Coal and Steel Community
EDC	European Defence Community
EEC	European Economic Community
EPU	European Payments Union
ERP	European Recovery Programme
FDP	Freie Demokratische Partei
FRG	Federal Republic of Germany
FRUS	Foreign Relations of the Unites States
GARIOA	Government Appropriations for Relief in Occupied Areas
GDP	Gross Domestic Product
GDR	German Democratic Republic
IHG	*Investitionshilfegesetz*
JCS	Joint Chiefs of Staff
KPD	Kommunistische Partei Deutschlands
MP	Member of Parliament
MSA	Mutual Security Agency

List of Abbreviations

NA PRO	National Archive, Public Record Office
NATO	North Atlantic Treaty Organisation
NSDAP	Nationalsozialistische deutsche Arbeiterpartei
OEEC	Organisation for European Economic Co-operation
OMGUS	Office of the Military Government, US, in Germany
POW	Prisoner of War
RM	Reichsmark
RWWA	Rheinisch-Westfälisches Wirtschafts Archiv
SED	Sozialistische Einheitspartei Deutschlands
SPD	Sozialdemokratische Partei Deutschlands
SRP	Sozialistische Reichspartei
StEG	Staatliche Erfassungsgesellschaft für öffentliches Gut
WEU	Western European Union

Chronology of events in post-war Germany

1945

4–11 Feb	Yalta Conference: The 'Big Three' decide to divide Germany into zones of occupation with a joint administration.
8 May	Unconditional surrender of the Wehrmacht.
23 May	Dönitz Government arrested.
5 June	'Berlin Declaration': Four Powers assume supreme authority over Germany.
17 July–2 Aug	Potsdam Conference: 'Big Three' (later joined by France) confirm Yalta; Announcement of the '4 Ds'; reparations from ongoing production and dismantling in respective zones but Germany treated as an economic unit; territories east of the rivers Oder and Neisse put under Polish and Russian administration respectively; resettlement of ethnic Germans from Poland, Czechoslovakia, Yugoslavia and Hungary (resettlement details confirmed in November).
10 Sept–2 Oct	First Conference of Foreign Ministers (CFM) in London: France demands separation of the Ruhr, the Russians a central German government and international control of the Ruhr.
17 Oct	Establishment of the *Länderrat* (council) in the US zone.

1946

26 March	Announcement of the (1.) Industry Plan: Allied Control Council limits German industrial output to 70–75 per cent of 1936; 1800 plants to be dismantled.
25 April–12 July	Second CFM in Paris, the US calls for a merger of the 4 zones (merger accepted by UK on 29 July); USSR demands $10 billion in reparations, 4-Power control of the Ruhr and hints at German reunification.
6 September	Byrnes's Stuttgart Speech

10 Sept–1 Oct	Treaties for the establishment of 5 (bizonal) Administrations signed (Food, Transport, Economics, Finance, Mail, all located in different places).
4 Nov–11 Dec	Third CFM in New York, Germany not being discussed.
2 Dec	Treaty for the economic merger of the US and GB zones signed by Bevin and Byrnes.

1947

1 Jan	Official start of the 'Bizone' *Vereinigtes Wirtschaftsgebiet* (Joint Economic Area).
1–3 Feb	CDU Ahlen Programme passed.
10 March–24 April	Fourth CFM in Moscow, terminated without agreement.
12 March	Truman Doctrine
29 May	Agreement signed by UK-US Military Governors to centralise the 5 German Administrations in Frankfurt and to establish a parliamentary body (Economic Council) and an Executive Council of states' representatives to direct the Administrations (takes effect 10 June).
6 June	Harvard Speech by US Secretary of State Marshall announces European Recovery Programme.
6–8 June	Munich Conference of Minister Presidents. Its failure symbolises the German division.
25 June	First meeting of the Economic Council (52 members sent by the 8 state Parliaments).
11 July	JCS 1779 allows for the economic reconstruction of (West) Germany.
24 July	First election of the Administrations' Directors (=Ministers). All posts go to CDU/CSU due to strategic blunder by the SPD.
29 Aug	Revised Industrial Plan allows industrial production of 1936.
16 Oct/7 Nov	New dismantling list: 682 plants in the Bizone, 236 in the French zone.
25 Nov–15 Dec	Fifth CFM in London terminated early.

1948

7–8 Jan	Conference of the Military Governors with the Minister Presidents on how to reform the Bizone.
9 Feb	'Frankfurt Charter' takes effect: doubling the number of Economic Council members to 104, established a *Länderrat* (State Council) as second chamber to

	replace the (old) Executive Council; (new) Executive Council made up of the Administrations' Directors with a Chairman of the Executive Council (*Oberdirektor*) as quasi head of government.
23 Feb–6 March	London 6 Power Conference (first phase) (US, UK, F, B, NL, Lux) recommends establishing a West German state based on a federal structure and accepting it into the Marshall Plan.
1 March	Establishment of the *Bank deutscher Länder* (from 1957 Bundesbank).
17 March	Brussels (Defence) Treaty by GB, F, B, NL, Lux.
20 March	Termination of Allied Control Council by the Soviet Union (SU) out of protest against the London 6 Power Conference and the Brussels Treaty – End of 4-Power control over Germany.
1 April	Beginning of the 'Little' Blockade of Berlin by the SU by implementing traffic inspections.
16 April	OEEC established.
20 April–4 June	London 6-Power Conference (second phase) ends with the 'London Recommendations': Military Governors to authorise Minister Presidents to set up a Constitutional Assembly.
20 April–8 June	'Rothwesen Conclave': German financial experts prepare the currency reform.
20 June	Currency Reform in 3 Western zones.
21/24 June	'*Leitsätze Gesetz*' abolishes all rationing and price controls (except for basic food, fuel, rent and steel).
24 June	Begin of the Berlin Blockade and subsequent Berlin Airlift.
1 July	'Frankfurt Documents' delivered to the West German Minister Presidents.
8–10 July	Koblenz Conference of Minister Presidents (*Rittersturz Conference*) accepts the Allied instruction for the creation of a new state but applies conditions which are refused by the Allies.
21/22 July	Niederwald Conference of German Minister Presidents finds compromise to accept Frankfurt Documents.
26 July	Final meeting over Frankfurt Documents between Military Governors and Minister Presidents in which the Germans concede on the substance and the Allies on the terminology.
10–23 Aug	West German experts drafts principles for a constitution (Basic Law) (*Herrenchiemseer Verfassungskonvent*).

Chronology of events in post-war Germany

1 September	First meeting of the Parliamentary Council (65 members, elected by the state Parliaments, plus five Berlin deputies without voting right); Chairman: Konrad Adenauer.
22 Nov	Military Governors' aide-mémoire to the Parliamentary Council.
28 Dec	Publication of the draft Ruhr Statute.

1949

17 Jan	Establishment of a Military Security Board for the 3 Western zones to satisfy French security concerns.
4 April	Foundation of NATO
5–8 April	Allied Conference on Germany decides on Occupation Statute, reduction in dismantling and the replacement of the Military Governors by High Commissioners.
22 April	Ruhr Statue takes effect: control of Ruhr's coal and steel production by the 6 Powers, Western zones represented by the Military Governors.
10 May	Parliamentary Council names Bonn provisional seat of government.
12 May	Berlin Blockade ends. Military Governors accept Basic Law.
23 May	Basic Law announced by the Parliamentary Council; (official) establishment of the Federal Republic of Germany.
23 May–20 June	Sixth CFM: SU proposes return to Potsdam Agreement, Western Powers offer *Anschluss* of the Soviet Zone to the Federal Republic.
15 July	CDU's Düsseldorfer *Leitsätze* (Principles) as economic election manifesto passed.
14 Aug	First Bundestag elections.
12 Sept	Federal Assembly elects Theodor Heuss first Federal President.
15 Sept	Bundestag elects Adenauer first Chancellor.
21 Sept	Occupation Statute takes effect.
31 Oct	Federal Republic joins OEEC.
22 Nov	Petersberg Agreement allows (among other things) to join Council of Europe and Ruhr Authority and consular relations.
15 Dec	Federal Cabinet accepts ERP Bilateral Agreement => first international treaty.

1950

13 Jan	Abolition of (Allied) licensing of political parties.
9 May	French Foreign Secretary Robert Schuman announces proposal for European Coal and Steel Community (Schuman Plan).
25 June	Beginning of Korean War.
29 Aug	Adenauer's memorandum for the defence of the FRG.
12–18 Sept	CFM of the Western Powers decide on a West German contribution to the European defence.
9 Oct	*Himmeroder Denkschrift.*
24 Oct	French Minister President Pleven outlines his plan for German troops for the European defence (Pleven Plan).
26 Oct	Theodor Blank appointed 'Plenipotentiary for Questions Relating to the Increase of Allied Troops'.

1951

25 Jan	Principle agreement between Adenauer and DGB chairman Hans Böckler about co-determination in the iron and steel industry.
6 March	Adenauer acknowledges German pre- and post-war foreign debts; First revision of the Occupation Statute, increased German authority for foreign affairs (=> re-establishment of Auswärtiges Amt (German Foreign Office) on 15 March, first Foreign Minister: Adenauer).
10 April	Bundestag passes bill on co-determination in iron and steel industry.
18 April	Treaty for the establishment of the European Coal and Steel Community signed.
24 Sept	Begin of Allied negotiations with Adenauer on the replacement of the Occupation Statute.
27 Sept	Federal Government declares willingness to pay compensation to Israel.
16/19 Nov	Federal Government calls for the ban of the KPD and SRP at the Constitutional Court (SRP banned 23 Oct 1952, KPD banned 17 Aug 1956).

1952

11 Jan	Treaty on ECSC ratified by Bundestag.
8 Feb	Bundestag agrees to EDC treaty.
28 Feb	Beginning of the London Debt Conference.
10 March	'Stalin Note' to the Western Allies proposes peace treaty with Germany on the basis of neutrality and unification.

20 March	Beginning of negotiations with Israel and the Jewish Claims Conference on compensation.
25 March	Western reply to Stalin Note: free all-German elections precondition for talks about a peace treaty.
16 May	Bundestag passes Law on the Equalisation of Burden (in force from 1 Sept).
26 May	Signing of the General Treaty in Bonn.
27 May	Signing of the EDC Treaty in Paris.
25 July	Treaty on the ECSC takes effect.
10 Sept	Compensation agreement with Israel and the Jewish Claims Conference signed.

1953

27 Feb	London Debt Agreement signed.
6 March	Stalin dies.
25 March	Bundestag passes Expellee Bill.
25 June	Bundestag passes new electoral law (with 5 per cent bar).
27 July	Ceasefire in the Korean War.
6 Sept	Second election to the Bundestag; Coalition government of CDU/CSU, FDP, DP and BHE.

1954

7 May	French defeat at Dien Bien Puh
4 July	'*Wunder von Bern*' Germany wins the football world cup.
30 Aug	French National Assembly rejects EDC treaty.
1 Oct	Beginning of Algerian uprising.
19–23 Oct	Paris Conference: 3 Powers and FRG negotiate the future status of West Germany, leading to Paris Treaties: end of Occupation Statute and NATO membership, Western guarantees for Berlin and claim for sole representation; Saar Statute (political autonomy, economically tied to France).

1955

27 Feb	Bundestag ratifies Paris Treaties.
5 May	Sovereignty proclaimed for FRG (still qualified!), end of Occupation Statute, FRG joins Western European Union (WEU).
9–11 May	FRG joins NATO.
1–3 June	Messina Conference.
7 June	Soviet offer for full diplomatic relations to FRG.
9–13 Sept	Adenauer's Moscow visit.

20 Sept	SU declares GDR independence and confirms '2 states' theory.
22 Sept	Hallstein Doctrine.
23 Oct	Saar Statute rejected with a 2/3 majority in a popular referendum.

1956

5 Jan	Adenauer's 80th birthday.
27 Oct	Signing of French-German Saar treaty.
4 Nov	Hungarian uprising squashed by Soviet troops.
5–6 Nov	Anglo-French troops invade the Suez Canal zone => Suez Crisis.

1957

1 Jan	Saar joins FRG.
15 March	Signing of the Treaty of Rome: Creation of EEC and Euratom.
1 April	First West German conscripts called up; General Speidel becomes CiC EU-CENT.
4 April	Adenauer calls in an interview for German nuclear weapons.
12 April	'Göttinger Declaration' by 18 leading German nuclear schientists.
4 July	Bundestag passes anti-cartel law.
15 Sept	Third Bundestag elections: CDU/CSU gain absolute majority.
19 Oct	Termination of diplomatic relations to Yugoslavia after its recognition of the GDR (first application of the Hallstein Doctrine).

1958

1 Jan	EEC and EURATOM treaties take effect.
1 June	Charles de Gaulle assumes power in France.
27 Nov	'Khrushchev Ultimatum' on Berlin.
14 Dec	Western Allies and FRG reject Khrushchev ultimatum.
31 Dec	Western Powers declare willingness to negotiate about Berlin and German unification.

1959

1 Jan	EEC countries lower internal tariffs by 10 per cent.
11 May–20 June	4-Power CFM on Germany in Geneva, FRG and GDR participate as 'observers'.
5 June	Adenauer declines to stand for Federal President.
13–15 Nov	SPD passes Godesberg Programme.

Chronology of events in post-war Germany

1960

30 June	SPD declares acceptance of 'Westintegration'.
29–30 July	Adenauer meets De Gaulle at Rambouillet.

1961

28 Feb	Constitutional Court declares Adenauer's plans for a state TV unconstitutional.
13 Aug	Building of the Berlin Wall.
22 Aug	Adenauer visits Berlin.
17 Sept	Fourth Bundestag elections, CDU loses absolute majority.

1962

18 March	France ends Algerian war.
2–8 July	Adenauer visits France.
4–9 Sept	De Gaulle visits Germany.
22 Oct	US naval blockade of Cuba – height of the Cuban Crisis.
26 Oct	*Der Spiegel* publishing house searched by police, editor/proprietor Augstein arrested for high treason.
19 Nov	FDP ministers resign from Cabinet because of *Spiegel* affair.

1963

12 Jan	Termination of diplomatic relations to Cuba (second application of Hallstein Doctrine)
14 Jan	De Gaulle vetoes British EEC membership.
22 Jan	French–German treaty on co-operation signed (Elysée Treaty).
22 April	CDU Parliamentary Group nominates Erhard to succeed Adenauer as Chancellor.
11 Oct	Adenauer hands his resignation to the Federal President.
16 Oct	Erhard elected new Chancellor.

Part I
Interregnum, 1945–49

The time from the unconditional surrender of Germany on 8 May 1945 to the establishment of the Federal Republic in spring and summer 1949 is crucial to one's understanding of the politics, social life and economic affairs of the so-called 'Adenauer era'. The Second World War that had been unleashed by the Nazis had eventually returned to Germany itself and had devastated the country. Towns and cities and all aspects of infrastructure had suffered large-scale destruction which would take years to mend; millions of people were bombed out, competing with displaced persons and refugees for a place to live; and from late 1945 onward, widespread hunger and even starvation appeared for the next two years, despite British and American efforts to sustain the population. Beyond the physical destruction, the reputation of the German people was badly tainted because of the war crimes that had been committed in their name, and by the holocaust. As a result, in 1945 the Germans were perhaps the most ostracised people in modern history. Yet only four years later, the 'interregnum period', a time without a German government, ended with the US-supported creation of the Federal Republic of Germany (FRG) in May 1949 and the subsequent creation of the German Democratic Republic (GDR) by the Soviet Union in October 1949. Although it was initially only a gradual rehabilitation, the speed with which West Germany was to be integrated into a newly-emerged Western alliance was amazing and only possible because of the increasing distrust between the Western Allies and the Soviet Union. In the summer of 1945 it was not foreseeable how much Allied relations, and in particular US-Soviet relations, would deteriorate. Serious strains in the relationship appeared in 1946; but it was in 1947 that Cold War tensions really increased. It is only in that period that US policy began to seriously contemplate and subsequently instigate the division of Germany. It can easily be

1

argued that being at the fault line of the Cold War in Europe was to determine many if not most aspects of West German domestic and foreign policy at least until the late 1960s, but more likely right up to the country's eventual reunification in 1990.

1

The Allies in control, 1945–46

The situation in Germany in the spring and summer of 1945 was totally different from the situation after the end of the First World War. In 1918, fighting ceased because of an armistice, with the German army still occupying large areas of foreign territory. In May 1945, when the Nazi war machine that once had occupied large parts of Europe had surrendered unconditionally, only small pockets of Germany in the north and the south of the country had not yet been conquered by Allied troops. This time, there could be no doubt that Germany had been defeated; and the Allies wanted to make sure that their mistakes in the post-First World War settlement – which eventually contributed to the rise of Hitler – were not repeated. The whole of Germany was to be occupied, rather than merely a small strip of land in the west of the country. In contrast to circumstances in the First World War, large parts of the civilian population in Germany had directly experienced the war, either through aerial warfare or because they witnessed for themselves the advance of Allied troops into Germany. In 1945, all Germans saw the defeat with their own eyes and experienced military occupation.

While the Second World War ended only in September 1945 with the capitulation of Japan, the fighting in Europe had come to an end with the unconditional surrender of the German Wehrmacht on 8 May 1945. For two more weeks, a German government under Admiral Dönitz, who had been appointed by Hitler shortly before his suicide on 30 April 1945, remained formally in charge until they were arrested on 23 May, bringing the Third Reich also nominally to an end. Another two weeks later, on 5 June, the four Allied governments officially took supreme control of Germany. This so-called 'Berlin Declaration' made it unequivocally clear that Germany and the defeated Germans now had to follow Allied directives and could expect little sympathies from the victorious powers.

Doc 1 'Berlin Declaration'

5 June 1945

The German armed forces on land, at sea and in the air have been completely defeated and have surrendered unconditionally and Germany, which bears responsibility for the war, is no longer capable of resisting the will of the victorious Powers. The unconditional surrender of Germany has thereby been effected and Germany has become subject to such requirements as may now or hereafter be imposed upon [it].

There is no central Government or authority in Germany capable of accepting responsibility for the maintenance of order, the administration of the country and compliance with the requirements of the victorious Powers.

It is in these circumstances necessary, without prejudice to any subsequent decisions that may be taken respecting Germany, to make provision for the cessation of any further hostilities on the part of the German armed forces, for the maintenance of order in Germany and for the administration of the country, and to announce the immediate requirements with which Germany must comply.

The Representatives of the Supreme Commands of the United Kingdom, the United States of America, the Union of Soviet Socialist Republics and the French Republic, hereinafter called the 'Allied Representatives', acting by authority of their respective Governments and in the interests of the United Nations, accordingly make the following Declaration:

The Governments of the United Kingdom, the United States of America and the Union of Soviet Socialist Republics, and the Provisional Government of the French Republic, hereby assume supreme authority with respect to Germany, including all the powers possessed by the German Government, the High Command and any state, municipal, or local government or authority. The assumption, for the purpose stated above, of the said authority and powers does not effect the annexation of Germany.

The Governments ... will hereafter determine the boundaries of Germany or any part thereof and the status of Germany or of any area at present being part of German territory.

In virtue of the supreme authority and powers thus assumed by the four Governments, the Allied Representatives announce the following requirements arising from the complete defeat and unconditional surrender of Germany with which Germany must comply:

...

Article 2
(*a*) All armed forces of Germany or under German control, wherever they may be situated, including land, air, anti-aircraft and naval forces, the SS, SA and Gestapo, and all other forces or auxiliary organizations equipped with weapons, shall be completely disarmed, handing over their weapons and equipment to local Allied Commanders or to officers designated by the Allied Representatives.
(*e*) Detachments of civil police to be armed with small arms only, for the maintenance of order and for guard duties, will be designated by the Allied Representatives.

Article 5
(*c*) At the demand of the Allied Representatives all facilities will be provided for the movement of Allied troops and agencies, their equipment and supplies, on the railways, roads and other land communications or by sea, river or air. All means of transportation will be maintained in good order and repair, and the labour, services and plant necessary therefore will be furnished ...

Article 8
There shall be no destruction, removal, concealment, transfer or scuttling of or damage to, any military, naval, air, shipping, port, industrial and other like property and facilities and all records and archives, wherever they may be situated, except as may be directed by the Allied Representatives.

Article 11
(*a*) The principal Nazi leaders as specified by the Allied Representatives, and all persons from time to time named or designated by rank, office or employment by the Allied Representatives as being suspected of having committed, ordered or abetted war crimes or analogous offences, will be apprehended and surrendered to the Allied Representatives.
(*b*) The same will apply in the case of any national of any of the United Nations who is alleged to have committed an offence against his national law, and who may at any time be named or designated by rank, office or employment by the Allied Representatives.
(*c*) The German authorities and people will comply with any instructions given by the Allied Representatives for the apprehension and surrender of such persons.

Article 13
(*b*) The Allied Representatives will impose on Germany additional political, administrative, economic, financial, military and other requirements arising from the complete defeat of Germany. The Allied Representatives,

or persons or agencies duly designated to act on their authority, will issue proclamations, orders, ordinances and instructions for the purpose of laying down such additional requirements, and of giving effect to the other provisions of this Declaration. All German authorities and the German people shall carry out unconditionally the requirements of the Allied Representatives, and shall fully comply with all such proclamations, orders, ordinances and instructions ...

Berlin, 5 June 1945.
Signed by the Allied Representatives:
B. Montgomery, F.M.
Dwight D. Eisenhower
G. K. Zhukov
J. de Lattre de Tassigny

From: *Military Government Gazette, Germany, British Zone of Control, 1945.*

The official US policy on occupied Germany, the Joint Chiefs of Staff directive JCS 1067, had been given to the American supreme commander, General Eisenhower, in April 1945 before the war had ended. JCS 1067 is a document that displays American 'missionary zeal' to democratise the world and one that was at least in part written in the spirit of the Morgenthau Plan which had called for the wholesale deindustrialisation of Germany. By imposing tough measures on Germany, the directive's aim was to drive the message home to the German people that their actions and those of the Nazis had brought this plight on them. A very significant point within JCS 1067 prevented the American occupiers from taking any steps to improve the German economic situation, or even repairing damaged infrastructure beyond the level necessary for the prevention of disease and starvation, or beyond their own needs as an occupying power. This stood in sharp contrast to the British occupational policy, which was aimed at utilising and even reviving parts of the German industry in order to pay for the British occupation costs. The overall tone of JCS 1067 was seen as so anti-German that the Americans did not dare to publish it before October 1945 for fear of negative German public reaction.

Doc 2 JCS 1067

April 1945

1. The Purpose and Scope of this Directive

This directive is issued to you as Commanding General of the United States Forces of Occupation in Germany. As such you will serve as United States member of the Control Council and will also be responsible for the administration of military government in the zone or zones assigned to the United States for purposes of occupation and administration. It outlines the basic policies which will guide you in those two capacities after the termination of the combined command of the Supreme Commander, Allied Expeditionary Force ...

PART I GENERAL AND POLITICAL

2. The Basis of Military Government

a. The rights, power and status of the military government in Germany are based upon the unconditional surrender or total defeat of Germany.

b. Subject to the provisions of paragraph below, you are, by virtue of your position, clothed with supreme legislative, executive and judicial authority in the areas occupied by the forces under your command. This authority will be broadly construed and includes authority to take all measures deemed by you necessary, appropriate or desirable in relation to military exigencies and the objectives of a firm military government ...

3. The Control Council and Zones of Occupation

c. The administration of affairs in Germany shall be directed towards the decentralization of the political and administrative structure and the development of local responsibility. To this end you will encourage autonomy in regional, local and municipal agencies of German administration. The German economic structure shall also be decentralized. The Control Council may, however, to the minimum extent required for the fulfilment of purposes set forth herein, permit centralized administration or establish central control of (a) essential national public services, such as railroads, communications and power, (b) finance and foreign affairs and (c) production and distribution of essential commodities.

d. The Control Council should adopt procedures to effectuate, and you will facilitate in your zone, the equitable distribution of essential commodities between the zones. In the absence of a conflicting policy of the Control Council you may deal directly with one or more zone commanders on matters of special concern to such zones.

4. Basic Objectives of Military Government in Germany

a. It should be brought home to the Germans that Germany's ruthless warfare and the fanatical Nazi resistance have destroyed the German economy and made chaos and suffering inevitable and that the Germans cannot escape responsibility for what they have brought upon themselves.

b. Germany will not be occupied for the purpose of liberation but as a defeated enemy nation. Your aim is not oppression but to occupy Germany for the purpose of realizing certain important Allied objectives. In the conduct of your occupation and administration you should be just but firm and aloof. You will strongly discourage fraternization with the German officials and population ...

d. Other Allied objectives are to enforce the program of reparations and restitution, to provide relief for the benefit of countries devastated by Nazi aggression and to ensure that prisoners of war and displaced persons of the United Nations are cared for and repatriated.

5. Economic Controls

a. ... You will be guided by the principle that controls upon the German economy may be imposed to the extent that such controls may be necessary to achieve the objectives enumerated in paragraph 4 above and also as they may be essential to protect the safety and meet the needs of the occupying forces and ensure the production and maintenance of goods and services required to prevent starvation or such disease and unrest as would endanger these forces. No action will be taken in execution of the reparations program or otherwise which would tend to support basic living conditions in Germany or in your zone on a higher level than that existing in any one of the neighboring United Nations.

b. In the imposition and maintenance of such controls, German authorities will to the fullest extent practicable be ordered to proclaim and assume administration of such controls. Thus it should be brought home to the German people that the responsibility for the administration of such controls and for any breakdown in those controls will rest with themselves and German authorities.

6. Denazification

a. A proclamation dissolving the Nazi Party, its formations, affiliated associations and supervised organizations, and all Nazi public institutions which were set up as instruments of Party domination, and prohibiting their revival in any form, should be promulgated by the Control Council ...

c. All members of the Nazi Party who have been more than nominal participants in its activities, all active supporters of Nazism or

8

militarism and all other persons hostile to Allied purposes will be removed and excluded from public office and from positions of importance in quasi-public and private enterprises such as (1) civic, economic and labor organizations, (2) corporations and other organizations in which the German Government or subdivisions have a major financial interest, (3) industry, commerce, agriculture and finance, (4) education, and (5) the press, publishing houses and other agencies disseminating news and propaganda ... No such persons shall be retained in any of the categories of employment listed above because of administrative necessity, convenience or expediency ...

PART II ECONOMIC
General Objectives and Methods of Control

16. You will assure that the German economy is administered and controlled in such a way as to accomplish the basic objectives set forth in paragraphs 4 and 5 of this directive. Economic controls will be imposed only to the extent necessary to accomplish these objectives, provided that you will impose controls to the full extent necessary to achieve the industrial disarmament of Germany. Except as may be necessary to carry out these objectives, you will take no steps (a) looking toward the economic rehabilitation of Germany, or (b) designed to maintain or strengthen the German economy.

18. In order to decentralize the structure and administration of the German economy to the maximum extent possible, you will
b. on no account propose or approve in the Control Council the establishment of centralized administration of controls over the German economy except where such centralization of administration is clearly essential to the fulfilment of the objectives listed in paragraphs 1 and 5 of this directive ...

30. In order to disarm Germany the Control Council should
a. prevent the production, acquisition by importation or otherwise, and development of all arms, ammunition and implements of war, ...
b. prevent the production of merchant ships, synthetic rubber and oil, aluminium and magnesium and any other products and equipment on which you will subsequently receive instructions;
c. seize and safeguard all facilities used in the production of any of the items mentioned in this paragraph and dispose of them as follows:
   (1) remove all those required for reparation;
   (2) destroy all those not transferred for reparation if they are especially adapted to the production of the items specified in

this paragraph and are not of a type generally used in industries permitted to the Germans (cases of doubt to be resolved in favor of destruction); ...

32. Pending final Allied agreements on reparation and on control or elimination of German industries that can be utilized for war production, the Control Council should
a. prohibit and prevent production of iron and steel, chemicals, non-ferrous metals (excluding aluminum and magnesium), machine tools, radio and electrical equipment, automotive vehicles, heavy machinery and important parts thereof; except for the purposes stated in paragraphs 4 and 5 of this directive;
b. prohibit and prevent rehabilitation of plant and equipment in such industries except for the purposes stated in paragraphs 4 and 5 of this directive; and
c. safeguard plant and equipment in such industries for transfer on reparation account ...

36. You will prohibit all cartels or other private business arrangements and cartel-like organizations, including ... the *Wirtschaftsgruppen* ...

Industry to be Dispersed

37. It is the policy of your government to effect a dispersion of the ownership and control of German industry. To assist in carrying out this policy you will make a survey of combines and pools, mergers, holding companies and interlocking directorates and communicate the results, together with recommendations, to your government through the Joint Chiefs of Staff. You will endeavor to obtain agreement in the Control Council to the making of this survey in the other zones of occupation and you will urge the coordination of the methods and results of this survey in the various zones.

Reprinted in: Oppen, *Documents on Germany under Occupation, 1945–54*.

JCS 1067 clearly stated that any individual American policy was to be superseded by decisions of the Allied Control Council made up of the four Allied Supreme Commanders, who would also act as Military Governors for their respective zones. During the Potsdam Conference (17 July–2 August 1945) the 'Big Three', Great Britain, the Soviet Union and the United States, later joined by France, confirmed most of the decisions on the future of Germany that the 'Big Three' had already taken at the Yalta Conference in February 1945. The agreements reached or confirmed at the conference were to have wide-ranging implications for the future of Germany.

The '4Ds' were one of the political aims that were announced; the term referred to the denazification and demilitarisation of Germany, along with the decartelisation of its economy and the democratisation of its population and institutional structures. The Potsdam Conference confirmed the division of the German Reich into four separate zones of occupation, with the former capital, Berlin, similarly divided into four sectors and becoming the seat of the Allied Control Council. It was further agreed that Germany should be treated as a single economic entity but with each power having full control over its respective zone of occupation. The practical implication of this decision meant that within the Soviet zone of occupation the Sovietisation of the zone could take place, while the Americans for their part wanted to impose their model of the polity onto their zone by trying to decentralise and 'federalise' political and economic structures. The British approach, very much in line with national tradition, wanted to change only what was really necessary while keeping in place as many of the proven German institutions as was possible. The French, whose zone had been carved from territories in the west of the British and American zones, had two main objectives: the first was to strip their zone of as many assets as possible without causing permanent economic damage. Secondly, their most important objective was to prevent the establishment of any form of administrative or other structure that could be used as a nucleus for a new central German administration of any kind. The Soviet policy was to obtain as much reparation as possible and to install pro-Soviet German Communists in positions of power. Very soon it became clear that this form of occupation would make the treatment of Germany as an economic unit impossible. As a matter of fact, it would allow each side to accuse the other of undermining this clause of the Potsdam Agreement once the ideological differences between the Soviet Union and the Western powers became prevalent. It is hardly surprising therefore, that in years to come the border between the Soviet zone of occupation and the Western zones of occupation become the main fault line of the Cold War in Europe.

Another significant decision that was confirmed at Potsdam is sometimes referred to as 'Poland's shift to the west'. This meant that

Poland lost its pre-World War Two territory east of the Curzon Line to the Soviet Union but was compensated with the southern part of East Prussia (the northern part going to the Soviet Union) and by receiving 'administrative control' of German territories east of the rivers Oder and Neisse. Up until the early 1970s the government of the Federal Republic would refer to those eastern territories as 'East Germany', while the territory that would become the German Democratic Republic, the GDR, was referred to as '*Mitteldeutschland*' or Central Germany. This distinction and the Federal Republic's claim of political representation of all these areas became a stumbling block for any talks about German reunification during the post-war years. The Allied decision to cede the land east of the rivers Oder and Neisse to Poland had a more serious short-term impact, since it meant that Germany was to lose its agricultural surplus region. With the secession came a further decision that would have a crucial impact on the society and politics of the future West German state.

Doc 3 FRUS map

	Population 1939 census	Percentage of Germans
	2,488,122	93.8 (1925)
	391,000	92.8 (1923)
	835,884	ca 99.0 (1925)

Area north of dotted line Pop.: ca 1,000,000

	Population 1939 census	Percentage of Germans
	2,104,553	100
	2,721,512	100

	Population 1939 census	Percentage of Germans
	1,527,491	57.0 (1914)

Proposed cession of territory by Germany	Area in Sq miles	Population 1939 census
Territory east of Line D	18,032	4,015,613
Territory added by Line C	6,812	835,884
Total east of Line C	24,844	4,851,497
Territory added by Line B	10,473	2,104,553
Total east of Line B	35,317	6,956,050
Territory added by Line A	8,106	2,721,512
Total east of Line A	43,423	9,677,562

Note: The former Free City of Danzig is not included in the above tables.

0 kilometres 200

From: *FRUS 1945, The Conference of Berlin (Potsdam)*, vol. 1.

The Munich Conference in 1938 had paved the way for the piece-meal swallowing up of Czechoslovakia by Nazi Germany. In 1945 the Allies sought to prevent any possible future repetition of German claims to territory on the basis that these territories were populated by ethnic Germans. For this reason the Allies had agreed at the Potsdam Conference to implement a 'population transfer' that would move ethnic Germans out of eastern and south-eastern Europe. In November 1945, the Control Council made a further and more detailed decision according to which ethnic Germans were to be removed from Poland, Hungary, Czechoslovakia and Austria altogether, and were to be resettled in one of the four occupation zones. While this form of ethnic cleansing was to be carried out in an organised, staged and humane manner, the reality on the ground was different. Considering how the Nazis had treated Poles and Czechs, it is of little surprise that both the authorities and the population of those countries had little sympathy for ethnic Germans. Subsequently most of the 'planned resettlements' turned into violent expulsions in the middle of winter. Many of the victims were given less than 24 hours' notice and allowed only one suitcase of belongings per person.

Doc 4 Expulsion plan for ethnic Germans

20 November 1945

1. The entire German population to be moved from Poland (three and a half million persons) will be admitted to the Soviet and British zones of occupation in Germany.

2. The entire German population to be moved from Czechoslovakia, Austria and Hungary (3,150,000 persons) will he admitted to the American, French and the Soviet zones of occupation in Germany.

3. Tentative (preliminary) allocation of the population between zones will be as follows:
(a) Into the Soviet zone from Poland, 2 million persons. Into the Soviet zone from Czechoslovakia, ¾ million persons.
(b) Into the British zone from Poland, 1½ million persons.
(c) Into the American zone from Czechoslovakia, 1¾ million persons. Into the American zone from Hungary, ½ million persons.
(d) Into the French zone from Austria, 150,000 persons.

The French zone will start acceptance not earlier than I5th April, 1946. Meanwhile, after the exchange of German refugees is completed according to the principle of one-for-one, the French zone will continue to accept approximately 250,000 refugees from the United States zone who were domiciled formerly in the French zone.

4. It is considered possible, immediately after the confirmation of this plan, to proceed with the admittance of population from the above-mentioned countries in accordance with the following schedule:
During December 1945, at the rate of 10 per cent of the total number.
During January and February 1946, at the rate of 5 per cent of the total number.
During March 1946, at the rate of 15 per cent of the total number.
During April 1946, at the rate of 15 per cent of the total number.
During May 1946, at the rate of 20 per cent of the total number.
During June 1946, at the rate of 20 per cent of the total number.
During July 1946, at the rate of 10 per cent of the total number.
Changes may be made on account of weather or transport, and after more information is received about the quantity of population transferred. The British zone will start acceptance of the above refugees into the British zone when the volume of the present exchanges on the head-for-head basis permits it. This date will be fixed by agreement between the chiefs of the Prisoners of War and Displaced Persons Division of the Soviet and British Elements.

5. The execution of this plan must not interfere with the carrying out of the previously reached agreement as regards the exchange of the German refugees between the zones on a one-for-one basis.

Reprinted in: Oppen, *Documents on Germany under Occupation, 1945–54.*

The Federal Government had estimated the number of Germans who perished in the process of expulsion or as they fled to be up to two million. Although this figure was produced at the height of the 1950s Cold War and thus was certainly somewhat exaggerated for political reasons, the overall number of those who perished, either in their attempt to flee the advancing Red Army after January 1945 or because of the expulsion, has to be estimated at between 1 million and 1.5 million.

Obviously, the sheer number of people affected by this expulsion would have a serious impact on any of the areas that were to receive them. In January 1945 alone, hundreds of thousands of Germans had fled westward from the advancing Red Army. Many of them had a brief stop in the area that would become the Soviet-occupied zone before they moved on into the Western occupation zones. The majority of the refugees from Poland and the Czech Republic chose to move into the Western zones immediately, in order to avoid the dreaded Soviet occupation in the future GDR. However, the French had not participated in the initial talks at Potsdam which had ratified this population transfer. Therefore they did not feel obliged to take an equal share of refugees. They admitted only some 250,000 people into their zone. Consequently the British and American zones bore the brunt of the exodus. By 1948 the share of refugees living in the territory of the American and British occupation zones was about 20 per cent of the total population.

One of the biggest issues for the Germans, and one which caused considerable concern for the occupation forces to deal with between the summer of 1945 and the summer of 1948, was insufficient food supply for the population. During the war, the majority of Germans had received a reasonably high calorie intake – at least up to late 1944 or even to early 1945 – due to the Nazis' ruthless exploitation of occupied Europe. With the German defeat, these resources had been lost; and so was Germany's own breadbasket in the east of the former Reich. Now hunger and starvation threatened the German population in the urban centres which were located mainly in the Western zones. The influx of the refugees meant that there were some eight to ten million extra mouths to feed in the US and British zones. Further to the loss of agricultural heartland to Poland, no food supplies came from the mainly agricultural Soviet zone to the western part of the country either, since the four zones were never treated as an economic unit, which effectively prevented intra-German trade. The insufficient size of many farms in the three Western zones made them economically unproductive. Furthermore, the lack of agricultural machinery, fertiliser and even work animals meant that the agricultural sector was unable to feed the population. Consequently, from late 1945 onwards, most Germans, in particular those in the larger towns and cities experienced daily hunger and starvation.

Doc 5 Food supply, 1946

At the world food conference in London the former American President Hoover indicated that a human needs a minimum daily intake of 2300 calories to sustain his vitality and capacity to work.

In the British Zone of Occupation the daily calorific value of a normal ration is 1040 calories. In the American zone it is 1275 calories, in the French zone daily allocation for 10–18-year-old juveniles and normal consumers are 927 calories and 1144 for heavy workers. There is no detailed information from the Russian-occupied zone, but it can easily be assumed that the average calorific intake there is not higher than in the western part of the Reich territory. That means that today the German people in the British and in the French occupation zones receive less than half, in the American occupation zone a bit more than half the calorific intake which, according to Hoover, is necessary to survive.

The consequences of such meagre rations, even if it is accepted that there are additional sources of supplies for a wider section of the population especially in the countryside, are: a gradual but ever more accelerating decay of the nation's physical powers and mental resistance. This decay will and must take hold of those segments of society on which the economic reconstruction of the new Germany and its political pacification will depend: the German workers. There is no doubt that the German worker fulfils his national duty to the full: he has surrendered himself to the hard task of national reconstruction with discipline, a willingness to work and to make sacrifices which deserves the highest recognition. But his willingness to work and his ability to work are inextricably linked to physical conditions. And these conditions are gradually beginning to crumble to a worrying degree.

Hamburger Freie Presse, 10.4.1946, translated from source in: Kleßmann, *Das Gespaltene Land*.

This press report highlighted one of the big problems that came along with the continuing short supply of foodstuffs and subsequent under-nourishment of the population: labour productivity declined and thus impacted negatively on any reconstruction effort. Constant hunger, certainly abetted by the erosion of social norms and values as a result of the war, had a significant negative impact on the population – who often resorted to crime in their struggle for food.

Doc 6 Hunger and crime

On 11 August, between 8 and 9 p.m. a number of boys aged between 10 and 13 years gained possession of bread in a rather original way. At the Bockmann bakery in Altona, Grosse Bergstrasse 218, they smashed a 50x80 cm big window with the help of a long stake they had wrapped in rags. They were able to spike six loaves of bread from inside the bakery onto the tip of the stake and got them out.
(*Kriminalpolizeiliches Meldeblatt für Groß-Hamburg*, 15.8.1945)

The murder of the 69 year old grocer Louise Z. who had been found battered and strangled to death in the cellar of her shop at Barmbecker-strasse 187 has been solved. Olga G., the 24 year old grandchild of the murder victim has confessed to it. She killed her grandmother with an axe in order to rob her beddings, cloth and foodstuff.
(*Hamburger Volkszeitung*, 13.4.1946)

On Thursday night it came to a shootout between a police patrol and three men when these tried to clear out a food store at Lehmweg in Hamburg. Nobody was injured in the gunfight.
(*Hamburger Echo*, 8.6.1946)

On Friday evening some ten to fifteen men climbed over the fence of the customs area at Ross railway station in Steinwärder so that they could break into three freezer cars which were loaded with frozen meat. Police officers who intervened saw themselves surrounded by an increasing crowd of pillagers who threatened them. With the support of the riot squad which had been called in the meantime, the robbery could be prevented.
(*Hamburger Volkszeitung*, 7.8.1946)

All trans. from sources in: Kleßmann, *Das gespaltene Land.*

According to The Hague Convention, the ultimate responsibility for the food supply and welfare of civilians in an occupied country rested with the occupying forces. The dire situation of the German population between 1945 and 1948 resulted not from Allied ill will, but was rather due to insufficient Allied planning for the post-war period, as well as their complete miscalculation of actual available German resources in their zones, combined with the lack of the traditional supplies from the East.

17

Because there was insufficient planning for the post-war period the military governments had no proper guidelines for their occupation authorities on the ground. This not only affected economic matters, but arguably had also a strong impact on political affairs. For example, while at the Potsdam Conference the Four Powers had agreed on a political vetting and denazification of all adult Germans, no details were agreed on the procedure. Subsequently, and because the Allies had different agendas for denazification, it was carried out differently in style and severity in each zone. What made the situation worse, however, was the fact that in the absence of clear guidelines, in particular within the American zone of occupation (to a lesser degree so in the British and French zones), the rigour with which the denazification process was carried out depended very much on the zeal or pragmatism of individual US Army officers in charge of the procedure. The resulting widespread inconsistency in the process caused considerable confusion among both Germans and Americans.

Doc 7 Chaos of denazification

... that in the first instance the occupational powers themselves and within the English zone the various agencies have to agree on a set of principles under which they want to readmit ordinary party members into the German administration. At present, we have the grotesque situation such that in the American zone this process is being conducted differently from the English and Russian zones. In addition, in each zone, the different personalities do not concur in their public statements at all. It is even the case that within these statements there can be ideas which appear contradictory to the uninitiated German ...

Here in Cologne we experience on a daily basis the grotesque situation whereby the city's military commander allows a person back to work only to be removed again some weeks later by the Field Security Service (FSS). It appears that here in Cologne the Military Government 622 and the FSS do not act on the same principles. If there is no agreement on the basic principles, things can only get worse when, beyond the general situation, the detailed question of readmitting members of trade and industry is looked at separately. Add to this the fact that every individual Military Government has its own views on the re-admission of former party members. In Cologne we saw 5500 officials who were party members being kicked out, leaving only 527 officials. In addition two-thirds of all white-collar workers were sacked and only one-third remained. In Düsseldorf all party members remained in their posts. In Wuppertal all those kicked out by the town administration had to be reinstated on the order of the Military Government. We are faced with the grotesque situation that the lower administrative bodies (town and district councils) sometimes act very stringently, sometimes very leniently; while in the higher administrative bodies (Chamber of Agriculture in Bonn, State Food Office, government, *Oberpräsident*) party members remain in the highest and most responsible posts. But the grotesque practice does not stop there. An American Lieutenant demanded that party members who lived as evacuees far outside Cologne in a children's home had to be removed from there immediately because of their dangerous influence on the children. At the same time, there is a philanthropic officer in charge of school affairs who not only readmits party members without trial or consulting with the Personnel Office in the school administration, but also allows the return of former party members into the teaching body.

As long as there is this kind of chaos, it seems to me fairly futile to even start a discussion on the particular case of readmitting any party members into trade and industry.

Letter by the City of Cologne Personnel Office to Mayor Suth, 21.11.1945, trans. from sources in: Kleßmann, *Das Gespaltene Land*.

This uncoordinated and even unpredictable process eventually created strong resentment among the German population, even among those who initially had welcomed denazification. A more structured approach was tried by the Allies with the introduction of the *Fragebogen* or questionnaire. Everyone above the age of 18 had to answer its 131 questions so that they could be classed in one of five categories: accused of major crimes, accused of crimes, accused of minor crimes, fellow traveller and person exonerated (*Hauptschuldige, Belastete, Minderbelastete, Mitläufer, Entlastete*). But once again, the thoroughness with which the process was carried out varied from zone to zone, with the Americans initially adopting the toughest approach; in contrast, the British vetting was the softest. From the outset, the Americans pursued minor Nazis quite rigorously and punished them severely. Those who were actually more involved with the Nazi regime or had committed crimes in the regime's name were usually not dealt with immediately, so that more evidence could be collected against them. However, lack of personnel meant that the process never went very far. As a result, when American policy changed with the emerging Cold War, fellow travellers and minor Nazis had been sentenced while those involved with the regime on a larger scale got away with either relative minor sentences or no punishment at all. Not surprisingly, by 1949 even German opponents of the Nazi regime were deeply dissatisfied with the whole process.

Doc 8 OMGUS report on denazification, 1949

Adverse criticism of the methods of denazification reached a high point in early 1949 as the denazification hearings approached completion. The predominant opinion (65 per cent in AMZON) was that the program had been badly carried out. Although exact comparisons with previously expressed attitudes were not possible because the question had been phrased differently, there was a strong indication that approval of the methods and procedures had declined over the years. In November 1945 50 per cent expressed satisfaction with the program. In March 1946 it rose to 57 per cent. By December of that year it had dropped sharply to 34 per cent, to 32 per cent in September 1947 and further to 17 per cent in May 1949. This decline does not necessarily imply hostility to the idea of denazification; critics based their objection on its laxness, rather than its harshness or unfairness.

Those who disapproved of the denazification procedures were most likely to come from upper income groups (83%), to be better educated (85%), have a higher socio-economic status (90%), and they were more likely to be native residents (69%) then expellees from elsewhere (47%), 'liberal' conservatives (84%), men (71%), and of course, former NSDAP members (78%) and their relatives (79%). Critics of the program claimed that it had treated the less important former members of the NSDAP more harshly than major offenders. People who approved the conduct of the hearings tended to talk primarily in terms of the justice of punishing the guilty for the past crimes and misdeeds.

Generally speaking, majorities in each American occupied area voiced their approval if the *idea* of denazification; 66 per cent in AMZON, 68 per cent in Berlin and 64 per cent in Bremen. Very revealing, however, is the fact that the opinion-leading and most vocal groups – the university-educated (49%) and the upper socio-economic groups (55%) – were most likely to express their opposition to the principle of denazification. Arguments of those who disapproved [of] even the idea of holding supporters of Nazism responsible for the regime were scattered. The argument most frequently mentioned was that these people had been idealists and were therefore not deserving punishment.

20

From: Merritt and Merritt (eds) *Public Opinion in Occupied Germany: The OMGUS Survey 1945–49.*

The democratisation of Germany was another of the four 'D's agreed at Potsdam. As early as 10 June 1945, the Soviet Military Government allowed the (re)-establishment of 'anti-fascist' parties and trade unions. The Americans permitted the formation of political parties in late August, the British in mid-September. However, in both cases their activities were limited to district level. At first democratisation was a slow process, and any German executive official, from the lowest village mayor to minister presidents of the newly-founded states – the *Länder* – was appointed by the occupying powers. The conflict between the Allies' distrust of the Germans on the one hand and their desire to introduce democratic structures on the other becomes clearly visible in the British Military Government directive of 15 September 1945 that allowed the establishment of political parties.

Doc 9 Establishment of political parties

Ordinance No. 12 Formation of Political Parties
In order to encourage the development of a democratic spirit in Germany and prepare free elections for a date yet to be appointed, the following directives are issued herewith:

Art. 1 Formation of Political Parties
(1) Political parties can be formed in a district (*Kreis*) according to the directives contained herein.
(2) The military government can allow parties which have been formed according to these directives to unite with one another in larger areas, thereby dispensing with certain rules and conditions.
(3) Membership in political parties must be voluntary.

Art. 2 Method of Application
(4) Every person or group of persons who has the wish to form a political party for a *Kreis* can apply to the military government for permission to form such a party. All such applications will be signed by the persons making them and will be accompanied by the following documents:
a) A draft of the terms of association and of the rules for the proposed political party;
b) A programme outlining its aims and objectives; ...

(6) Notification of permission, whether to form a party or unite already established ones, will be delivered to the applicants by the military government. This permission (in future to be called military government permission) will be issued in writing and will contain the rules and conditions according to which the political party is to be formed or according to which already established parties can be united. Neither the formation nor the union of political parties can take effect before the military government permission is granted.

(7) The grant of a military government permission according to this regulation does not include the right to hold political meetings without a permission according to Regulation No. 10 or to organize public processions without a permission according to Regulation No. 11.

Art. 6 Penalties

(12) Any person:

a) who takes part in political activities, whether as a member of a political party or not, which have as their objective or which tend towards

   (i)   the undermining of the authority of the Military Government, or
   (ii) the creation of dissension between the Allied Powers, or
   (iii) the glorification of or the preparation for war or militarisation, or
   (iv) the restoration of the Nazi regime or the establishment of any similar regime, or
   (v)   the introduction of discrimination against any person or group of persons on the grounds of race, colour, nationality or religious beliefs, ...

Shall upon conviction by a Military Government court suffer such punishment (including death) as the court may determine.

From: *Military Government Gazette – Germany, British Zone of Control, 1945.*

There were some younger Germans involved in the political process who had learned their lessons from war and Nazism, but it was mainly carried out by those who had been politically active before 1933 and who had survived the Nazi regime. The old Communist Party, the KPD, which had been severely persecuted by the Nazis, as had the country's oldest political party, the Social Democratic Party (SPD), were the first ones that received Allied permission to reconstitute themselves. On the conservative side of the political spectrum one man who would soon come to prominence in West German (party) politics, even though he himself had not originally participated in the founding of his future party, was the 69-year-old former Lord Mayor of Cologne, Konrad Adenauer. A leading figure of the Catholic Centre Party in the Weimar years, he had been forced into retirement by the Nazis in 1933. Adenauer did not join the re-founded Centre Party in 1945, becoming instead a member of the newly-formed Christian Democratic Union (CDU). The party had been founded initially in Berlin in the spirit of Christian socialism, and had as its aim to combine the political forces of all Christian denominations and end the split between political Catholicism and Protestantism. This was a lesson most Christian politicians had learned from the collapse of the Weimar Republic. In the early years, Adenauer's position within the party was certainly not undisputed. What set him above the rest of his fellow party grandees and eventually secured his unrivalled position within the CDU was not his political experience but his cunning as a political operator combined with his (sometimes Machiavellian) political pragmatism. Adenauer proved himself to be a *Realpolitiker* par excellence who was able to analyse a political situation without much sentimentality or illusion. At the same time he was able to develop a political vision for his country. A letter he wrote to a political friend in late October 1945 regarding Germany's foreign policy situation displays both of these attributes.

Doc 10 Adenauer on Germany's foreign policy situation, 1945

Russia holds the eastern half of Germany, Poland, the Balkans, apparently Hungary, a part of Austria. Russia is withdrawing more and more from co-operation with the other great powers and directs affairs in the countries dominated by [itself] entirely as [it] sees fit.

In those countries occupied by Russia are already totally different economic and political principles applied than in the rest of Europe. Therefore, the division into Eastern Europe, the Russian area and Western Europe has become reality.

England and France are the leading great powers in Western Europe. The part of Germany not occupied by Russia is an integral part of Europe. If it remains weak [*krank*], it will have the most severe consequences for the whole of Western Europe, including England and France. It lies in the most inner self-interest of the part of Germany not occupied by the Russians, but even more so in the interests of England and France, to ally Western Europe under their leadership and to pacify, rebuild and return to its former health, politically and economically, that part of Germany which is not occupied by the Russians.

23

A separation of the Rhineland and Westphalia does not serve this purpose, and it would have the opposite effect. It would direct the political orientation of the non-Russian occupied part of Germany towards the East.

In the long run the French and Belgian demand for security can only be achieved through the economic interconnection of West Germany, France, Belgium Luxemburg and Holland. If England would decide to participate in this economic interconnection [*Verflechtung*], then one would be much closer to the ultimate aim of a 'Union of Western European States'.

Regarding the constitutional structure of the non-Russian occupied part of Germany: at the moment a sensible constitutional structure does not exist, and it has to be restored. The creation of a centralised unified state [*Einheitsstaat*] will be neither possible nor desirable, the constitutional link can be looser than before, perhaps in a federal form.

Trans. from: Adenauer, *Briefe 1945–47*.

The split of Europe which Adenauer was predicting in late 1945 and the accompanying split of the war-time alliance and the creation of two antagonistic power blocks did not happen overnight. Developments in the wider world as well as events in, and Allied disagreements over, Germany contributed to increasing tensions and increasing mutual distrust. At Potsdam, the Allies had agreed not to create or establish a German central government but to run their respective zones as if the country were an economic unit. The Control Council, a body made up of the four Allied Supreme Commanders, was supposed to be the organisation with which the Four Powers jointly administered the occupation. To enable Germany to be run as an economic unit, proposals were brought before the Council to establish a number of German 'central administrations' which would be in charge of mail, transport and food supplies. However, these proposals were all vetoed by the French representative, with the result that each zone was left to fend for itself. Commenting on, and warning against, the increasing Sovietisation of those countries under Soviet influence, the British opposition leader in the House of Commons, Winston Churchill, on 5 March 1946 made his famous 'Iron Curtain' speech at Fulton, Missouri. Significantly, the British Foreign Office had been warning throughout the spring of 1946 of an increasing Soviet threat. On

3 May General Lucius D. Clay, the US Deputy Military Governor, stopped all deliveries of reparation goods from the American occupation zone to the other zones. Although this was a move mainly directed against French obstruction of the Potsdam Agreement and French unwillingness to Four-Power co-operation, to a lesser extent it was also seen at the time as a move against the Soviet Union to make them, too, comply with the Potsdam Agreement. The Soviets, whose infrastructure and economy had been severely hit by the German invasion and who were desperate to rebuild their country, certainly interpreted the decision as directed against them. By the summer of 1946, the three Western Allies could not agree on the future policy on Germany. The British wanted the German economy revived as far as possible so that their occupation costs and obligations could be covered from the proceeds of German exports and not by the British taxpayer. The French were categorically opposed to any form of central administration in Germany or any large-scale economic revival. Within the American administration, the State Department still fought with the Treasury Department and the Pentagon's Army Department over how to treat Germany. The Soviets stalled on the fulfilment of some aspects of the Potsdam Agreement but were even more exasperated by the French blockade policy. They saw it as a deliberate attempt by all Western powers to prevent the Soviet Union from achieving the greatest possible economic benefit for their battered country. Then, during the second stage of the Paris Conference of Foreign Ministers, on 10 July, after having a claim for $10 billion worth of reparations from Germany rejected by the Americans, Soviet Foreign Secretary Molotov dropped a bombshell. He stated that the Soviet Union did not want to destroy Germany as a state, nor its industry. Instead the Soviet Union favoured the future creation of a central German government, implying that the Soviet Union was willing to allow the establishment of a single German state.

Doc 11 Molotov's Paris speech

M. Molotov then made the following statement:
'The time has come when we should discuss the fate of Germany and a peace treaty with that country.

The Soviet Government has always held that the spirit of revenge is a poor counsellor in such affairs. It would be just as incorrect to identify Hitler Germany with the German people though the German people cannot divest themselves of the responsibility for Germany's aggression and for its gravest consequences ... I proceed from the fact that in the light of the interests of world economy and tranquillity in Europe it would be incorrect to adopt the course of Germany's annihilation as a state or that of its agrarianization, including the annihilation of its main industrial centres. Such a course would result in undermining the economy of Europe, in the dislocation of world economy and in a chronic political crisis in Germany which would spell a threat to peace and tranquillity ...

I think therefore that our purpose is not to destroy Germany but to transform Germany into a democratic and peace-loving state which beside its agriculture will have its own industry and foreign trade but which will be deprived of economic and military potentialities to rise again as an aggressive force ...

Germany has long held an important position in the world economy. While continuing as a single state Germany will remain an important factor of world trade which also corresponds to the interests of other people ...

It has of late become fashionable to talk about the dismemberment of Germany into several 'autonomous' states, about the federalisation of Germany and about the separation of the Ruhr from Germany. All such proposals originate in the same policy of destruction and agrarianization of Germany, for it is easy to understand that without the Ruhr Germany cannot exist as an independent and viable state. But I have already said that if the interests of peace and tranquillity are dear to us the destruction of Germany should not be our objective ...

Such is the view of the Soviet Government regarding war industry and war potential of Germany. These considerations cannot hamper the development of peaceful industries in Germany.

In order that the development of German peaceful industries may be of benefit to other peoples who need German coal, metal and manufactured products, Germany should be granted the right of export and import and if this right of foreign trade is to be effectuated we should not put obstacles in the way of the increase in the output of steel, coal and manufactured products of a peaceful nature in Germany, naturally within certain bounds and provided that an inter-Allied control shall inevitably be established over German industry and over the Ruhr industries in particular ...

It goes without saying that we raise no objection to the setting up of a German central administration as a transitional step towards the establishment of a future German government ...

From: *FRUS 1946*, vol. II.

This statement was a direct Soviet challenge for the hearts and minds of the German people. If the proposal for national unity and sovereignty appealed to the Germans it could result in their taking a more pro-Soviet and a more anti-Western (i.e. anti-American) stance which ultimately could have led to Soviet control of the whole of Germany. After inter-Allied tensions had been simmering below the surface for some time, Molotov's speech can be seen as the opening shot of the Cold War in Germany. Now it was up to the Americans to come up with a more constructive occupation policy, a policy that would bring some hope for a better future to the Germans.

2

Growing division, 1946–49

In the two years following Molotov's Paris speech the relationships between the Soviet Union and the Western Powers deteriorated quickly, reaching a low point on 20 March 1948 with the Soviet withdrawal from the Four-Power Control Council. Three months later, the outbreak of World War Three seemed very close when after the American-inspired currency reform in the Western zones the Soviets imposed a blockade on Berlin. Fortunately, the Americans did not respond with military force but instead initiated the Berlin Airlift, the biggest air transport operation the world had ever seen. Between the summer of 1946 and mid-1948 the East-West tensions helped to fundamentally change American policy on Germany. At the end of this process, which had considerable positive implications for the treatment of the German population by the Western Allies, the division of the country had become a fact. Despite all verbal statements to the contrary from all sides, Cold War logic would determine that the division would remain and even deepen during the coming decades.

Since early 1946, even before Molotov's Paris speech, the Americans had realised that things had not gone at all well in Germany. In particular food supply had become a major concern. The worst-hit zone was the British, where the situation was close to developing into a vicious circle that afflicted the other zones as well: the lack of food had a direct detrimental impact on labour productivity. But without the basic production of the Ruhr, in particular coal, there was no hope for any improvement of the economic situation anywhere in Germany. Without an organised and meaningful reconstruction, there was no way to improve the dire food and housing situation. How desperate the situation was and the possible consequences that loomed become clear in a memo from February 1946, written by General Clay, the American Deputy Military Governor.

Doc 12 Food supply in the British zone

27 February   1946CC 23681 SECRET
From Clay for Hilldring

[Lt. Gen. Sir Brian] Robertson announced today a cut in the ration in the British zone to 1000 calories with corresponding cuts for heavy workers to include coal miners. This ration will of course barely maintain life and is far below any minimum standard or the average consumer to maintain health for even a short period. He has been unable to get any assurances from his Government as to food supplies for a greater ration, and indigenous sources would provide him only about 700 calories per person. I do not believe that such a ration could be continued in British zone without a repercussion in all other zones, particularly if we continue a ration of 1500 calories ...

I am not advised here whether the British position is due to inability to obtain food supplies or to financing problems; if the former, I am inclined to withdraw my opposition to pooling insofar as it applies to the food supplies still to be brought into Germany. Stocks on hand should not be pooled as they are insufficient to help the existing situation and would involve transportation difficulties. In view of my statement to German officials that we would support 1500 calorie ration, I would prefer to take any change up with them prior to action. I believe that they would volunteer a further reduction to prevent what looks like possible mass deterioration in the British zone ...

From: *The Papers of General Lucius D. Clay*

How desperate the situation really was came to light just four weeks later in another memo from Clay to the administration in Washington. It demonstrated that in early 1946 the USA, despite all their potential resources, had not begun to tackle the problem of insufficient food supplies for the German population. Further cuts in the already insufficient rations seemed unavoidable. In Clay's opinion this would inevitably mean that out of sheer desperation the German population would switch their allegiance away from the Western powers and the USA towards the Soviet Union – and pave the way for the spread of Communism.

Doc 13 Consequences of insufficient food supplies

27 March 1946   CC 2124 SECRET
From CLAY for Echols and Petersen

The 150,000 tons of food in the next three months would provide approximately 1115 calories per day until next harvest season if distribution is perfect. However, it is doubtful if such an average ration should be established without some assurance that additional stocks would be available later. All of our assumptions have assumed that some food would be available to Germany from the next crop season in the United States ...

Certainly there is some non-rationed food available. However, it goes largely to farm and small village people and the great mass of population in the large cities probably do not have access to more than 50 calories per person per day. We cannot delay further in reducing present ration allowance. Our Minister Presidents will be advised on Friday to reduce the ration to 1275 calories. They will be further advised that the commitment which we now have for 150,000 tons will not support even this ration and that they must be prepared for further cuts by 1 May unless we have received additional commitments. This is not in the interest of good government, as the uncertainties involved will not only be disturbing to our German officials but will unquestionably reach the German people in distorted rumours. However, there is no other recourse at this time. If additional commitments are not received during the coming month, the ration for the remaining period would have to be reduced to something just over 1000 calories. This will be in the face of the commitment made in good faith to support a ration of 1550 calories.

It is our belief that the Russian zone is feeding approximately 1500 calories and will continue to do so until the next harvest season.

We have insisted on democratic processes in the U.S. zone and have maintained a strict neutrality between political parties. As a result the Communist Party has made little inroad. However, there is no choice between becoming a Communist on 1500 calories and a believer in democracy on 1000 calories. It is my sincere belief that our proposed ration allowance in Germany will not only defeat our objectives in middle Europe but will pave the road to a Communist Germany ...

As the occupying power in our own zone we have assumed some obligations even though the Germans are an enemy people. It would seem to me that we are making the accomplishment of our objectives impossible.

From: *The Papers of General Lucius D. Clay*

In particular the American State Department had recognised Molotov's Paris speech as a direct appeal to the German population in order to win them over to the Soviet camp. They feared that if the plan were successful, the whole of Germany could fall under the Soviet sphere of influence. It was from this point on that US policy on Germany became determined by the accelerating Cold War hostilities. More and more US policy became guided by the State Department's *Realpolitik* approach, which began to replace the previous, more punitive measures that had been influenced partly by the Treasury Department under Henry Morgenthau. The first clear sign of this change came in the speech given by Secretary of State, James F. Byrnes on 6 September 1946 to the Minister Presidents and other high-ranking German officials of the US occupation zone in Stuttgart. The tremendous impact the speech had on the German public can be seen from the fact that even today it is regarded as the beginning of America's reconstruction effort and called 'The Speech of Hope'. Although Byrnes made it clear that the agreements reached at Potsdam, in particular those concerning territory, would not be changed the speech committed the USA to the reconstruction of Germany for the first time. Thus the speech has to be understood as a direct response to Molotov's Paris statement on possible reunification.

Doc 14 Byrnes's 'Stuttgart speech'

I have come to Germany to learn at first hand the problems involved in the reconstruction of Germany and to discuss with our representatives the views of the United States Government as to some of the problems confronting us.

We in the United States have given considerable time and attention to these problems because upon their proper solution will depend not only the future well-being of Germany, but the future well-being of Europe …

Freedom from militarism will give the German people the opportunity, if they will but seize it, to apply their great energies and abilities to the works of peace. It will give them the opportunity to show themselves worthy of the respect and friendship of peace-loving nations, and in time, to take an honorable place among members of the United Nations.

It is not in the interest of the German people or in the interest of world peace that Germany should become a pawn or a partner in a military struggle for power between the East and the West …

After considerable discussion the Allies agreed upon levels to which the principal German industries should be reduced to carry out the Potsdam Agreement. These levels were agreed to upon the assumption that the indigenous resources of Germany were to be available for distribution on an equitable basis for all of the Germans in Germany and that products not necessary for use in Germany would be available for export in order to pay for necessary imports ...

The German people were not denied, however, the possibility of improving their lot by hard work over the years. Industrial growth and progress were not denied them ...

The conditions which now exist in Germany make it impossible for industrial production to reach the levels which the occupying powers agreed were essential for a minimum German peacetime economy. Obviously, if the agreed levels of industry are to be reached, we cannot continue to restrict the free exchange of commodities, persons, and ideas throughout Germany. The barriers between the four zones of Germany are far more difficult to surmount than those between normal independent states ...

Important as economic unification is for the recovery of Germany and of Europe, the German people must recognize that the basic cause of their suffering and distress is the war which the Nazi dictatorship brought upon the world ...

It is also essential that transportation, communications, and postal services should be organized throughout Germany without regard to zonal barriers. The nationwide organization of these public services was contemplated by the Potsdam Agreement. Twelve months have passed and nothing has been done ...

Germany must be given a chance to export goods in order to import enough to make [its] economy self-sustaining. Germany is a part of Europe and recovery in Europe, and particularly in the states adjoining Germany, will be slow indeed if Germany with [its] great resources of iron and coal is turned into a poorhouse ...

The American Government has supported and will continue to support the necessary measures to de-Nazify and demilitarize Germany, but it does not follow that large armies of foreign soldiers or alien bureaucrats, however well motivated and disciplined, are in the long run the most reliable guardians of another country's democracy.

All that the Allied governments can and should do is to lay down the rules under which German democracy can govern itself. The Allied occupation forces should be limited to the number sufficient to see that these rules are obeyed ...

Security forces will probably have to remain in Germany for a long period. I want no misunderstanding. We will not shirk our duty. We are not withdrawing. We are staying here. As long as there is an occupation army in Germany, the American armed forces will be part of that occupation army.

The United States favors the early establishment of a provisional German government for Germany. Progress has been made in the American zone in developing local and state self-government in Germany, and the American Government believes similar progress is possible in all zones.

It is the view of the American Government that the provisional government should not be hand-picked by other governments, but should be a German national council composed of democratically responsible minister presidents or other chief officials of the several states or provinces which have been established in each of the four zones ...

While we shall insist that Germany observe the principles of peace, good-neighborliness, and humanity, we do not want Germany to become the satellite of any power or powers or to live under a dictatorship, foreign or domestic. The American people hope to see peaceful, democratic Germans become and remain free and independent ...

With regard to Silesia and other eastern German areas, the assignment of this territory to Poland by Russia for administrative purposes had taken place before the Potsdam meeting. The heads of government agreed that, pending time and determination of Poland's western frontier, Silesia and other eastern German areas should be under the administration of the Polish state and for such purposes should not be considered as a part of the Soviet zone of occupation in Germany. However, as the Protocol of the Potsdam Conference makes clear, the heads of government did not agree to support at the peace settlement the cession of this particular area.

The Soviets and the Poles suffered greatly at the hands of Hitler's invading armies. As a result of the agreement at Yalta, Poland ceded to the Soviet Union territory east of the Curzon Line. Because of this, Poland asked for revision of [its] northern and western frontiers. The United States will support revision of these frontiers in Poland's favor. However, the extent of the area to be ceded to Poland must be determined when the final settlement is agreed upon.

The United States does not feel that it can deny to France, which has been invaded three times by Germany in 70 years, its claim to the Saar territory, whose economy has long been closely linked with France. Of course, if the Saar territory is integrated with France [the latter] should readjust [its] reparation claims against Germany.

Except as here indicated, the United States will not support any encroachment on territory which is indisputably German or any division of Germany which is not genuinely desired by the people concerned. So far as the United States is aware the people of the Ruhr and the Rhineland desire to remain united with the rest of Germany. And the United States is not going to oppose their desire.

While the people of the Ruhr were the last to succumb to Nazism, without the resources of the Ruhr Nazism could never have threatened the world. Never again must those resources be used for destructive purposes. They must be used to rebuild a free, peaceful Germany and a free, peaceful Europe ...

From: *FRUS 1946.*

Western commentators at the time described the distribution of occupation zones and inter-Allied co-operation sarcastically with the following words: 'The Russians have the food, the Americans have the scenery, the British have the rubble and the French have objections.' Although Britain had prevailed in the war against Nazi Germany, the cost for this was near-bankruptcy. Since Germany was in no position pay for the costs of the occupation, Britain had to find those funds in its own depleted coffers. In particular the costs of food supply for the German urban population in the industrial cities of the Ruhr had to be bought for hard dollars on a tight world food market. In other words, because of the occupation, Britain was haemorrhaging hard currency to a degree it could ill afford in its own dire economic situation. When, after Molotov's Paris speech, the Americans proposed to economically merge their zone with that of any of the other occupying powers in order to fulfil the Potsdam Agreement, the British instantly took up the offer. By December 1946 an agreement was reached that arranged for the sharing of the economic burden of the occupation. Before the agreement on the zonal merger could take effect on 1 January 1947, the food situation in the Ruhr had become so desperate that the British government was forced to introduce bread and potato rationing at home – a step not even undertaken during the war years – in order to sustain the insufficient food rations in Germany.

Doc 15 US/UK Zonal merger

2 December 1946

Representatives of the two Governments have met at Washington to discuss the questions arising out of the economic fusion of their zones of occupation in Germany. They have taken as the basis of their discussion the fact that the aim of the two Governments is to achieve the economic unity of Germany as a whole, in accordance with the Agreement reached at Potsdam on 2nd August, 1945. The arrangements set out hereunder, for the United States and United Kingdom Zones, should be regarded as the first step towards the achievement of the economic unity of Germany as a whole in accordance with that Agreement. The two Governments are ready at any time to enter into discussions with either of the two occupying Powers with a view to the extension of these arrangements to their zones of occupation. On this basis, agreement has been reached on the following paragraphs:

1. Date Of Inception
This Agreement for the economic fusion of the two Zones shall take effect on 1st January, 1947.

2. Pooling Of Resources
The two Zones shall be treated as a single area for all economic purposes. The indigenous resources of the area and all imports into the area, including food shall be pooled in order to produce a common standard of living.

3. German Administrative Agencies
The United States and United Kingdom Commanders-in-Chief are responsible for setting up under their joint control the German administrative agencies necessary to the economic unification of the two Zones.

4. Agency For Foreign Trade
Responsibility for foreign trade will rest initially with the Joint Export Import Agency (United States–United Kingdom) ...

5. Basis Of Economic Planning
The aim of the two Governments is the achievement by the end of 1949 of a self-sustaining economy for the area.

6. Sharing Of Financial Responsibility
Subject to the provision of the necessary appropriations, the Governments of the United States and the United Kingdom will become responsible on an equal basis for costs of approved imports brought into account after 31st December, 1946 ... in so far as those cannot be paid for from other sources, in accordance with the following provisions:

(A) For this purpose the imports of the area shall be divided into two categories: those imports required to prevent disease and unrest (Category A), which are financed in decreasing amounts by appropriated funds; and those further imports (including raw materials), however financed, which will he required if the economic state of the area is to recover to an extent sufficient to achieve the aim laid down in paragraph 5 of this Agreement (Category B).

(B) It is the intention of the two Governments that the full cost of Category A imports shall be defrayed as soon as possible, subject to sub-paragraph (C) below, from the proceeds of exports. Any portion of the cost of Category A imports which is not met by export proceeds will be defrayed by the two Governments in equal shares from appropriated funds.

(C) The proceeds of exports from the area shall be collected by the Joint Export-Import Agency and shall be used primarily for the provision of Category B imports until there is a surplus of export proceeds over the cost of these imports.

(E) The costs incurred by the two Governments for their two Zones before 1st January, 1947, and for the area thereafter, shall be recovered from future German exports in the shortest practicable time consistent with the rebuilding of the German economy on healthy non-aggressive lines.

7. Relaxation Of Barriers To Trade

With a view to facilitating the expansion of German exports, barriers in the way of trade with Germany should be removed as rapidly as world conditions permit. To the same end the establishment of an exchange value for the mark should be undertaken as soon as this is practicable; financial reform should be effected in Germany at an early date; and the exchange of full technical and business communications between Germany and other countries should be facilitated as soon as possible. Potential buyers of German goods should be provided access to both Zones to the full extent that facilities permit, and normal business channels should be restored as soon as possible.

8. Procurement

The determination of import requirements shall be the responsibility of the Joint Export-Import Agency. The procurement of these requirements shall be dealt with as follows:

(i) Procurement of Category A imports to the extent that they are financed from appropriated funds of either Government shall be the responsibility of that Government.

(ii) Procurement of Category B imports and of Category A imports to the extent that they are not financed by appropriated funds shall be the responsibility of the Joint Export-Import Agency, with such assistance from the two Governments as may be desired.

Unless otherwise agreed, subject to the provisions of this paragraph, procurement shall be from the most economical source of supply. However, the sources shall be selected to the fullest extent practicable so as to minimise the drain on the dollar resources of the United Kingdom. [...]

10. Food
The two Governments will support, to the full extent that appropriated and other funds will permit, an increase in the present ration standard to 1800 calories for the normal consumer as soon as the world food supply permits. This standard is accepted as the minimum which will support a reasonable economic recovery in Germany. However, in view of the current world food supply, a ration standard of 1550 calories for the normal consumer must be accepted at present.

11. Imports For Displaced Persons
Subject to any international arrangements which may subsequently be made for the maintenance of Displaced Persons, the maintenance of Displaced Persons within both Zones from the German economy shall not exceed the maintenance of German citizens from this economy. Supplementary rations and other benefits which may be provided for Displaced Persons in excess of those available to German citizens must be brought into Germany without cost to the German economy.

(Signed) Ernest Bevin
(Signed) James F. Byrnes

Reprinted in: Oppen, *Documents on Germany under Occupation, 1945–54.*

Almost exactly one year later, on 17 December 1947, the treaty was revised, with the US taking on almost all the costs, which also increased their say in the political and economic administration of both zones. Obviously, the creation of the 'Combined Economic Area' – usually referred to as the 'Bizone' – on 1 January 1947 is one of the crucial points in the following process of the division of Germany and the subsequent establishment of two German states. Some of the underlying American political and geo-strategic thinking in the Cold War context are revealed in a Joint Chiefs of Staff memorandum in May 1947. Although this was 'only' a secret military study and not an official policy document, it succinctly explains both American fears and actions resulting from these fears in Germany and Europe in the face of a Soviet Union that seemed ever more threatening and expansionist.

Doc 16 Germany's strategic importance

Top Secret   [Washington,] May 12, 1947.

Subject: Policies, Procedures and Costs of Assistance by the United States to Foreign Countries
Enclosure: J.C.S. 1769/1 (Copy No. 39)
                              Appendix

United States Assistance To Other Countries From The Standpoint Of National Security

Report By The Joint Strategic Survey Committee
     [Washington, April 29, 1947.]
                              The Problem

1. On the assumption that the next war will be ideological, to prepare a study, from the standpoint of national security, to determine the countries of the world, in the order of their urgency and their importance, to which the United States should, if possible, give current assistance.
                              Discussion
2. See Enclosure.
                              Conclusion

3. a. A sound program of United States assistance to other countries along the line indicated in the remainder of these conclusions will greatly assist in the realization of the major objectives currently supported by the Joint Chiefs of Staff in the interest of strengthening the national security of the United States ...
h. The nations it is desirable to aid *because of their need*, listed in order of the urgency of current need, are as follows:

Greece	Austria	Netherlands-NEI
Italy	China	The Philippines
Iran	Turkey	Portugal
Korea	Great Britain	The Latin American
France	Belgium and Luxembourg	Republics
	Canada	

i. The nations it is desirable to aid *because of their importance to the national security of the United States*, arranged in order of importance are:

Great Britain	Italy	Spain
France	Canada	Japan
Germany	Turkey	China
Belgium	Greece	Korea
Netherlands	Latin America	The Philippines
Austria		

[...]

Enclosure

1. At the outset, it should be firmly fixed in mind that the mere giving of assistance to other countries will not necessarily enhance the national security of the United States. The results obtained by such assistance will determine whether our national security is strengthened thereby. What, then, are the desired results? These are firm friends located in areas which will be of strategic importance to the United States in the event of war with our ideological enemies, and with economies strong enough to support the military establishments necessary for the maintenance of their own independence and national security ...

6. Potentially, the strongest military power in this area is Germany. Without German aid the remaining countries of western Europe could scarcely be expected to withstand the armies of our ideological opponents until the United States could mobilize and place in the field sufficient armed forces to achieve their defeat. With a revived Germany fighting on the side of the Western Allies this would be a possibility. Further, the complete resurgence of German industry, particularly coal mining, is essential for the economic recovery of France – whose security is inseparable from the combined security of the United States, Canada, and Great Britain. The economic revival of Germany is therefore of primary importance from the viewpoint of United States security.

7. France is, however, still the leader of those countries of Europe west of Germany and all indications are that France will vigorously oppose any substantial revival of German heavy industry. The fear of a revived Germany is still strong in France and this fear is compounded by the activities of French communists who, in accordance with Soviet desires, seek to make post-war Germany weak industrially and militarily. Yet the German people are the natural enemies of the USSR and of communism. If treated without undue harshness by the Western Allies they would in all probability align themselves with the Western Allies in the event of ideological warfare unless the countries of Europe to the west

of Germany had previously fallen under communist domination. In this latter case Germany would be between two hostile factions and [its] alignment in such a war would be problematical.

8. From the viewpoint of the security of the United States it appears that our efforts should be directed toward demonstrating both to the leaders of France and to the leaders of Germany that the emergence of a principal world power to the east of them, ideologically opposed to all of their traditional way of life, whose ultimate aim is world conquest, and which they can successfully oppose only if both are strong and united against the new eastern menace, makes them interdependent just as France, England, Canada, and the United States are interdependent. Further, France, as one of the victors of the past war, must be made to see that diplomatic ideological warfare is now going on and that if the diplomatic war can be won the shooting war will be delayed and perhaps even avoided. Most important of all, France and the United States and Great Britain must acknowledge that the decisive diplomatic contest between totalitarian Russia and the democracies of the West is taking place in Germany today. The Western democracies can win this contest only if there is drastic change in their economic policies for Germany. Further, Germany can aid in European recovery and become an ally of the West against their ideological opponents only if [its own] economy is restored. In fact, such a course should appeal to France and Great Britain as well as to the United States in view of the high cost that devolves upon these countries for the mere feeding of the German population so long as German industry and foreign trade are paralyzed. This cost to Great Britain and the United States has been estimated by Mr. Herbert Hoover to be $950,000,000 before July of 1948 ...

From: *FRUS 1947*, vol. I, pp. 734 ff.

How much American thinking in regard to Germany had changed by the summer of 1947 becomes even more apparent in a letter General Clay sent to the Secretary of the Army, Petersen, in which he spoke out against the British plans of nationalising the coal mines of the Ruhr. For the British Labour Government, this was an attempt to prevent a future war by transferring Germany's key raw material into public ownership. The previous year, Clay had vetoed the nationalisation of basic and key industries in Hesse, although voters there had expressed their desire for such a move in a popular referendum by a two-thirds majority. Clay's argument

was that nationalisation would predetermine the question of ownership of the German industries but that such a step should be left to
be decided by the Germans themselves. The flawed logic of Clay's
argument is obvious. Preventing the nationalisation of industries
predetermined the future economic system in at least the same way
as nationalisation would have done, so the reason for Clay's opposition lay somewhere else. For one, it should not be forgotten that
the Americans already had to accept the nationalisation programme
in Great Britain which the Labour government had announced in
1945. The Americans would have found it very hard to accept that
Europe's biggest industrial region, the Ruhr area, was to be nationalised, as well. Furthermore, as G. and J. Kolko had pointed out, by
preventing nationalisation of German industry Clay was protecting
direct American business interests in Germany.

Doc 17 Ruhr coal socialisation

24 June 1947   CC 9661
From CLAY for PETERSEN

[Maj. Gen. William] Draper in writing of Bipartite Economic Panel
presented our proposal for five year trusteeship of coal mines. Yesterday
[Christopher Eden] Steel, acting Political Adviser for British military
government advised Murphy informally that Sir Cecil Weir [British
member Bipartite Economic Panel] had informed [Foreign Secretary]
Bevin of the proposal. Steel stated that Mister Bevin was very much
upset as British plan for Germany visualizes the early socialization of
the coal mines on a Land basis, with ownership being vested in Land
North Rhine-Westphalia. Apparently General [Sir Brian] Robertson had
advised Mister Bevin that I had agreed to the socializing of the mines
provided it was done on a Land basis and by vote of the German people.
   This is rather a liberal interpretation of what I said to General
Robertson. I have told him repeatedly that I believed it would be a great
mistake for British military government to undertake nationalization of
industry within Germany and that I doubted if such action would be
acceptable to the United States. I have told him that the United States
might accept socialization in Germany if it were undertaken on a state
and not a national basis as a result of the freely expressed desire of the
German people. However I did not anticipate that conditions could be
created in Germany which would permit such a free expression until its
future political structure had been determined and central government

established. Moreover, I have never expressed any views as to the desirability of socializing coal and steel industry of the Ruhr in Land North Rhine-Westphalia. Obviously this would give to one Land the control of the major resources of Germany and a dominant position therewith in German government.

Nevertheless, Steel has indicated that British conversations with German officials have gone too far for this movement to be stopped now. If this is the case, the American side has not been advised of these discussions.

It seems clear that we may expect immediate adverse British reaction to the proposed trusteeship with a corresponding energetic move for the immediate transfer of ownership of the coal mines to Land North Rhine-Westphalia.

For some time I have found it difficult to know what position to take with respect to socialization in western Germany. While I realize that our policy in general is not to oppose socialist measures if freely adopted by the German people, it seems apparent that we must determine what constitutes a free expression of German opinion. Certainly the present economic and political conditions in Germany are not sufficiently stable to permit this question to be resolved with intelligent and protracted discussion of its merits before the German people. Nevertheless it is my conviction that unless our Government is prepared now to take a strong position that the question must be deferred until reasonable stability has been attained in Germany, it will in fact become the pattern for western Germany. If our Government is prepared to accept socialism now and without an effort to maintain a reasonable degree of free enterprise while the issue is deferred, then I am creating an unnecessary opposition in our Bipartite Board which does prevent complete harmony in our operations. It seems to me that we must either accept or reject socialization now or else agree to defer the issue for a definite period of time if our Bipartite Board is to function effectively. This question is immediate and therefore I request advice and instructions urgently.

From: *The Papers of General Lucius D. Clay*

For the German population, the severe winter of 1946–47 had brought further misery. Despite the Allies' best efforts official rations in some places were reduced for a short period to as little as 800 calories for normal consumers – less than a third of the 2500 calories necessary to sustain an adult. At the same time, the small successes that had been achieved in the reconstruction process were wiped out by the severe winter weather and thrown back months. On 12 March 1947, US President Truman raised Cold War tensions by announcing what would become known as the Truman Doctrine. With US-Soviet tensions having increased to such an extent, it is not surprising that the Moscow Conference of Foreign Ministers (10 March–24 April 1947) failed to produce any positive results. The Moscow Conference can be seen as the last chance for the wartime Allies to improve their relationships. In Germany the meeting's failure was seen as a further setback for the country's reconstruction. So the German political leadership, with American backing, became active themselves and the Bavarian Minister President invited his fellow *Länder* chiefs – including those from the Soviet occupation zone – for a meeting in Munich in order to discuss solutions to the dire situation.

Doc 18 Invitation to the Munich conference of Minister Presidents

On 7 May 1947 the Bavarian Minister President, Hans Ehard, in the name of the Bavarian Government, has invited the Minister Presidents of the states [*Länder*] of all four zones to Munich for a meeting in early June. The result of the Moscow Conference of the four Powers' Foreign Ministers is perceived as a failure by the whole of the German people. The German people are physically and mentally unable to withstand another winter, waiting with hunger and cold, living in the squalor of the destroyed cities, in economic emaciation and political hopelessness. Therefore it is the duty of responsible German governments not to let the time pass with idle waiting until the London Conference, scheduled for the beginning of the next winter. In the light of all these considerations, the Bavarian Government has taken the initiative by calling for a meeting of all German Minister Presidents so that measures can be considered that will prevent a further slide of the German people into a hopeless economic and political chaos ... The Bavarian Government is aware of its duty not only to Bavarians, but to the entire German people. It is full of the conviction that the aim of these endeavours has to be to gradually undertake in a timely manner all the measures necessary, so that we are prepared for the next winter and can survive it in a tolerable way.

In Germany the failure of the Moscow Conference to bring about the merger of the four zones into an economic union has been perceived as a heavy blow, and even more so that the prospect for the creation of a political superstructure has been further postponed ...

Trans. from: *Akten zur Vorgeschichte der Bundesrepublik Deutschland*, vol. 2, *Jan.–June 1947*.

If there were high hopes before the meeting, those were dashed when the conference ended in failure. It would come to symbolise the early split of Germany into a part occupied by the Soviet Union and a part occupied by the three Western powers. However, while the Bavarian government's official press communiqué on the withdrawal of the East German delegates blamed their dogmatic insistence on a 'political' agenda, this claim could easily be turned around. In the tense atmosphere of 1947, the decision by the Minister Presidents of the Western zones to avoid a 'political' agenda was in itself a political decision, and one that had been encouraged by the Americans.

Doc 19 Press communiqué after the Munich Conference, 7.6. 1947

During the preliminary talks by the German *Länder* chiefs on 6 June on the agenda of the Conference of Minister Presidents to remedy the German economic plight, the Minister Presidents of the Eastern zones surprisingly put forward the following resolution: 'We propose as a decisive precondition for the conference's negotiations that the first point on the agenda be the establishment of a central German administration. This administration should be ratified by the democratic German parties and trade unions for the creation of a unified German state [*Einheitsstaat*].'

During the previous extensive and repeated commission talks, to which the representatives of the Eastern zones were invited, though did not attend, Minister President Ehard announced a particular and solemn pledge for German unity. He immediately pointed this out to the representatives of the Eastern zones. The other heads of the *Länder* agreed in their expressions that during the conference the necessity for German unity had to be stressed in every point of the agenda. Opinions differed as to whether this aim should be a special, separate point of the agenda and if it should be in the form of a request to the political parties. Even during this debate ... the *Länder* heads of the Russian zone withdrew for special deliberations lasting more than an hour. After they had finished they made a statement through the Brandenburg Minister President Steinhoff who had appeared in the meantime, that ... they felt forced to take no further part in the conference. Following this, the gentlemen left the conference room. The remaining heads of government continued their deliberations and agreed on the agenda in which the food emergency, the economic emergency and the plight of the refugees would be in the foreground.

Trans. from: *Akten zur Vorgeschichte der Bundesrepublik Deutschland, vol. 2, Jan.–June 1947.*

The Minister Presidents of the three Western zones knew that France would have vetoed any proposal for a central German government anyway. Such a veto would have been used by the Soviet Union to accuse the Western Powers of preventing German unity. On the other hand, just five days before the meeting, General Clay had informed the *Länderrat* – the Minister Presidents of the American-occupied zone – that the British and the Americans were to establish a German administrative body in the Bizone. Clay went out of his way to stress that such a move did not constitute a political merger of the two zones, only an economic union. Saying otherwise would have enabled the Soviet Union to accuse Britain and the USA of breaching the Potsdam Agreement by unilaterally establishing a separate political entity and thus splitting Germany. Such a step would have been resented by many Germans as well.

Doc 20 Economic Council announced by Clay

I am very glad to be down here today for the regular monthly meeting of the *Länderrat*. Last week I sent by special messenger to the Minister President a copy of an agreement for the further integration of the American and the British zones worked out by the American and British Military Governments ... The document ... has been approved and is now an agreement between the British and the American Military Government.

As you know, both you and ourselves have been conscious of the difficulty in obtaining economic integration without political integration. Nevertheless, we have not been willing to unify the American and British zones politically in the fear that it might be harmful to the early unification of Germany as a whole. Thus the agreement we have reached still does not provide for political unification of the American and British zones. On the other hand, within the fields of economics, and under strictly defined powers, it does provide an arrangement where the views of the German people can be given to the American and British Military Governments on the economic policies to be followed by the two governments.

There is established an Economic Council which is composed of representatives elected by the *Landtage* of the several *Länder* ... To the extent possible within each Land the representatives the Economic Council will be proportioned to the political party strengths at the last election. The Economic Council will be charged with the enactment of policies and ordinances within the field of economics, subject, of course, to the approval of the British and American Military Governments.

In addition to the Economic Council and to assure coordination among the bizonal economic agencies there is also established an Executive Committee. This Executive Committee will be composed of one representative from each of the *Länder*. It will nominate the heads of the Executive Agencies for confirmation by the Economic Council. It will be authorised to issue implementing regulations under the policies and laws of the Economic Council. It will sit continuously and will be responsible for the coordination and supervision of the several economic agencies ... However, it is not subordinate to the Economic Council and it is charged with coordination and supervision of economic agencies in its own right. There will, of course, be reporting to this Executive Committee, the executive Directors of the several economic agencies whose duties and functions will be roughly comparable to that of State Secretaries. The law will become effective on the tenth of June ...

Trans. from: *Akten zur Vorgeschichte der Bundesrepublik Deutschland, vol. 2, Jan.–June 1947.*

It is obvious that despite its name the Economic Council could – and would – be something more than just a body concerned with economic affairs. In fact it was a parliamentary body in all but name that would become the legislative nucleus for a separate West German state.

The decisions on the developments in the Western zones have to be seen against wider Cold War events. Once Britain and the USA had identified the Soviet Union as a threat, the political decision to integrate the Western zones into their camp became nearly inevitable. The failure of the Moscow Conference of Foreign Ministers would certainly have had an impact on the drafting of the JCS Memorandum of May 1947 (Doc 16). For the Americans, it had now become imperative that Germany's (or at least West Germany's) economic and military potential should not fall into the hands of the Soviets. The easiest way to prevent this from happening was to integrate the Western zones fully into the Western camp. For this to be successful, it was crucial to prevent the German population from falling under the influence of communist propaganda. The answer to both issues was the rehabilitation of the German economy within the European economic framework. With better food supplies and increased industrial production the German standard of living would improve and the danger of the Germans being lured towards Communism out of sheer desperation would decline. The way forward to fight the economic misery would be the famous Marshall Plan, named after the US Secretary of State, George C. Marshall. Although he did not refer to Germany at all when he was talking about European reconstruction in his famous Harvard Speech of 5 June, the inclusion of the Western zones in an American programme of economic aid for Europe was only logical. There could be no European recovery without (West) German recovery, and vice versa.

America's new political and economic thinking regarding German reconstruction was fully expressed for the first time in JCS 1779, which replaced the much more punitive JCS 1067 on 11 July 1947.

Doc 21 JCS 1779

1. Purpose of this Directive
This directive, issued to you as Commanding General of the United States forces of occupation and as Military Governor in Germany consti-tutes a statement of the objectives of your Government in Germany and of the basic policies to which your Government wishes you to give effect from the present time forward. It supersedes JCS 1067/6 and its amend-ments.

2. Authority of Military Government
b. Pending arrangements for the effective treatment of Germany as an economic and political unit, you will exert every effort to achieve economic unity with other zones.

3. United States Policy Toward Germany
The basic interest of the United States throughout the world is just and lasting peace. Such a peace can be achieved only if conditions of public order and prosperity are created in Europe as whole. An orderly and prosperous Europe requires the economic contributions of a stable and productive Germany as well as the necessary restraints to insure that Germany is not allowed to revive its destructive militarism ...

4. Demilitarization
There should be no relaxation of effort to complete and effectively to maintain the disarmament and the demilitarization of Germany.

6. German Self-Government
b. It is the view of your Government that the most constructive development of German political life would be in the establishment throughout Germany of federal German states (Laender) and the formation of a central German government with carefully defined and limited powers and functions. All powers shall be vested in the Laender except such as are expressly delegated to the Central Government ...

15. General Economic Objectives
The economic objectives of the United States Government in Germany are:
a. to eliminate industry used solely to manufacture and to reduce industry used chiefly to support the production of arms, ammunition and implements of war;
b. to exact from Germany reparation for the losses suffered by United Nations as a consequence of German aggression; and
c. to encourage the German people to rebuild a self-supporting state devoted to peaceful purposes, integrated into the economy of Europe.
Although the economic rehabilitation of Germany, within the framework of these objectives, is the task and responsibility of the German people, you should provide them general policy guidance, assist in the development of a balanced foreign trade and ensure that German efforts are consistent with, and contribute to, the fulfilment of your Government's objectives.

18. Economic Unity and Recovery
a. Your Government is desirous of securing agreement in the Control Council to the treatment of Germany as an economic unit, the formulation of common policies in all matters affecting Germany as a whole, and the establishment of central Germany administrative agencies for the purpose of implementing such common policies in the fields of finance, transport, communications, agriculture, economics (including industry and foreign trade) and such other fields as the Control Council may consider necessary and appropriate.
b. Your Government likewise desires to secure the adoption of a production and foreign trade program for Germany as a whole which should be directed toward an increasing standard of living in Germany and the attainment at the earliest practicable date of a self-sustaining German economy. Such a program should give highest priority to increased production of coal, food and export goods, provide for such allocation and distribution of German indigenous output and approved imports throughout Germany as are necessary to carry out the production program and attain the agreed standard of living; ensure full payment for all goods and services exported from Germany (other than reparations

or restitutions) in approved imports or in foreign exchange which can be utilised for the payment of approved imports, and to provide for the pooling of all export proceeds to be made available, first to meet the import needs of Germany as a whole for such time and in such amount as may hereafter be determined, and secondly to compensate the occupying powers for past expenditures pursuant to terms and conditions to be established hereafter ....

19. Finance
b. 3) You will take such action as may be necessary to prevent the establishment of a centralized German banking system and an undue concentration of financial power but will encourage the establishment of a central authority for the production, issuance and control of currency and for technical banking supervision. You will also encourage the Germans to re-establish normal banking facilities within the mutation prescribed above and within the present blocking of assets and accounts under Military Government law No. 52; ...

From: US Department of State (ed.), *Documents on Germany 1944–1985*

Although Allied trust in the Germans built up only gradually, and although JCS 1779 still called for demilitarisation and certain controls of the German economy, less then seven weeks after the publication of JCS 1779, the Americans revised the limits of most German industrial production upwards. Since these limits (75 per cent of 1936 industrial output) had been agreed by the Four Powers in the 1946 (first) industrial plan this bilateral British-American move caused furious reactions from the French and the Soviets, although there was little they could do to stop it from happening. While in 1946 it had been the British who had called for higher German production quotas, in another reversal of roles it was now the US which was the driving force for an expansion of West German industrial capacity and output.

Doc 22 Revised (2nd) industry plan

29 August 1947

PREAMBLE

In March, 1946, the four occupying powers, acting through the allied control authority, adopted a plan for reparations and the level of post-war German economy. The objectives of the plan were to eliminate Germany's war potential, to provide reparations and yet to leave within Germany the necessary plants and equipment to permit the rebuilding of a viable peaceful economy.

Experience has shown the necessity for revision of the plan which was based on specific assumptions that have not been fulfilled. Neither the bizonal area nor all of Germany can regain economic health under the plan as it now stands. Moreover, it has become increasingly apparent that under present conditions Germany cannot contribute [its] indispensable part to the economic rehabilitation of Europe as a whole.

... Consideration has been given throughout to the necessity for ensuring that the bizonal plan can be assimilated into a plan for Germany as a whole. The offer to the other occupying powers to join the bizonal area in developing a unified German economy still stands. The plan has been developed with due regard to the hope that this offer will be accepted.

I. GENERAL CONSIDERATIONS
The industrial capacity retained under the March 1946 plan was estimated to provide production equal to 55% of 1938, which would have been about 70–75% of 1936 production. The effect of the new plan will be to retain sufficient capacity in the bizonal area to approximate the level of industry prevailing in Germany in 1936, a year that was not characterized by either boom or depressed conditions.

A. The old plan provided for very sharp cuts in production capacities in the metals, machinery and chemicals industries, from which the bulk of reparations were to be obtained. It is impossible to provide a self-sustaining economy in the bizonal area without materially increasing the levels in these industries. Substantially the entire difference between the original and revised plan is in these reparations industries since the original plan already provided for maximum, and in some cases unrealistic, levels for the non-reparations industries. Under the revised plan, capacities in the metals, machinery, and chemical industries will be sufficient to permit production at levels averaging about 5 or 10% less than [those] in 1936. As compared with the war year 1944, the proposed levels represent a reduction of 55 to 60%.

B. It must be borne in mind that the bizonal area already has a population at least 6 million more than in 1936 and by 1952 it may be expected to have a population from 8 to 10 million greater than pre-war. On the basis of an expected population of 41 to 44 million in the bizonal area in 1952, the per capita production capacity provided in the new plan would be approximately 75% of 1936.

II. REQUIREMENT FOR A BALANCED ECONOMY

In addition to pre-war foreign trade, the bizonal area must produce a surplus over its internal requirements for trading with the remainder of Germany; this particularly affects requirements for the industrial capacity of steel and steel products, which are the most needed and, therefore, the most dependable trade commodities required by the rest of Germany in exchange for key products essential to the bizonal economy.

A. Change in Price Relationships. World food and raw material prices have increased more rapidly than the prices of manufactured goods since 1936 and this situation seems likely to continue. Consequently, the bizonal area must be prepared to exchange in foreign trade proportionately larger quantities of industrial products in return for necessary food and raw material imports.

B. Imports in the general way. The bizonal area accounted for the whole of Germany's pre-war food deficit, as the remainder of Germany was about self-sufficient in foodstuffs. It is estimated that imports of food, seed and fertilizer sufficient to make possible an essential diet will amount to 1.00 to 1.15 billion dollars at current prices ...

3. The foregoing considerations lead to the conclusion that the total bizonal requirements from outside of Germany will approximate at least 2.0 billion dollars at current prices. Repayment of advances by the occupying powers would be an addition to these estimates.

C. Exports. The 1936 exports from the bizonal area were approximately RM 2.6 billion, which is estimated to represent about 1.75 billion dollars at current prices ...

1. These estimates, therefore, indicate that, in addition to trade requirement for the rest of Germany, the bizonal economy will need to export to other countries at least 15% more in volume than in 1936. Since trade between the bizonal area and the rest of Germany is subject to greater uncertainty than former internal trade, the result may be to increase still further the need for trade with other countries.

2. Before the war, the broad fields of metals, machinery, and chemicals accounted for two-thirds of the total exports ... Therefore, the level of exports from the restricted industries will need to be greater than pre-war.

III. INCREASED LEVELS IN RESTRICTED INDUSTRIES

The following determinations have been reached with respect to the industries restricted under the original Level of Industry Plan.

A. *Steel.* Under the March, 1946, level of industry plan, steel capacity for all of Germany is limited to 7.5 million tons, with actual production in any single year not to exceed 5.8 million tons. Careful calculations show that this level would be clearly insufficient even to support the level of industry contemplated in the original plan, and it is far too low to provide for the needs of the economy under the revised plan. It has been determined that in order to support the revised level of industry in the bizonal area and to permit that area to become self-supporting, the limit of annual steel production in the bizonal area shall be fixed at 10.7 million ingot tons per annum and sufficient capacity to produce that tonnage shall be retained.

B. *Mechanical engineering industries:*
1. *Heavy machinery industry.* Sufficient capacity will be retained to produce RM 500 million, which is about 80% of pre-war production. This leaves 35% of the present capacity to be removed as reparations as against 60% under the previous plan.
2. *Light machinery industry.* The capacity in the bizonal area is estimated at about RM 1,195 million. Capacity will be retained to produce RM 916 million, which is 119% of pre-war production. This leaves 23% of present estimated capacity available for reparations, as compared with 33% under the old plan ...
4. *Fine mechanics and optics.* In the field of precision optics, no plants will be made available for reparations. The capacity is to be retained to provide for internal needs and to attain exports of the same products equal to those from the bizonal area in 1936.

  In the case of photo-technics, no plants are to be made available for reparations and the retained capacity will be used to attain 150% of pre-war exports in this field from the bizonal area as well as to provide for internal requirements ...
5. *Machine tools.* The March, 1946 level of industry plan permits the production of RM 74 million in all of Germany, or 11.4% of 1938 output. The bizonal area, before the war, produced about 43% of Germany's machine tools. Present capacity is estimated at RM 119 million. It has been determined that capacity sufficient to produce

RM 170 million must be retained in order to support the revised level of industry. This will leave about 35% of present capacity for reparations ...

E. *Electrical engineering.* The present capacity of the electrical industry in the bizonal area is required with the exception of three war-time plants. Capacity is estimated to be about one-half greater than pre-war. This increase is necessary because pre-war requirements of the bizonal area were in large part met from capacities in Berlin, which have been almost totally dismantled ...

F. *Chemicals:*
1. Approximately the 1936 capacity will be retained in the chemical industry which is about 42% more than that provided in the old plan. However, a large number of explosive and other chemical plants were developed for war purposes. Between 40 and 50% of the total chemical capacity, including war explosives will, therefore, be removed as reparations or destroyed ...

G. *Cement.* All of the cement capacity in the bizonal area is required and will he retained ...

IV. PROHIBITED INDUSTRIES
The production of aluminium, beryllium, vanadium, and magnesium is prohibited under the previous level of industry plan. No plants in these industries will be made available for reparations purposes pending further review. No change is proposed in the arrangements made under the previous plan in regard to ball bearings, synthetic ammonia, synthetic rubber, and synthetic gasoline and oil.

Reprinted in: Oppen, *Documents on Germany under Occupation, 1945–54.*

The Soviet Union certainly could not offer the Germans economic promises or improvements of any kind. Their only chance to respond to the changes in America's policy was to invoke, through the Communist Party in their zone of occupation, anti-fascist sentiments; and to appeal to the German desire for national unity and to attack the democratic parties for failing to work for this national unity. For this purpose, the Eastern zone's Communist-dominated Socialist Unity Party, the SED, on 26 November 1947 called for a 'People's Congress', in which delegates from all over Germany would meet. In a show of 'grass-roots democracy' the Congress would then be authorised to put forward German wishes and resolutions for consideration at the Conference of Foreign Ministers that was to meet in London.

Doc 23 Invitation to a 'People's Congress'

Unfortunately, all attempts for the creation of an all-German party consultation on the representation of the interests of the German people at the Conference of Foreign Ministers have failed due to the resistance of leading men within the Social Democratic Party and the bourgeoisie parties in the western zones of occupation. Eventually even the leader of the Christian Democratic Union in the Soviet Zone of Occupation refused to give his consent. In one of the most decisive moments the leaders of these parties fail and abandon the people.

The Socialist Unity Party cannot and will not accept this situation. They regard it as their duty to give the German people the opportunity to make their will public at the London Conference and make their voice heard. In the final hour the Socialist Unity Party calls to abandon all dividing issues.

It is not about parties but about the whole people!

Based on the already given consent of many organisations we suggest: all anti-fascist-democratic parties, trade unions and other mass organisations, shop stewards and the work force of large companies, peasant's organisation, deputies of science and the arts from all over Germany should raise their voice together for the German people.

We invite to a *German People's Congress for Unity and Just Peace* on the 6. and 7. December 1947 at the Berlin Staatsoper, Friedrichstrasse 101/102.

Agenda:

1) *The will of the German people for a just peace, for democracy and German unity.* – Presentations and discussions.

2) *Election of a delegation to the London Conference of Foreign Ministers.*

We recommend to all parties, organisations and large companies to respond immediately to our proposal and make preparations to send delegates to the People's Congress. Further communications between organisations willing to participate shall happen immediately.

Trans. from: *Dokumente der Sozialistischen Einheitspartei Deutschlands*, vol. 1.

The success of the appeal is open to question. Out of more than 2,200 delegates, only some 660 came from the Western zones. The next direct step in the process of Germany's division came once more from the West. From 23 February to 6 March 1948, the first phase of a six-power meeting comprising the USA, Great Britain, France and the Benelux countries took place in London to discuss the future of the western part of Germany. Two days after the Six Powers had begun their deliberations a Communist coup in Czechoslovakia will have increased Western anxiety and influenced the outcome of the meeting. On 8 March the Six Powers announced the results of their talks in a communiqué. For the first time, the logical consequences of the increasing Cold War tensions were spelled out. A separate West German state should be established that was to participate in, and would benefit from the European Recovery Programme, the Marshall Plan. In other words, France, the Benelux and Britain sanctioned the American initiative for the division of Germany.

Doc 24 London 6-Power communiqué

The informal discussions of German problems which began in London on 23rd February between the representatives of the United States, United Kingdom and France, and as from February 26th with the representatives of the Benelux countries, went into recess today.

... At the first meeting it was agreed to invite the Benelux countries to take part, on an equal footing, in the discussions of all items on the agenda, except those dealing with administrative matters which are the direct responsibility of the occupying powers controlling the three occupied areas ...

Important progress has been made and it has been decided that these discussions will be resumed during April for the purpose of reaching conclusions on the remaining question, so that the delegations may be in a position to submit to their governments, at the end of the next session, their recommendations over the whole field. In the meantime various aspects of certain of these problems will be the subject of more detailed examinations.

The continuous failure of the Council of Foreign Ministers to reach quadripartite agreement has created a situation in Germany which, if permitted to continue, would have increasingly unfortunate consequences for western Europe. It was therefore necessary that urgent political and economic problems arising out of this situation in Germany should be solved. The participating powers had in view the necessity of ensuring the economic reconstruction of western Europe including Germany, and of establishing a basis for the participation of a democratic Germany in the community of free peoples. While delay in reaching these objectives can no longer be accepted, ultimate Four Power agreement is in no way precluded ...

The relationship of western Germany under the occupying powers to the European Recovery Programme was also discussed by the U.S., U.K. and French delegations. It was agreed that for the political and economic well-being of the countries of western Europe and of a democratic Germany there must be a close association of their economic life. Since it has not proved possible to achieve economic unity in Germany, and since the eastern zone has been prevented from playing its part in the European Recovery Programme, the three Western powers have agreed that close co-operation should be established among themselves and among the occupation authorities in western Germany in all matters arising out of the European Recovery Programme in relation to western Germany. Such co-operation is essential if western Germany is to make its full and proper contribution to European recovery. It was also agreed to recommend to the three governments that the combined zone and the French zone should be fully associated in the European Recovery Programme and adequately represented on any continuing organization. Proposals in this sense will be presented at the forthcoming meeting of the CEEC [Conference for European Economic Co-operation]. Agreement in principle has been reached on recommendations for the association of the Benelux countries in policy regarding Germany. Consideration was given of all delegations to the establishment of an international control of the Ruhr on which Germany would be represented. The purpose of this international control would be to ensure that the economic resources of this area should not again be used for the purposes of aggression and that there should be adequate access to the coal, coke and steel of the Ruhr for the benefit of extensive parts of the European community including Germany. Agreed recommendations in this respect will be submitted to the governments concerned on the scope and form of this control.

From: US Department of State (ed.), *Documents on Germany 1944–61.*

The communiqué still spoke of re-establishing a united Germany, but this was only a verbal fig leaf for political and propaganda reasons. A statement of this kind was necessary to deny Stalin a propagandistic advantage in which he could accuse the West of dividing Germany. Such an accusation could antagonise the more nationalistic sections of the German population against US policies. In reality all four of the 'big' powers, as well as the smaller European states, were faced with the century-old 'German question' about the size and status of that country. In May 1948 R.M.A. Hankey, head of the British Foreign Office Northern Section summed up the Western position on Germany's future.

Doc 25 British view on Germany

3. It is indeed painfully obvious … that the division of Germany will bring great difficulties and dangers. But given the measure of Sovietisation that will be inevitable in the Eastern zone I do not think the Germans in the West will tend to regard Berlin as their proper capital as much as they do now while quadripartite rule is established there …

4 … In my opinion a united Germany would be a far greater menace to peace than a divided Germany for the following reasons:
a) A united Germany is bound to be regarded as a real menace by Russia. [It] must always fear that [Germany] will be controlled by hostile powers and in [Russian] eyes any non-Communist power *is* hostile. Therefore [Russia] must inevitably try to control or ally itself with Germany.
b) If Russia controls, or directs, or is allied with the whole of Germany, it will always be tempted to encourage Germany to expand westwards in order to keep German eyes away from the East. The combination of Russia and Germany would be an almost irresistible menace to the Western world. We should therefore have indefinitely more trouble with Russia than we do now.
c) A united Germany of 62 million people or more *cannot* in my opinion be adequately controlled or directed by any methods the Western Powers can use, as we saw between the wars. Only the Russians can direct a united Germany through the Communist Party and Secret Police system.
d) A united non-Communist Germany allied to the Western Powers will I suggest start trouble at the earliest opportunity to regain their lost territories in the east. The Western Powers could not allow such a Germany be destroyed by Russia. As an ally a united Germany would therefore be a most dangerous asset.
e) A united non-Communist Germany, even allied to the West will, in my opinion, always be tempted to blackmail us by threatening to join Russia and, if c) is correct, we could not be sure of preventing this.

f) A Western Germany of 40 million inhabitants all afraid of Russian aggression and penetration will depend on co-operation with the Western powers for protection and will depend completely on Western Powers for raw materials, food and markets; it will be less liable to invade Eastern Germany than a united Germany would be to invade Poland; in short, it would be far more amenable and far less of a danger to France.

g) In any case there obviously cannot be a united Germany. Neither we nor the Russians can allow the other to control Germany and it is plain, after the experience of the last three years, that we cannot agree to control Germany jointly. Given Russia's ideology this has seemed inevitable for a long time but obviously we had to try the experiment.

h) ... The Russians obviously intend to run their zone in their own way, possibly with a German Government in it. I suspect that they are waiting for us to start the first German Government so that they can blame us [*handwritten insert*: to the people of the Soviet orbit for rebuilding Germany & recreating a German danger, & to the German people for] dividing Germany. The only question for the French to consider is whether a Balkanised and therefore indigent Western Germany will give the Russians more chances to intrigue against us than a united and prosperous Western Germany. The answer is as plain as a pikestaff. Prosperity and unity in Western Germany may in some degree represent a payment by the Western powers at the expense of their own security, but if the Russian aspect is taken into account it is a very worthwhile insurance premium.

From: NA PRO FO 371 70587/C3653/71.

Under the circumstances Hankey's logic was flawless. Unification, in whichever form, was out of the question. From now on, any Allied statement – and for that matter, many German statements, too – that called for unification would be nothing but a rhetorical exercise in lip service. Only six weeks later the next step towards the division of Germany occurred. Following the currency reform in the Western zones of occupation, the Soviet Union on 24 June blocked all surface access routes from the West to Berlin under the pretext of 'technical difficulties'. The US Military Governor General Clay was ordered by his superiors not to break through the blockade with military force. Instead Clay initiated the relief of the city through air transport. The US Military Government's political advisor, Murphy, informed Secretary of State George C. Marshall on 26 June on the endeavour.

Doc 26 US plans for the airlift

Secret   Berlin, June 26, 1948
General Clay, in cooperation with General Le May, Commanding
General USAFE, gave orders this morning for the organization of air
lifts between the Western Zones and Berlin on the basis of an estimated
daily supply of 225 tons. 70 planes are immediately available which
will make an estimated 100 trips daily. There is under consideration the
question of adding an additional 30 planes which if brought into the
service would enable the shipment eventually of up to 500 tons daily.
For the supply of the UK and US forces only 50 tons daily are necessary.
The balance will be devoted to the needs of the German population and
Military Government is establishing a priority list of commodities. As a
comparative figure, the daily food supply for the population of the three
western sectors of Berlin is 2,000 tons ...

From: *FRUS* 1948, vol. 2.

Murphy's telegram indicated the scale of the task ahead. Supplying
a few thousand Allied military personnel and their dependents was
the easy part, but supplying the 6,000 tons of goods a day necessary
to sustain a city of 2 million people through air transport seemed
impossible at the time. After a very moderate start the daily tonnage
delivered into the city increased on a weekly basis. By spring of 1949,
more goods were flown into West-Berlin than had reached the city
by road, rail or canal transport before the blockade. By this time,
the airlift itself had become a propaganda weapon in the Cold War.
This fact was pointed out by Undersecretary of State Robert Lovett
at a meeting of the National Security Council in December 1948.

Doc 27 Significance of the airlift

Mr Lovett stated emphatically that the airlift, which had started out
merely as a difficult embarrassment for us, had now become a vital
part of our foreign policy. It had had the effect of welding the western
Germans into a unity that we had been unable to get otherwise. He
mentioned how one old-time Communist in the Ruhr area had recently
been beaten [in elections] and pointed out that in the Western sectors
of Berlin there was an 82.6% turnout of voters. He stressed the fact
that the airlift was just not a mechanism but a symbol of American

determination and ingenuity. He agreed with Mr Draper's remark that it was now the greatest political symbol in Europe ...

From: US National Archive RG59, 740.00119, reprinted in: G. Gerhardt, *Das Krisenmanagement der Vereinigten Staaten während der Berliner Blockade 1948/1949.*

As a result of the American-led Berlin Airlift, the Soviets' blockade of Berlin was a failure and was abandoned in May 1949. By this time the Americans had imposed a counter-blockade that prevented goods from Western Europe to cross the Iron Curtain, a blockade that in different forms lasted until the 1990s. What was more important for the Americans in the Cold War context of the late 1940s and early 1950s was the fact that because of the Berlin Blockade most West Germans changed their view on the Americans. They now were seen no longer as occupiers but more as protectors and friends, which made it easier for them to implement policies that had been agreed on during the second phase of the London Six Power Conference (20 April–2 June 1948). The most important result of the second phase were the 'Frankfurt Documents', which the three Western Military Governors handed over to the German Minister Presidents on 1 July 1948. In the documents the Germans were instructed to set up a constituent assembly which was tasked, in accordance with strict Allied guidelines, to draft a constitution for a federal state.

Doc 28 Frankfurt Documents

1 July 1948

DOCUMENT I: Constituent Assembly

The Military Governors of the US, UK and French Zones of Occupation in Germany, in accordance with the decisions of their respective Governments, authorize the Ministers President of the states of their respective zones to convene a constituent assembly to be held not later than September 1948.

...

The constituent assembly will draft a democratic constitution which will establish for the participating states a governmental structure of federal type which is best adapted to the eventual re-establishment of German unity at present disrupted, and which will protect the rights of the participating states, provide adequate authority, and contain guarantees of individual rights and freedoms.

If the constitution as prepared by the constituent assembly does not conflict with these general principles, the Military Governors will authorize the submission for ratification ... When the constitution has been ratified by two-thirds of the states, it will come into force and be binding upon all states ...

DOCUMENT III: Occupation Statute

A. The Military Governors will grant legislative, executive and judicial power to German governments and reserve to themselves such powers as are necessary to ensure the fulfilment of the basic purpose of the occupation. Such powers are those necessary to enable the Military Governors to:

(a) Conduct or direct for the time being Germany's foreign relations;
(b) Exercise the minimum control over German foreign trade, and over internal policies and measures which could adversely affect foreign trade, necessary to ensure a respect for obligations entered into by the Occupying Powers in regard to Germany and the proper use of funds made available to Germany;
(c) Exercise such controls as have been or may be agreed upon, as for example, regarding the international authority for the Ruhr, reparations, the level of industry, decartelisation, disarmament and demilitarisation, and certain aspects of scientific research.
(d) Protect the prestige and ensure the security of the occupation forces and the satisfaction of their requirements within defined limits agreed upon between the Military Governors;
(e) Ensure the observance of the constitutions which they have approved.

B. The Military Governors will resume their exercise of their full powers in an emergency threatening security, and if necessary to secure compliance with the constitutions or the occupation statute.

C. The Military Governors will exercise the above-mentioned controls according to the following procedure:
(a) Any amendments to the constitutions will be submitted to the approval of the Military Governors;
(b) In the fields mentioned in (a) to (e) of paragraph A above, the German authorities will comply with the decisions or directions of the Military Governors;

(c) Unless otherwise provided, in particular for implementation of paragraph (b) above, all laws and regulations emanating from the federal government shall come into force automatically within 21 days unless disapproved by the Military Governors.

The Military Governors will have special responsibility to observe, advise and assist the federal and state governments in regard to the democratization of political life, social relations and education. This shall not imply any restriction of the legislative, executive and judicial competence accorded to such governments in these matters.

The Military Governors request the Ministers President to submit their observations on the above principles. The Military Governors will then communicate these broad principles, modified as they may then agree, to the constituent assembly, as a guide to that body in its work of preparing the constitution and will receive from it the observations which it may wish to put forward. When the Military Governors announce their approval for the submission of the constitution to the states they will publish simultaneously an occupation statute incorporating these principles as finally modified in order that the people of the states may understand that they accept the constitution within the framework of this occupation statute.

Reprinted in: Oppen, *Documents on Germany under Occupation, 1945–54.*

While the Minister Presidents were prepared in principle to accept the Allied instructions for the creation of a separate West German state they attached conditions which were rejected by the Military Governors. Eventually a linguistic compromise was reached which allowed the Germans to claim that the creation of a West German state would not threaten national unity since the new state would only be a temporary creation on the road to the re-establishing of a sovereign and united Germany. On 1 September 1948 the Parliamentary Council – not a constitutional assembly – met for the first time to discuss the drafting of a 'basic law' that would take the place of a constitution. Konrad Adenauer became chairman and he used the position to install himself as the eventually most authoritative politician of the future Federal Republic.

The Allies did not get involved in the proceedings of the Parliamentary Council except for an aide-memoire they sent on 22 November to Adenauer as Parliamentary Council chairman to remind him of the basic principles they expected of the new constitution.

Doc 29 Allied aide-mémoire

22 November 1948

As you are well aware, the Parliamentary Council was convened in order to draft a democratic constitution which will establish for the participating states a governmental structure of federal type, will protect the rights of the participating states, provide adequate central authority and contain guarantees of individual rights and freedom. During the last eleven weeks the Parliamentary Council in plenary session as well as in its several committees has freely discussed those principles and drafted a basic law (provisional constitution) which is now before the main committee. In view of the advanced stage now reached in the work of the Parliamentary Council, the Military Governors consider it advisable at this time to give the Council some indication of the interpretation which they will apply to the general principles set out in document number 1, since there are several ways in which democratic federal government can be obtained. They intend to consider the provisions of the basic law (provisional constitution) in their whole context. Nevertheless they believe that the basic law (provisional constitution) should to the maximum extent possible provide:

(i) for a Bicameral legislative system in which one of the houses must represent the individual states and must have sufficient power to safeguard the interests of the states;

(ii) that the executive must only have those powers which are definitely prescribed by the constitution and that emergency powers, if any, of the executive must be so limited as to require prompt legislative or judicial review;

(iii) that the powers of the federal government shall be limited to those expressly enumerated in the constitution and in any case, shall not include Education, Cultural and Religious Affairs, Local Government and Public Health (except in this last case to secure such coordination as is essential to safeguard the health of the people in the several states); that its powers in the field of Public Welfare be limited to those necessary for the coordination of social security measures; that its powers in the Police field be limited to those especially approved by the Military Governors, during the Occupation period;

(iv) that the powers of the federal government in the field of Public Finance shall be limited to the disposal of moneys including the raising of revenue for purposes for which it is responsible; that the federal government may set rates and legislate on the general principles of assessment with regard to other taxes for which uniformity is essential, the collection and utilisation of such taxes being left to the individual states; and that it may appropriate funds only for the purposes for which it is responsible under the constitution;

(v) that the constitution should provide for an independent judiciary to review federal legislation, to review the exercise of federal executive power, to adjudicate conflicts between federal and Land authorities as well as between Land authorities and to protect the civil rights and freedom of the individual;

(vi) that the powers of the federal government to establish federal agencies for the execution and administration of its responsibilities should be clearly defined and should be limited to those fields in which it is clear that state implementation is impracticable;
(vii) that each citizen has access to Public Office with appointment and promotion being based solely on his fitness to discharge the responsibilities of the position and that the civil service should be non-political in character;

(viii) that a public servant, if elected to the federal legislature, shall resign his office with the agency where he is employed before he accepts election.

The Military Governors will be guided by these principles in their final examination of the basic law (provisional constitution) and any subsequent amendments thereto, and they will consider the basic law (provisional constitution) as a whole in order to determine whether or not the broad requirements of the document have been met.

From: US Department of State (ed.), *Documents on Germany 1944–85*.

The Allied insistence on a federal structure with strong regional states was their attempt to prevent the resurgence of an all-powerful central government, and some question of detail on the matter nearly prevented the Allies' acceptance of the Basic Law. The issues could be solved only in last-minute discussions and, after the Military Governors accepted the German draft on 12 May 1949, the Federal Republic of Germany was officially established on 23 May with the enacting of the Basic Law.

Doc 30 Basic Law

23 May 1949

Preamble

The German People in the Länder of Baden, Bavaria, Bremen, Hamburg, Hesse, Lower Saxony, North Rhine Westphalia, Rhineland-Palatinate, Schleswig-Holstein, Württemberg-Baden, and Württemberg-Hohenzollern, Conscious of its responsibility before God and Men, animated by the resolve to preserve its national and political unity and to serve the peace of the World as an equal partner in a united Europe,

Desiring to give a new order to political life for a transitional period, has enacted, by virtue of its constitutional power, this Basic Law of the Federal Republic of Germany.

It has also acted on behalf of those Germans to whom participation was denied. The entire German people is called on to achieve by free self-determination the unity and freedom of Germany.

Article 1

1) The dignity of man is inviolable. To respect and protect it is the duty of all state authority.

2) The German people therefore acknowledge inviolable and inalienable human rights as the basis of every community of peace and of justice in the world.

3) The following basic rights bind the legislature, the executive and the judiciary as directly enforceable law.

Article 2

1) Everyone has the right to the free development of his personality insofar as he does not violate the rights of others or offend against the constitutional order or the moral code.

2) Everyone has the right to life and to inviolability of his person. The freedom of the individual is inviolable. These rights may only be encroached upon pursuant to law.

Article 4

1) Freedom of Faith and of conscience, and freedom of creed, religious or ideological, are inviolable.

2) The undisturbed practice of religion is guaranteed.

Article 5

1) Everyone has the right freely to express and to disseminate his opinion by speech, writing and pictures and freely to inform himself from generally accessible sources. Freedom of the press and freedom of reporting by radio and motion pictures are guaranteed. There shall be no censorship.

2) These rights are limited by the provisions of the general laws, the provisions of law for the protection of youth and by the right to inviolability of personal honour.

3) Art and science, research and teaching are free. Freedom of teaching does not absolve from loyalty to the constitution.

Article 6

1) Marriage and family enjoy the special protections of the state.

2) Care and upbringing of children are the natural right of the parents and a duty primarily incumbent on them. The state watches over the performance of this duty ...

Article 7

1) The entire educational system is under the supervision of the state.

2) The persons entitled to bring up a child have the right to decide whether it shall receive religious instruction ...

Article 8

1) All Germans have the right to assemble peacefully and unarmed without prior notification or permission.

2) With regard to open-air meetings this right may be restricted by or pursuant to a law.

Article 9

1) All Germans have the right to form associations and societies.

2) Associations, the objects or activities of which conflict with the criminal laws or which are directed against the constitutional order or the concept of international understanding, are prohibited.

3) The right to form associations to safeguard and improve working and economic conditions is guaranteed to everyone and to all trades and professions. Agreements which restrict or seek to hinder this right are null and void; measures directed to this end are illegal.

Article 14

1) Property and the rights of inheritance are guaranteed. Their content and limits are determined by the laws.

2) Property imposes duties. Its use should also serve the public weal.

3) Expropriation is permitted only in the public weal ... In case of dispute regarding the amount of compensation, recourse may be had to the ordinary courts.

Article 15

Land, natural resources and means of production may for the purpose of socialization be transferred into public ownership or other forms of publicly controlled economy by a law which provides for kind and extent of the compensation. With respect to such compensation Article 14, paragraph 3, ... apply *mutatis mutandis.*

Article 18
Whoever abuses freedom of expression of opinion, in particular freedom of the press (Article 5, paragraph 1), freedom of teaching (Article 5, paragraph 3), freedom of assembly (Article 8), freedom of association (Article 9), the secrecy of mail, posts and telecommunications (Article 10), property (Article 14), or the right of asylum (Article 16, paragraph 2) in order to attack the free democratic basic order, forfeits these basic rights. The forfeiture and its extent are pronounced by the Federal Constitutional Court.

Article 20
1) The Federal Republic of Germany is a democratic and social federal state.
2) All state authority emanates from the people. It is exercised by the people by means of elections and voting and by separate legislative, executive, and judicial organs.
3) Legislation is subject to the constitutional order; the executive and the judiciary are bound by the law.

Article 21
1) The political parties participate in the forming of the political will of the people. They may be freely formed. Their internal organization must conform to democratic principles. They must publicly account for the sources of their funds.
2) Parties which, by reason of their aims or the behaviour of their adherents seek to impair or destroy the free democratic basic order or to endanger the existence of the Federal Republic of Germany are unconstitutional. The Federal Constitutional Court decides on the question of unconstitutionality.

Article 31
Federal law overrides *Land* law.

Article 39
1) The Bundestag is elected for a four-year term. Its legislative term ends four years after its first meeting or on its dissolution. The new election takes place during the last three months of the term or within sixty days after dissolution.
2) The Bundestag assembles within thirty days after the election, but not before the end of the term of the previous Bundestag ...

Article 54

1) The Federal President is elected, without debate, by the Federal Convention. Every German is eligible who is entitled to vote for the Bundestag and who has attained the age of forty.

2) The term of office of the Federal President is five years. Re-election for a consecutive term is permitted only once.

3) The Federal Convention consists of the members of the Bundestag and an equal number of members elected by the representative assemblies of the *Länder* according to the rules of proportional representation.

Article 59

1) The Federal President represents the Federation in its international relations. He concludes treaties with foreign states on behalf of the Federation. He accredits and receives envoys.

Article 62

The Federal Government consists of the Federal Chancellor and the Federal Ministers.

Article 63

1) The Federal Chancellor is elected, without debate, by the Bundestag on the proposal of the Federal President.

2) The person obtaining the votes of the majority of the members of the Bundestag is elected. The person elected must be appointed by the Federal President.

3) If the person proposed is not elected, the Bundestag may elect within fourteen days of the ballot a Federal Chancellor by more than one half of its members.

4) If there is no election within this period, a new ballot shall take place without delay, in which the person obtaining the largest number of votes is elected. If the person elected obtained the votes of the majority of the members of the Bundestag, the Federal President must appoint him within seven days of the election. If the person elected did not receive this majority, the Federal President must within seven days either appoint him or dissolve the Bundestag.

Article 65

The Federal Chancellor determines, and is responsible for, general policy. Within the limits of this general policy, each Federal Minister conducts the business of his department autonomously and on his own responsibility. The Federal Government decides on differences of opinion between the Federal Ministers. The Federal Chancellor conducts the business of the Federal Government in accordance with rules of procedure adopted by it and approved by the Federal President.

Article 67

1) The Bundestag can express its lack of confidence in the Federal Chancellor only by electing a successor by the majority of its members and by requesting the Federal President to dismiss the Federal Chancellor. The Federal President must comply with the request and appoint the person elected.

Article 68

1) If a motion of the Federal Chancellor for a vote of confidence is not assented to by the majority of the members of the Bundestag, the Federal President may, upon the proposal of the Federal Chancellor, dissolve the Bundestag within twenty-one days. The right to dissolve lapses as soon as the Bundestag, by the majority of its members, elects another Federal Chancellor.

Article 116

1) Unless otherwise provided by law, a German within the meaning of this Basic Law is a person who possesses German citizenship or who has been admitted to the territory of the German *Reich*, as it existed on December 31, 1937, as a refugee or expellee of German stock or as the spouse or descendant of such person.
2) Former German citizens who, between January 30, 1933 and May 8, 1945, were deprived of their citizenship for political, racial or religious reasons, and their descendants, shall be re-granted German citizenship on application. They are considered as not having been deprived of their German citizenship if they have established their domicile in Germany after May 8, 1945 and have not expressed a contrary intention.

Article 131

Federal legislation shall regulate the legal status of persons, including refugees and expellees, who, on May 8, 1945, were employed in the public service, have left the service for reasons other than those arising from civil service regulations or collective agreement rules, and have not until now been employed or are employed in a position not corre-sponding to their former one. The same applies *mutatis mutandis* to persons, including refugees and expellees, who, on May 8, 1945, were entitled to a pension or other assistance and who no longer receive any assistance for reasons other than those arising from civil service regula-tions or collective agreement rules ...

Article 146

This Basic Law shall cease to be in force on the day on which a constitu-tion adopted by a free decision of the German people comes into force.

Bonn/Rhine, May 23, 1949.

Reprinted in: *The German Question: A Documentary.*

The Basic Law enshrined basic human rights, guaranteed the demo-cratic order against political extremists and laid out the principles of the division of power within the polity. It became one of the great successes of the post-war German state, even to the degree that Germans were described once as 'constitutional patriots'.

Part II
'The Allies' Federal Chancellor', 1949–55

After the Cold War-driven events up to 1948, the period 1949–55 saw the logical conclusion of these developments. For West Germany, the two most significant events in this process were the establishment of the Federal Republic of Germany (FRG) in 1949 and its eventual integration into NATO in 1955. The latter completed the advance of a state that had started out with very limited sovereignty to become an (almost) equal member of the Western camp. The years 1948/49 were also the period in which some of the Federal Republic's lasting myths were born. For example, even very few contemporaries today remember that the immediate effect of the currency reform was increased hardship for many ordinary people; a hardship that was even more difficult to bear in the face of shop windows that were full once more. The social, economic and political challenges the FRG was confronted with right from its 'conception' in 1948/9 up to its eventual sovereignty in 1955 were staggering. However, in retrospect it is fair to say that through Cold War developments the odds were staged in West Germany's favour. In contrast to practice in his later years, Adenauer conducted his foreign policy – especially vis-à-vis the Allies – in a pragmatic and sometimes cunning way, very often against strong domestic opposition. It is during these years that his reputation changed from being 'the Allies' Chancellor' to being the 'greatest German' of modern times, according to a TV poll conducted in 2003. During the process of rehabilitating Germany and integrating it into the Western community, as well as in the early stages of European integration, Adenauer skilfully and successfully used the Cold War situation to gain more leeway in his negotiations with the Western powers, and this found its climax in the FRG's rearmament and NATO membership in 1955.

71

3

Founding myth and 'economic miracle'

As Werner Abelshauser has pointed out, the Federal Republic lacks a political 'founding myth' that most other countries have. France has the Great Revolution of 1789, the USA has the War of Independence and Great Britain has a whole selection of events, from the Magna Carta to the Glorious Revolution, events that all stand significantly in the national memory. Since the Federal Republic was to a large extent an Allied creation and seen by many Germans only as a temporary arrangement prior to the country's eventual re-unification, no such political myth could emerge. For example, few people in Germany today know the date the country's constitution, the Basic Law, was enacted, although West Germans were once described as '*Verfassungspatrioten*' or 'constitutional patriots'. This lack of a political myth, so Abelshauser argues, has been compensated for by the creation of an economic myth. The currency reform, the Marshall Plan and eventually the 'economic miracle' initiated by the bizonal Director for Economics and later Federal Minister for Economics and in 1963 Adenauer's successor as Federal Chancellor, Ludwig Erhard, take the top three places among these myths. In particular, the currency reform of 20 June 1948 has not only achieved but also retained its mythological status in post-war German history more than any other event. What is usually forgotten about the currency reform is the fact that it was an American operation, and that it has to be seen at least as much in the context of the Marshall Plan as in a purely German context. Without a German currency reform a German economic recovery was doubtful, but without German economic revival the recovery of Europe, which was the overall aim of the Marshall Plan, would most likely have failed, as well.

Among the myths it is the status and significance of the Marshall Plan which is less clear-cut. It was only in the late 1970s that the orthodox view of the Marshall Plan's economic significance was challenged for the first time, causing a debate about what impact the Plan had on West German reconstruction which lasted more than ten years. Today it is generally accepted that the European Recovery Programme (the Plan's official name), was not as crucial to German recovery as initially thought. In West Germany, long-term investment for the reconstruction could have been raised in different ways. The Marshall Plan's prime benefit therefore was the narrowing of the dollar gap that had plagued the reconstruction in Europe as a whole, and which had severely restricted the importation of raw materials.

The 'economic miracle' and with it the 'social market economy' are the most memorable – and mainly misinterpreted – features of the Adenauer era. The phrase 'economic miracle' had already been used twice before in German history. It first emerged in the second half of the 1920s when Germany recovered from the political turmoil and the 1923 hyperinflation and experienced a brief economic boom before the Wall Street crash. The term was then used again in the 1930s when the Nazis eliminated mass unemployment. In contrast to those in the 1920s and 1930s the economic recovery in the 1950s was longer-lasting and did not threaten state bankruptcy as the Nazi boom did. Considering the widespread devastation of Germany after the war, the economic recovery – and with it the spread of mass consumption – must have indeed appeared as a miracle to most contemporaries. But far from being caused by divine intervention, as the word 'miracle' would imply, the process can be attributed to far more worldly causes. One of those was identified by contemporaries as the German work ethic. Although working hours of 48 and more per week combined with modest wage claims did help the recovery, the emphasis on hard work has long since been seen as a German attempt to distract from the Nazi past. The argument goes that by becoming the role model of hard work, the Germans wanted to demonstrate to the world (and themselves) that decent people like themselves could not have been involved in Nazi atrocities.

The 'social market economy', finally, is the most misunderstood aspect of the myths. The label was created by economics professor and later State Secretary of Economics, Alfred Müller-Armarck. The success of the label derived most certainly from the impression it created, i.e. the successful combination of a 'social' economy, that took care of the citizens' welfare (as some aspects of the Weimar economy had done), with a (free) market economy, ruled by nothing but market forces – thus implying something of a 'third way' between pure capitalism and socialism. The reality was quite different from the phrase and expectation. Ludwig Erhard himself did not believe in state welfare: actually he was what is now called a neo-liberal, fighting against the expansion of the welfare state at every turn. On the other end of the label, – 'market economy' – things were not what they should have been either. There was widespread state intervention, due partly to the legacy of the war, partly to German economic policy tradition; and many industrialists preferred a system of cartels that controlled their economic sector. The 'social market economy' was at worst neither 'social' nor 'market', or, at best, a bastardisation of both its elements. Seen more positively, the 'social market economy' can be regarded as the twentieth-century high point of 'Rhineland Capitalism', when from the mid- to late 1950s onwards the booming economy allowed the state to be more generous with all sorts of benefits.

A different explanation to describe the West German economic model is given once again by Abelshauser who speaks of a 'corporate economy' in which the state, industrial associations and trade unions worked closely together to the mutual benefit.

Part of the FRG's political fiction is that the SPD was the working-class party stuck to socialist dogma; that the Liberal Party, the FDP, was the party of economic liberalism and traditional nationalism; and that the CDU was the business-friendly, conservative party. In the case of the SPD and the FDP, the statements are oversimplifications. In the case of the CDU's early years, the image is plainly wrong. The party had been founded regionally, first in late June 1945 in Berlin and then in other areas; and it was strongly influenced by Christian-socialist ideas. The strength and dominance of these ideas manifested itself in the party's first official programme, the so-called Ahlen Programme of February 1947. It was an attempt to find a third way between the pure forms of socialism and capitalism by denouncing both socialist class dogma and unlimited capitalism, where it went so far as to suggest public ownership of certain industries.

Doc 31 Ahlen Programme

The capitalist system has not fulfilled the expectation in the national and social interests of the German people. Following the terrible political, economic and social collapse caused by criminal power politics, a fundamental reorganisation is the only way forward.

The subject and aim of this social and economic reorganisation can no longer be the capitalist strive for profit and power, but only the welfare of our people. By a common order the German people shall receive an economic and social constitution that fulfils the right and dignity of men, that serves the spiritual and material reconstruction of our people and that secures the inner and outer peace ...

The economy has to serve the development of the creative powers of the nation, of men and of the community. Starting point of the economy has to be the acknowledgement of personality. The freedom of the individual in economic matters and freedom of the individual in political matters are closely linked. The structuring and leadership of the economy shall not take away the personal freedom of the individual. Therefore the following measures are necessary:

The strengthening of the individual's economic position and freedom, the prevention of the accumulation of economic power in the hands of individual persons, companies, private or public organisations which could threaten the economic or political freedom. Coal is the crucial product of Germany's national economy. We demand the socialisation of the coal mines ...

The new structure of the German economy has to assume that the time of the unlimited rule of private capitalism is over. But one should also avoid a situation where private capitalism is replaced by state capitalism, as this would be even more dangerous for the political and economic freedom of the individual. A new economic structure has to be found which avoids the shortcomings of the past and which allows the possibility of technical progress and the creative initiative of the individual.

1. Large companies [*Konzerne*] and similar economic organisations which are not entirely necessary for technical, social or economic reasons are to be split up [*entflochten*] and transformed into separate companies. Technical development demands a certain minimal size from certain enterprises, especially in order to maintain competitiveness abroad. This minimum size has to be granted to those companies.

2. Companies with a monopolistic character, companies which have to be larger than a certain size create economic and thus political power which can threaten the freedom within the state. This danger has to be

prevented by passing relevant cartel laws. Furthermore, the principle of division of power is to be introduced in these companies so that any domination of essential economic sectors by the state, private individuals or groups which would be detrimental for the common good can be prevented.

a) For this reason public bodies, such as central government, regional government [*Staat, Land*], municipalities and municipal associations, as well as co-operatives and the employees working there, take a share in those companies; the essentially required entrepreneurial initiative is to be given the necessary space.

b) In addition, private share ownership of those companies, which is centralised in one hand, either in ownership or voting rights, shall be limited by law.

3) Mining. Coal mines have a monopolistic character simply because of the basic product [*Urprodukt*] they produce and which is vital for the whole nation. Therefore the application of the principles named in II/2 is urgent, thus they are to be socialised. If, in special cases, the form of state ownership appears to be advisable, then the aforementioned basic principles shall not prevent this.

...

Trans. from: Konrad-Adenauer-Stiftung www.KAS.de/wf/de/33.813.

It was only during 1948/49 that the political outlook of the CDU began to change when it began attracting more politically conservative elements and influential members of the business community. More important for the future economic course of West Germany, however, was the appointment of Ludwig Erhard as Director for Economics in the Executive Committee (the *Verwaltung des Vereinigten Wirtschaftsgebietes*), the Bizonal Economic Council's equivalent to a Cabinet. During Erhard's time in office the Americans carried out 'Operation Bird Dog' – the currency reform in the three Western zones. The planning for the replacement of the old Reichsmark with the new Deutsch Mark was a solely American affair, with no German input other than the physical exchange of bank notes, which was carried out by German personnel. However, it was Erhard who the following day, and against American intentions, passed the '*Leitsätzegesetz*' that abolished all rationing. The ordinance also lifted price controls for all goods except basic foodstuffs, fuel, rent and basic materials. It was this measure that helped to stimulate economic activity. Although he was not yet a party member, by 1949 the CDU had convinced Erhard to stand for them as a candidate in the first election to the national parliament, the Bundestag. The slogan of the 'social market economy' that was associated with him would be the base of the CDU's economic policy programme for the election. For that purpose, on 15 July 1949 the Ahlen Programme was replaced by the Düsseldorf Principles. The promise of a better economic future would be the key for the CDU's electoral success in the years to come.

Doc 32 'Düsseldorf Principles'

After the war, the economic and social life of the German people moved ever more towards total dissolution. The 20 June 1948 brought the turn-around. The currency reform on its own did not achieve this. It only created the technical requirement. The essential impulse, however, derived from the free market [*marktwirtschaftliche*] principles coming into effect. On 20 June 1948 these free-market principles came to form the basis of Germany's economic policy through the 'social market economy' advocated by the CDU/CSU.

What does the CDU/CSU Mean by Social Market Economy?
The 'social market economy' is the socially controlled constitution of industry [*gewerbliche Wirtschaft*] in which the work of free and efficient people is brought into a kind of order which provides maximum economic benefit and social justice for all. This order is created by freedom and control [*Freiheit und Bindung*] which is expressed within the 'social market economy' by real competition and independent monopoly control. Real competition exists when a competitive order guarantees that under equal opportunities and fair competitive conditions without interference [*Wettkampfbedingungen in freier Konkurrenz*], the best performance will be rewarded. The co-operation of all participants is controlled by prices geared to market requirements [*marktgerecht*]. 'Social market economy' stands in sharp contrast to a system of planned economy, which we reject regardless of whether the planning bodies are organised at the centre, decentralised, state run or self-administered.

However, the 'social market economy' is also in contrast to a 'free economy' of liberalist character. To avoid a relapse into the 'free economy' it is necessary to secure competition by controlling monopolies. For in the same way that the state or semi-public bodies should have no directing influence on the economy or individual markets, so the capacity of private individuals and private organisations to exert such an influence should also be limited.

The 'social market economy' does without planning and directing production, labour and sales. However, it approves the planned influencing of the economy with the organic means of a comprehensive economic policy based on an elastic adaptation on the observation of the markets. This economic policy leads in a sensible combination of monetary, credit, trade, tariff, tax, investment and social policy as well as other measures towards the economy fulfilling its ultimate aim of serving the welfare and satisfaction of the nation's needs. This satisfying of needs [*Bedarfsdeckung*] includes of course an adequate supply of that part of the population that suffers hardship.

The basic principles of the Ahlen Programme which are mainly concerned with right of property and socio-political [*gesellschaftspolitisch*] issues are acknowledged but expanded and developed further towards a market economy.

To realize the social market economy we draw up the following basic principles [*Leitsätze*]:

1. Competition has to be secured by law. Monopolies and representatives of market forces are to be subjected under an institutionally established, independent monopoly control which is responsible only to the law.

2. We strive towards legal measures to deepen a real responsibility in the economy.

3. Legal measures to increase publicity have to be introduced especially with joint stock companies.

4. A centrally organised body with authority over monetary affairs is necessary for the protection of the currency.

5. Market conform prices have to be created which shall not be fudged by state or private arbitrariness or dictate. Such interventions push the goods off the market. However, we welcome the organic influence of prices by means of economic policy, especially monetary, credit and fiscal policy so that when prices are falling goods are increasingly pushed onto the market.

6. In the interest of German competitiveness on the world market we aim for a lowering of German prices. This will also lead to a rise in real incomes.

7. The setting of wage levels and working conditions has to be left to the collective bargaining system. Piece rates and wage increase within the framework of proper market prices are to be welcomed. They increase purchasing power and demand as it is done through the lowering of prices.

8. Technology and science are to be emphatically promoted. They create new desires and employment opportunities [*Arbeitsmöglichkeiten*]. They lower production costs.

9. The 'social market economy' includes the free choice of profession, free setting up of business, freedom of trade and freedom of movement [*freie Berusfwahl, Niederlassungsfreiheit, Gewerbefreiheit und Freizügigkeit*]. In the trades the certificate of qualification (*Meisterprüfung*) will still be required. The same is true for all professions the practice of which, for good reasons, demands a certificate of qualification.

10. The 'social market economy' endorses and encourages private property ownership. A just distribution of economic proceeds and a social legislation has to turn those within society without property into property owners. Alongside the largest possible dispersal of property, in the industrial sector we do approve company forms in public ownership, provided that these companies are economically useful, fit into the production process [*betriebstechnisch möglich*] or are politically necessary.

11. We want to actively support the creation of savings capital.

12. We demand a wide-ranging reform of the tax system, in particular the reduction of current tax rates on all levels as well as the simplification of the whole tax system.

13. Effective safeguards against economic crisis and mass unemployment have to be created. Such means are for example a constructive credit and currency policy as well as an investment policy by the government.

14. We want to support foreign trade by all means possible. We approve the Marshall Plan (ERP).

15. A German merchant navy has to be recreated.

16. The 'social market economy' can only be created if it has the trust of all sections of society, i.e. when entrepreneurs, workers, white-collar staff and consumers become actively involved in its implementation.

...

Trans. from: Konrad-Adenauer-Stiftung www.KAS.de/wf/de/33.814.

On 1 March 1948 the Americans had set up the *Bank deutscher Länder* as the new central bank for the Bizone. This was a clear sign beyond rumours that a currency reform was on the cards. By late spring of 1948 the West Germans were anticipating the reform and companies began to change their business attitudes. The pending reform mean that money would regain its value; thus for businesses it made sense to hold back at least some of their goods and products, rather than bartering them or selling them for Reichsmark which would soon become worthless. If companies unofficially began build up stocks before the reform, these could later be sold off for the 'new' money. Economics Director Erhard even encouraged the hording of goods for exactly that purpose, which had an obvious negative effect on the supply for the population and appeals had to be made by the authorities to guarantee basic supplies.

Doc 33 Currency reform in Bochum

To the People of Bochum

According to all announcements, monetary reform will be implemented soon. What matters now is that during these last days the orderly conduct of economic life in the vital sectors will be upheld. *Our urgent exhortation to industry, especially to the producers, the wholesalers and retailers is that they guarantee the vital supply of the population through the normal sale of the goods in stock.* This will be controlled by the increased deployment of food-control committees and price-control authorities. In cases of sharp violation of this warning the Food and Economic Office will hand out harsh punishments in accordance to the measures announced.

We also urgently warn consumers to only purchase the vital supplies for the next couple of days. Any attempt to create advantages through stocking up on goods will be regarded as damage to the common good and will be prohibited. When all parts of the population keep their common sense and stay calm we will successfully get through these last days before the currency reform. There is no need to worry about the food supply.

Bochum, 15 June 1948

The City Council	German Trade Union Association
SPD Group [Fraktion]	Chamber of Industry and
CDU Group	Commerce
KPD Group	Retail / District Trade Association
The Lord Mayor	Consumers Co-operative Bochum
The Town Clerk	

Trans. from source reprinted in: Kleßmann, *Das Gespaltene Land.*

The more or less clandestine holding back of output prior to the reform had a twofold effect on the production statistics. Before the reform a dip appeared in the output figures; after the reform output seemed to accelerate even faster since the hoarded goods appeared again, seemingly boosting the official production figures. Abelshauser ironically described this process with the sentence

'After the currency reform, even the cows gave more milk'; indicating that with the arrival of the new money farmers had an incentive to sell their produce on the official market and no longer on the black market. To the consumers' amazement, on the day after the currency reform, shop displays were again full of all sorts of goods that had not been available for years. An exceptionally good harvest in 1948, as well as American food supplies under the army's Government Appropriations and Relief in Occupied Areas (GARIOA) programme – and of course, the Marshall Plan – helped to stabilise the food situation. For the first time since 1944, people were no longer threatened by starvation. However, despite the improvements and because the *Leitsätzegesetz* did not abolish fixed prices for basic foodstuffs, the black market continued to exist for some goods. Even under the 'social market economy' some illegal trading remained considerably more profitable than officially permitted trade.

Doc 34 Black Market Prices before and after the Currency Reform and Official Prices

Commodity	Quantity	Dec 1947 RM	Dec 1948 DM	Official Retail Price, Dec '48
Butter	500g	200	16	2.56
Lard	500g	180	18	1.68
Bacon	500g	170	16–18	n/a
Meat	500g	40	6–10	1.5 (beef)
Flour	500g	40	1.3–1.5	0.32
Sugar	500g	60	2.6	n/a
Oil	1 ltr.	200	18–20	n/a
Schnaps	1 ltr.	120–180	10–12	n/a
Tobacco	50g	25–30	1.8–3	n/a
Cigarettes (US)	1	7	0.7	n/a
Cigarettes (German)	1	3	0.2–0.3	n/a
Cigarettes (British)	1	6	0.7	n/a

Trans. from sources in: Annette Kuhn (ed.), *Frauen in der Deutschen Nachkriegszeit*.

In one respect the comparison between black market prices before and after the currency reform were somewhat misleading. By converting 100 Reichsmark into less than10 Deutsch Marks the currency reform had reduced the supply of money by about 90 per cent. But for the scarcest products – especially fats – prices remained considerably above the official fixed price. After the currency reform, a profit-inflation appeared for goods with non-fixed prices since traders now could cash in on the pent-up consumer demands. What is largely forgotten in the German collective memory of the post-currency period is the fact that not everybody benefited from the reform and experienced an instant economic miracle. Although no longer threatened by starvation because of meagre rations, most ordinary people now had to count every *Pfennig* to get on day by day, as an article in a trade union paper in late 1948 shows.

Doc 35 Frau Schäfer goes shopping

Frau Schäfer has been a housewife for 15 years. You can see it from her worn hands and her worried face. Her husband is a worker at Conti. They have two children, Liselotte and Heinz. They live in living-room, bedroom and kitchen – somewhere in a grey tenement block.

If you have been a housewife for 15 years you have had all kinds of worries. Frau Schäfer keeps her tiny flat in good order, the kids are out of the woods now but the worries – they never end.

'Never before has it been so difficult to feed the family, especially now after the currency reform', says Frau Schäfer. She puts the shopping bag on the kitchen table. She has brought potatoes, onions and a large Savoy cabbage. Nothing of the other pretty things one can see in the grocer shops: white firm cauliflower, long green cucumbers, dark juicy cherries, mushrooms which still give off the aroma of the forest. None of these are in her shopping net. Those things are not for her. Even the onions are too expensive: this bundle of 15 cost 85 Pfennigs! The Savoy cabbage cost 90 Pfennigs. If you think about it she couldn't afford the delicious new potatoes. But Herr Schäfer has to eat something after spending eight hours in the factory. Something has to be there when the kids come home from school. Once, when the Schäfers were just married, Herr Schäfer had said: 'Hilde, you stood behind a shop counter since you left school. Now you shouldn't have to work any more! We are plain people but it would be ridiculous if I couldn't earn what we need. You will take care that we have a comfortable, cosy [*gemütlich*] home.' Herr Schäfer has kept his word. But now she wonders if she should secretly take a job as a charwoman.

The kids need shoes. The beds need new cambric duvet cover and sheets. Frau Schäfer would love to buy some new plates and a few bits and pieces for the household. They haven't been able to buy anything new for such a long time. Sometimes she dreams of new stockings, of a new light summer dress. She isn't that old yet … and there are such pretty things.

But the biggest worry is how they are going to get the potatoes for the winter? The price for coal is said to have risen. Hopefully that is not true. If one adds up what Herr Schäfer is paid out at Conti on the four Fridays of each month then the family has 160 marks at their disposal. The rent is 32 marks. Then there is the gas bill and electricity has to be paid and there are other regular payments to be made. Frau Schäfer keeps a household book. If they are to get by she must have 33 marks for a ten-day period. Every day they need a loaf of bread. Herr Schäfer takes six slices to work. The children have a hearty appetite as well, there is nothing else for them. 'Bread is the main thing with us and a loaf costs 60 Pfennigs. That is far too expensive. And look here, a litre of skimmed milk costs 24 Pfennigs! Has that ever happened before?'

Trans. from source reprinted in Kleßmann, *Das Gespaltene Land.*

As a matter of fact, Erhard nearly lost his job over his reforms. Because he had freed most of the prices but kept wages fixed, in November 1948 the trade unions called for a 24-hour general strike. It was observed by more than ten million people, who protested not only against price rises and profiteering but also, implicitly, against Erhard's economic policy. He had to face two votes of no confidence in the Economic Council and only narrowly survived the second one. During 1949, the profit inflation eventually eased and then turned into a deflation which caused serious concern, in particular among the American Marshall Plan experts who saw the success of the whole programme in Germany under threat.

One group that benefited from the currency reform, or more precisely from the accompanying DM *Eröffnugsbilanz Gesetz,* were businesses. The *Eröffnugsbilanz Gesetz,* the Law on DM Opening Balances, allowed companies to revalue their assets – i.e., old machinery and equipment could be put on the books as if they were brand new. This enabled the companies to claim considerable annual depreciations which they could write off against tax claims. The supervisory board of *Vereinigte Glanzstoff Fabriken,* the country's biggest producer of artificial fibres, discussed the law for years in their annual meeting.

Doc 36 Effect of the 'Opening Balance' law

'... Herr Abs and Herr Merton pointed out that the company had to be in a position to earn the depreciation which is required with the new balance sheet, as well as a moderate dividend.

(CEO) Herr Dr Vits explained that the increased DM balance sheet estimates would allow the company increased depreciations for nearly five years. From the qualifying date for the DM opening balance sheet (*DM Eröffnungsbilanz*) to the present day, i.e. a period of two years, the necessary results have been achieved ....'

Trans. from: RWWA 195/B/5/1/15, Meeting of the Supervisory Board, 18.7.1950.

While the Law on the Opening of DM Balance Sheet was necessary to kick-start the economy, its immediate beneficiaries were holders of non-monetary assets. Individuals who only had monetary assets, i.e. bank savings, faced a nominal loss of more than 90 per cent of their possessions. Nothing could be further from the truth than the mythical claim 'On the day of the currency reform, we all started out with only DM 40'.

Immediately after US Secretary of State George C. Marshal had outlined the European Recovery Programme, hope in Europe and in Germany had been unrealistically high and these high hopes would soon be frustrated. For one, the USA was not prepared to throw money into the seemingly bottomless pit of European reconstruction, in particular in view of European hopes of tens of billions dollars of US aid. The US Congress insisted that every participating country had to sign a bilateral treaty with the USA in which clear conditions for the aid were given. In 1948, the three Military Governors had signed those treaties on behalf of their respective occupation zones, but with the establishment of the Federal Republic it was necessary that a redrafted treaty be signed by West Germany. One of the first crucial tasks the Adenauer government faced in late 1949 was to sign this new American treaty. However, in contrast to what one might expect, the reactions towards such a treaty were far from enthusiastic and Cabinet agreement was not at all certain. The usually dull Cabinet minutes give a glimpse of how much persuasion was necessary to get the treaty agreed.

Doc 37 Cabinet meeting on Bilateral Agreement

The Federal Minister for the Marshall Plan explains the treaty in detail. In particular he points out its main problems and the main differences in regard to the treaties of the other participating countries. For example, in the Federal Republic's treaty, the question of counterclaims had been dealt with separately. To the United States it is very important that the counterclaims [*Gegenforderungen*] be expressly determined, since the existence of such claims meant a certain protection for the Federal Republic against demands by other creditors from older debts. After heavy and tough negotiations, the German participants had to accept the claims under this aspect since the German side could not close their eyes to the fact that counterclaims would arise out of the substantial deliveries which had already occurred.

Then the Federal Minister for the Marshall Plan explains the significance of article 7 which deals with the Berlin question in detail. Looked at in its entirety, the treaty signified a success and would bring the Federal Republic the maximum of what had been achievable.

Agreeing with the opinion of the Federal Minister for the Marshall Plan, the Federal Minister for Finance welcomed the result of the negotiations. He pointed out that the conclusion of the treaty would finally mean the release of ERP funds and that rejection of the treaty was out of the question. If the treaty failed, the long-awaited funds to combat unemployment and to reconstruct the economy would be lost. To cover the debited accounts some DM 700 million are needed. This sum would be raised by loans, using the grain reserves as collateral; by demanding the payment of the subsidies from the regional states [*Länder*]; and by taking up a new loan of some DM 250–300 million.

The Federal Minister for Transport declared that he had received the papers only 24 hours ago and that it was therefore impossible for him to give a final declaration of support for the treaty.

The Federal Chancellor and the Ministers for the Marshall Plan and Finance asked expressly for consent since, after the arduous and lengthy negotiations, changes of any kind would not be possible. It was all about achieving the release of the counterpart funds and to prevent a disruption of the grain supply. It was inconceivable to get more out of the treaty.

The Cabinet agreed to the submitted treaty.

… The signing of the treaty needed constitutional ratification.

Trans. from: *Kabinettsprotokolle der Bundesregierung*, vol 1, 1949).

The Economic Co-operation Agreement, as the treaty was officially called, gave the USA considerable leverage and means to intervene indirectly in the West German economy and the reconstruction process through the allocation of the so-called counterpart funds. (This was one of the reasons why the USSR had declined to participate in the Marshall Plan in the first place.) Furthermore, the treaty told the Germans what kind of economic policy they had to conduct and, at a time when the future prosperity was not even a distant dream, made direct American demands to the German treasury. Finally, in contrast to any other country participating in the Marshall Plan, the Americans had inserted a paragraph stating that any assistance given to Germany constituted an US claim against the Federal Republic.

Doc 38 Economic Cooperation Agreement between the United States of America and the Federal Republic of Germany

Article 1
1) The Government of the United States of America undertakes to assist the Federal Republic of Germany by making available to the Government of the Federal Republic or to person, agency or organisation designated by the latter Government aid under the terms and conditions and termination provisions of the Economic Cooperation Act of 1948 ... Such aid will be provided upon the approval by the Government of the United States of America of requests made by the Government of the Federal Republic of Germany .... The Government of the United States of America undertakes further to extend assistance to the Federal Republic under applicable provisions of the Appropriation Act for Government in Occupied Areas.
2) The Government of the Federal Republic of Germany ... will exert sustained efforts ... speedily to achieve through a joint recovery programme economic conditions in Europe essential to lasting peace and prosperity and ... to become independent of extraordinary outside economic assistance within the period of this agreement ...
3) All assistance ... to the Federal Republic of Germany pursuant to this agreement shall constitute a claim against Germany ...

Article 2
1) ... The Government of the Federal Republic of Germany will use its best endeavours:
c) to stabilise its currency, establish and maintain a valid rate of

exchange, balance its governmental budget as soon as practicable, create or maintain internal financial stability and generally restore or maintain confidence in its monetary system.

3) The Government of the Federal Republic of Germany will take appropriate measures ... to prevent ... business practices or business arrangements ... which restrain competition, limit access to markets or foster monopolistic control ...

Article 4

2) The Government of the Federal Republic of Germany will establish a special account (hereafter called the ERP Special Account) in the Bank deutscher Länder in the name of the Government of the Federal Republic and will make deposits in Deutsche Mark to this account as follows:

d) Amounts in Deutsche Mark commensurate with the indicated dollar cost to the Government of the United States of America on commodities, services and technical information ... made available after the effective date of this agreement, to the Federal Republic of Germany in the form of assistance under the Economic Cooperation Act of 1948 ...

4) Five per cent of each deposit made pursuant to this article shall be allocated to the use of the Government of the United States of America for its expenditure in the Federal Republic of Germany ...

6) The Government of the Federal Republic of Germany may draw upon any remaining balances in the ERP Special Account for such purposes as may be arranged from time to time with the Government of the United States of America ...

Article 5

2) The Government of the Federal Republic of Germany will establish a special account (hereafter called the GARIOA Special Account) in the Bank deutscher Länder in the name of the Government of the Federal Republic and will make deposits in the account as follows: ...

Article 6

1) The Government of the Federal Republic of Germany will facilitate the transfer to the United States of America ... of materials originating in the Federal Republic which are required by the United States as a result of deficiencies or potential deficiencies in its own resources ... and in such quantities and for such period of time as may be agreed between the Governments of the United States of America and the Federal Republic, after due regard for the reasonable requirements of the Federal Republic .... The Government of the Federal Republic will take such specific measures as may be necessary to carry out the provisions of this paragraph, including the promotion of increased production of such

materials within the Federal Republic .... The Government of the Federal Republic will, when so requested by the Government of the United States of America, enter into negotiations for detailed arrangements necessary to carry out the provisions of this paragraph ...

Article 7
The Federal Republic agrees to make available to the US, UK and French sectors of Berlin, to the maximum extend possible, such assistance as may, in consultation between the Governments of the Federal Republic and the City of Berlin, be determined to be required for the economic maintenance of that area.

Article 10
1) The Government of the United States of America and the Federal Republic of Germany recognise that it is in their mutual interest that full publicity be given to the objectives and progress of the joint programme for European recovery and of the actions taken in furtherance of that programme. It is recognised that wide dissemination of information on the progress of the programme is desirable ...
4) The Government of the Federal Republic of Germany will make public in the Federal Republic in each calendar quarter full statements of operations under this agreement, including information as to the use of funds, commodities and services received.

Trans. from: *Bundesgesetzblatt 1950* (I).

Today perhaps more than ever, the workings of the Marshall Plan is little understood. The Americans did not give money to the European countries to their free disposal. Europe received American goods and services. As Alan Milward has pointed out, more than 40 per cent of all ERP deliveries to Germany were made up of foodstuffs, with only a slightly smaller share comprising raw-material deliveries. This aid was not given without charge to German companies or wholesalers. They had to pay the dollar equivalent (or 'counterpart') in local currency into special accounts held with the central bank (Articles 4 and 5 of the Bilateral Agreement). The Federal Government then could apply with the Americans for the release of the funds for reconstruction purposes. After the currency reform, about DM 5.3 billion were paid in this way into the counterpart accounts which were then used for long-term investments in reconstruction projects. The crucial question is of how important these investments were for Germany's reconstruction process. At first glance it becomes clear that during the period 1949 to 1956, ERP investments did not reach 10 per cent of total investments, and in most sectors it even remained below 5 per cent.

Doc 39 ERP share in investment

ERP Share in Gross capital Investment (in per cent)

Econ. Sector	1949	1950	1951	1952	1953	1954	1955	1956	1949–1956
Industry	7.1	13	4.5	2.3	2	1.9	2.1	0.6	3.2
Coal Mining	47	40	13	4.9	3	1.3	3	1.5	8.4
Iron & Steel	–	18	14	2	2.3	4	6.8	1.1	4.8
Non-ferrous Metals	5	27	10	2.1	2.2	3.8	1.9	0.6	3.9
Mach. tools	2.3	15	3.1	1.4	1.2	1.1	0.6	0.3	2.2
Vehicles	0.7	1.2	0.4	0.1	0.1	0.0	0.0	0.1	0.2
Precision & Optics	6.4	35	4.7	2.6	5.7	1.8	1.9	0.2	4.3
Con'mer gds	0.5	5.7	3.2	2.3	1.4	1.1	1.4	0.9	2.0
E-Power	18	25	27	6.2	4.9	2.0	1.1	0.6	8.3
Communication & Transport	20	7.1	3.3	2.2	5.4	3	4.9	3	5.5
Housing	0.7	4.6	2.9	2.3	0.9	0.3	0.3	0.3	1.2
Agriculture	2	13	2.7	3.7	2.3	1.2	2.6	1.8	3.2

Trans. from: Baumgart, *Investitionen & ERP Finanzierung*.

West Germany's total gross investment made during this time amounted to DM 226 billion. This does not mean that the DM 5.5 billion from the counterpart funds were insignificant. Especially in the early years of 1949–51, the funds constituted a vital 'manoeuvrable mass' for crucial investments into strategic reconstruction bottlenecks, with coal being the best example. (The reason why the share of ERP investment dropped considerably after 1951/2 has largely to do with the Auxiliary Investment Law which will be explained in Chapter 12). The funds had a further significant psychological impact. Germans still suffered from the traumatic experience of the 1923 hyperinflation and the losses of savings it had caused. Although it is now generally accepted that despite its weakness the German economy after 1949 could have raised investment funding through credits, the fact that the government could publicly point to 'those Marshall Plan funds' being used for investments instead of borrowing helped to ease the German public's fear of a repeated inflation. The very existence of the funds helped to strengthen the public's initial shaky trust in the new currency.

While the highest share of ERP counterpart funds in total investment in any sector was in the coal-mining industry, the actual biggest amount of money went to the electrical power industry, which had been made a top priority by American planners. Indeed, during 1949–51 they were so eager to get electrical power supply expanding that in 1952 the Mutual Security Agency (MSA), the successor body to the Marshall Plan administration, criticised that one power company in particular was still receiving large loans while at the same time they were already paying out huge dividends and lending money on their own. In other words, reconstruction credits were given to a sector that did not really need them while other sectors were still desperate for funds.

Doc 40 MSA investment report

Report No. MC-437, Appendix B
...
Results:

1) ... The total loans for the six projects authorised by the ECA [European Co-operation Administration] amounts to DM 280.95 million. Since 21 June 1948 the company has contributed some DM 17.6 million while the payments from counterpart funds up to 31 July 1952 amounted to DM 222.15 million; they will rise to DM 247.05 million by 31 December 1952.

Considering the substantial depreciations (DM 64.8 million on power plants) it appears that this company could have contributed a larger share of own funds to the financing of projects authorised by the ECA. Acquisitions from 21 June 1948 to 30 June 1951 amounted to DM 455 million for installations and DM 1.4 million for shares of subsidiary companies, making a total of DM 456.4 million.

2) From 21 June 1948 to 30 June 1951 the RWE has paid out dividends of DM 14.76 million.
Up to 30 June 1951, the RWE supplied financial loans of about DM 10,000,000.
...

Trans. from: *Historisches Archiv der Kreditanstalt für Wiederaufbau*, HA VS 118.

Looking more closely at key indicators of West Germany's economic performance for the first five years after the currency reform, the observer will note trends that reflect political and economic developments, some of which appear curious at first. Apart from the seasonal fluctuations, the growth of industrial production was fairly robust but not spectacular, considering the low starting point. The largest quarterly increase happened in the fourth quarter of 1950, but this was followed by two years with an increase of 'only' 12 index points. Employment remains stagnant between the currency reform and mid-1950, while at the same time the share of unemployed nearly trebled. From mid-1950 onwards, both employment figures and industrial production began to rise and unemployment figures slowly fell (except for seasonal fluctuations). A similarly uneven development can be seen with the cost-of-living index.

Two events played a major role in these trends: the currency reform caused unemployment to rise, since with the new money labour costs became a significant factor again, and under-employed workers who previously had received worthless Reichsmark were therefore laid off. The peak of this development was reached in February 1950 with more than 2 million people – or 12 per cent of the workforce – unemployed. The cost-of-living index shows the inflationary pressure created by the currency reform, which by 1949/50 had turned into deflation. The second significant event was the outbreak of the Korean War on 25 June 1950. It caused a strong external demand for German goods but also sparked off a spike in inflation. This was caused to a large part by a worldwide surge in the demand for raw material which also affected German prices. The somewhat contradictory development on the labour market, i.e. the fact that the share of unemployed did not fall more quickly in face of rising numbers of people in employment was due in the first place to the return of POWs and secondly because of a steady stream of people fleeing from the German Democratic Republic, the GDR. Overall, the table demonstrates that the currency reform and Marshall Aid on their own did not cause an instant 'economic miracle' – on the contrary, they actually had a negative short-term effect.

Doc 41 Economic development, 1948–53

Economic data 1948–53 by quarter

Year	Industrial Production (1936=100)	Employed (million)	Unemployed (in per cent)	Cost of Living	Gross wages/h
				(1950=100)	
1948					
II	57	13.5	3.2	98	77
III	65	13.3	5.5	104	84
IV	79	13.7	5.3	112	89
1949					
I	83	13.4	8.0	109	90
II	87	13.5	8.7	107	94
III	90	13.6	8.8	105	95
IV	100	13.6	10.3	105	95
1950					
I	96	13.3	12.2	101	97
II	107	13.8	10.0	98	98
III	118	14.3	8.2	99	100
IV	134	14.2	10.7	103	105
1951					
I	129	14.2	9.9	115	108
II	137	14.7	8.3	119	117
III	133	14.9	7.7	108	118
IV	146	14.6	10.2	112	–
1952					
I	136	14.6	9.8	111	120
II	143	15.2	7.6	109	122
III	144	15.5	6.4	109	123
IV	158	15.0	10.1	110	124
1953					
I	146	15.2	8.4	109	125
II	158	15.8	6.4	108	128
III	160	16.0	5.5	108	128
IV	174	15.6	8.9	107	128

Trans. from: Abelshauser, *Die langen 50er Jahre*, p. 78.

While in later years the situation did improve significantly, initially the 'market' side of the social market economy did not work properly either. The Kreditanstalt für Wiederaufbau, a bank that had been established to finance reconstruction projects and handle the counterpart funds for the investment process, gave a sobering statement in its first annual report which had been drafted in early 1950. Although the report spoke specifically of the dysfunctional financial market, the market situation in the national economy as a whole did not fare much better.

Doc 42 KfW Annual Report 1949

In the face of the massive discrepancy between the as yet unproductive supply from the domestic capital market as a result of the so-called currency re-ordering and the national economy's urgent need for investment funds caused by the degree of damage and the loss of German capital of production, the distribution of Marshall Plan loans could not have been left to free markets forces. Instead the distribution had to be carried out according to a predetermined plan (*planmäßig erfolgen*), not least to create a counterbalance to the mis-direction of capital funds caused by, for example, self-financing. The re-establishment of a free market economy in the area of capital appears to be justified only when the fundamental gaps in the supply of investment funds can be closed through increased capital formation. Apart from that, the ECA Administration as the fund provider demands the submission of individual investment project plans that correspond with the aims of the Marshall Plan. Only after those have been checked and authorised can the release of counterpart funds happen.

Trans. from: *Kreditanstalt für Wiederaufbau, 1. Jahresbericht 1949.*

As this report shows, even in early 1950 the reality did not yet match the theories the economists had and things had to get considerably worse before they got better. By 1950 West German exports were totally insufficient to pay for its essential imports of raw material and foodstuffs; the FRG depended heavily on Marshall Aid to acquire those commodities. At the same time and very much to Ludwig Erhard's delight and pleasure, the Americans used West Germany as the pacemaker for European and world trade liberalisation.

This meant that West Germany had lower tariffs and less import restrictions than any other Western country. When the Korean War broke out and world food and raw material prices skyrocketed, the FRG's balance of payment deficit did so as well, bringing the country close to insolvency. In early 1951 things had deteriorated so much that US High Commissioner John McCloy, now acting as America's Marshal Plan representative, had to write the following memorandum to Adenauer.

Doc 43 McCloy memorandum to Adenauer

Economic Cooperation Administration
Office of the Special Mission to Germany
6 March 1951
Dear Chancellor,
I have the honour to refer to the meetings that took place over the last few days between some of your ministers and Mr Cattier, which were concerned partly with West Germany's critical foreign-exchange situation and partly with the serious concerns which had arisen recently in the American administration, regarding the current and future consideration of West Germany in the continuation of dollar aid. In view of West Germany's foreign-exchange situation, you were without doubt informed that the deficit to other EPU [European Payments Union] countries has once again reached worrying levels. For February alone the deficit amounted to nearly 60 million dollars. You will recall that the EPU member states had granted West Germany a special credit under the assumption that Germany's position vis-à-vis the EPU would improve over time and that Germany would achieve a positive balance against the EPU by the spring of this year.

The development that has since taken place is not only running contrary to the expectations of the United States government and those EPU member countries', but indeed seriously threatens the ability of the Federal government to continue to fulfil its international obligations ...

First I want to emphasise that the Economic Co-operation Administration, after due consideration, agrees with the current intentions of Congress and takes the same view that, as a matter of principle, dollar aid should only be made available to cover deficits which arose due to direct links to defence. This principle has to serve as a guideline for the drawing up of a programme to eliminate West Germany's current payment difficulties. I am, of course fully aware of the economic progress West Germany had made within the framework of the free-market economy. I am also aware of the leading role West Germany has taken among the OEEC countries in the implementation of trade liberalisation and the redirection of imports from non-dollar areas. But without a doubt you will agree with the view that, faced with the latest dramatic international developments and the resulting efforts by the United States for an increased defence contribution, only a significant modification of the free-market economy can do justice to the changed situation ...

In view of the exceptional economic efforts that are now being undertaken by the American people, the government of the Federal Republic must intervene directly with economic control measures if West Germany wants to be considered for further dollar aid. Otherwise we can no longer guarantee that scarce raw materials, which are now supplied in the United States to military and associated purposes, can be provided for West Germany in the future ...

I am fully aware that under the circumstances I have described, both the Government and the West German people will have to make considerable sacrifices. But if measures are not taken immediately in the direction suggested then there is little prospect that the United States' government can be persuaded to continue the dollar aid and support the Federal government in the acquisition of indispensible raw materials ...
Yours faithfully
John J. McCloy

Trans. from: Bundesarchiv Koblenz B 136/1309.

The US plainly and simply threatened to cut West Germany off from the world market by suspending Marshall aid if the Adenauer government was not prepared to implement severe economic restrictions on its economy and population. For political and ideological reasons respectively, Adenauer and Erhard had no intention of implementing economic restrictions, and the Chancellor told McCloy so in fairly straight language in his reply. Eventually, the German side made some minor concessions but was able to abstain from any significant intervention in the economy, and by late 1951 the situation changed dramatically for the better. The 'Korea boom' which now developed for the German economy has to be seen as the real take-off point for the 'economic miracle'. German refusal to accept economic controls, and the subsequent improvements, were seen as a victory for the 'social market economy'.

The vision of a 'social market economy' had been advocated by the so-called Freiburg School of economic thinking which had developed in the late 1920s. In May 1948, Professor Alfred Müller-

Armarck, one of the school's leading theorists, outlined what the social market economy should involve. The point which he totally agreed with Ludwig Erhard concerned a competitive market economy, thus ruling out the existence of monopolies or cartels. But what he also called for was a strong component of social security measures, which was an evolution and further development of some of the social security measures introduced in the Weimar Republic.

Doc 44 The realisation of the social market economy

...

10. Replacing the collapsing system of total economic planning with a social market economy.

The situation of our economy forces us to realise that in future we have to decide between two basically different economic systems, namely the system of the anti-market economic planning and the system of market economy – which is based on free prices, real competition and social justice. The desired market economy shall be distinctly social in orientation and commitment. Its social character lies already in the fact that it is able to offer a larger and more diverse variety of goods at prices which are decisively determined by consumer demand. As a result lower prices raise real wages and thus allows for a better and broader satisfaction of human desires.

If there is already a strong social moment inherent in the productivity of the market economy, it will be necessary nevertheless to carry out, with all determination, a number of measures which guarantee social security and which can be realised within the framework of the market economy.

To outline the size of the social market economy, the following field of social activity is named:

a) Creation of a social order in the firms [*soziale Betriebsordnung*] which values the employee as human being and colleague, allowing him some influence in social affairs [*soziales Mitgestaltungsrecht*] without limiting the entrepreneurial business initiative and responsibility.

b) Realisation of a competitive order that is seen as a public responsibility so that the individual's striving for gainful employment [*Erwerbsstreben*] is necessarily pointed in a direction in which it can usefully serve the community.

c) Compliance with an anti-monopolistic policy to fight possible misuse of power within the economy.

d) The implementation of an employment policy which serves the needs of the economic development [*konjunkturpolitische Beschäftigungspolitik*] with the aim of giving the employer as much security as possible against setbacks caused by economic crises. To this end, besides credit and fiscal policy measures, a public investment programme, but with a sensible budget limit, is to be proposed.

e) A market economic income equalisation to abolish unhealthy income and ownership differentials to be achieved by taxation and by family supplements, child and rent support for those in social need.

f) Settlement policy and social housing schemes.

g) A policy of social structure of company sizes [*soziale Betriebsstruk-turpolitik*] through the promotion of small and medium companies and the creation of social mobility.

h) The inclusion within the economic order of co-operative self-help – for example in housing construction.

i) Expansion of the social security system.

j) Urban development/town planning.

k) Minimum wages and securing of individual wages through free collective bargaining.

...

12. Immediate lifting of fixed prices and rationing for all goods and services except bread, fat and milk as well as rents for old flats, the management of which has to be improved. Only through a real price and value structure will it be possible to reliably establish the urgency of the needs of the national economy on the one side and the level of scarcity of means of production on the other.

13. Liberalising of wages and salaries and the re-establishment of the free movement of workers, especially in regard to the choice of work place and kind of employment.

14. Germany's re-integration as an equal partner into international trade by re-establishing Germany's freedom of action in the field of foreign trade.

Trans. from source reprinted in: R. Löwenthal, H.P. Schwarz (eds), *Die Zweite Republik. 25 Jahre Bundesrepublik Deutschland*.

Obviously, an economic theory on its own does not create an economic boom, regardless how beneficial the implementation of this theory is supposed to be for ordinary people. The rapid expansion of the West German economy in the 1950s can to a large extend be attributed to the industrial infrastructure the Nazis had created for their war economy. As Abelshauser has demonstrated for the

Bizone, Allied bombing had destroyed only a small part of German industry while a huge industrial expansion had taken place between 1936 and 1944. The United States Strategic Bombing Survey which had been carried out in 1945 concluded that the air raids may have destroyed factory buildings, but the Americans expressed surprise how little machinery had actually been destroyed or damaged. This initial extremely negative assessment of the effectiveness of aerial warfare has been somewhat qualified by the studies of Overy and others, but the fact remains that far less damage had been inflicted on German industry than Bomber Command had promised. Similarly, the restitution and dismantling of industrial equipment about which the Germans at the time complained so bitterly concerned only a small share of assets. Even if one takes into account that the removal of a single piece of machinery could have had significant further negative implications on the production process, the impact of dismantling was grossly exaggerated by the Germans. By 1948 the industrial equipment in the British-American zone of occupation was, despite all negative impacts, larger and more modern than it had been in 1936.

Doc 45 Industrial gross fixed assets in the Bizone, 1936–48

Industrial Gross Fixed Assets in the British-American Occupation Area, 1936–48
(1936 = 100)

Gross Fixed Assets 1936	100
Gross Industrial Investment 1936–45 as % of 1936	+ 75.3
Depreciation 1936–45 as % of 1936	– 37.2
Destruction by War as % of 1936	– 17.4
Gross Fixed Assets 1945	120.6
Gross Industrial Investment 1946–8	+ 8.7
Depreciation 1946–8 as % of 1936	– 11.5
Restitution 1945–8 as % of 1936	– 2.4
Dismantling 1945–8 as % of 1936	– 4.4
Gross Fixed Assets 1948	111.1

Trans. from: W. Abelshauser, *Wirtschaftsgeschichte der Bundesrepublik 1945–1980.*

By 1953 West Germany's overall economic situation had significantly improved and businesses were thriving. The idea of a free market economy gained more and more popularity, particularly in business circles, which defined 'free' first and foremost as free from any kind of state interference in the way they conducted their business. Although there was a significant difference between businesses' and Erhard's definition of 'free market' there were vested interests that wanted to keep him in the post of economics minister. Business associations therefore financed various media campaigns on behalf of the social market economy. The following newspaper advertisement appeared on the eve of the second general election on 6 September 1953.

Doc 46 Advertisement for the social market economy

Prosperity by Our Own Efforts
For five years the German economy has been growing and regaining strength at a rate that has astonished the world. At a personal level, everyone of us has experienced this, in regard to clothing and food. Professor Dr Ludwig Erhard stands before us as being responsible for the German economy. He has done decisive things for us.

1948 A country destroyed, a people weakened by hunger, a wrecked currency. Honest work had lost its meaning. With a quick decision on the day of the currency reform Erhard rips apart the ration cards and coupons of the planned economy. His idea spurs on the economy: Everyone shows what he can do! Everyone should secure his own existence through his own creative work. Professor Erhard announces: Only free competition [*Wettbewerb*] increases production and the quality of our products. Only hard competition [*Konkurrenz*], not police

1953 Five years of hard work lie behind us but they were not in vain. The grey spectre of unemployment has been banished. Nearly three million new jobs were created. Housing for more than five million people had been built. Erhard watches relentlessly over the value of the currency. The D Mark today is as healthy to the core as is the dollar and the Swiss Franc. German exports, without which we would have starved, have risen seven fold in four years. We have seven billion DM in gold and foreign currencies. In Germany the human being has and summary court push prices lower and increase the purchasing power of the currency. We create work, not by inflation but through reconstruction. Only if social convictions and personal effort to achieve high performance [*Leistungs-streben*] combine can we look toward lasting prosperity.

not been nationalised [*verstaatlicht*] but the state and the economy have been utilised for the good of man. That is the 'fraudulent bankruptcy' which Ludwig Erhard's enemies had predicted. But he knows that by now he has the overwhelming majority of the population behind him.

Even today not all wounds caused by the war have healed, not all dangers that threaten our economic recovery are yet banished. Therefore we have to safeguard our peaceful reconstruction and tomorrow cast our vote for a party that declares themselves for ERHARD'S SOCIAL MARKET ECONOMY

Trans. from: *Rhein-Neckar-Zeitung*, 5 September 1953.

The advertisement did not call for an outright vote for the CDU or for Chancellor Adenauer and his policy but rather for '*a party supporting the social market economy*'. By so doing it appeared to put economic improvement before party politics, not least because some of Adenauer's domestic and foreign policies at this time were still contentious, even within sections of his own party. Instead the advertisement highlighted the economic success in which the overwhelming majority of the population already participated or at least hoped to benefit from soon. The economic boom was a growing reality and it had begun to trickle down into the middle and even to the working classes, as can be seen from the increase in use of motor vehicles taking place at the time.

Doc 47 Motor vehicle ownership

New Registration and Change of Motor Vehicle Ownership in per cent of all Cases During the Year

	Motorbikes			Cars		
	1952	1953	1954	1952	1953	1954
New Registration						
Workers	58.0	62.5	64.6	0.8	1.5	2.9
White Collar & Civil Servants	16.9	17.4	17.5	8.9	11.2	13.5
Agriculture	9.5	7.1	6.4	6.4	6.2	6.1
Trade	4.0	3.3	2.6	33.5	33.0	31.2
Industry	1.1	0.9	0.9	18.5	16.0	15.6
Others	10.5	8.8	8.0	31.9	32.1	30.7
Change of Ownership						
Workers	61.9	64.4	65.8	5.4	8.5	12.0
White Collar & Civil Servants	14.5	14.1	13.5	15.0	17.6	20.3
Agriculture	8.2	7.3	7.5	6.3	5.6	6.0
Trade	4.1	3.4	3.0	32.2	29.9	26.2
Industry	0.6	0.5	0.5	7.1	6.2	5.7
Others	10.6	10.3	9.7	34.0	32.2	29.8

Trans. from: *Der Arbeitgeber* 1955.

This process of growing mass consumption was closer to Erhard's own definition of 'social market economy' than any talk of social security. As he explained at the time in his most famous book *Wohlstand für Alle!* (the English translation's title 'Prosperity Through Competition' is closer to his real intention), the most important, even sole, role of the state was to guarantee free competition in the market place. This would lead to lower prices, which in turn would lead to more consumption and thus higher standards of living for everyone, since the increased prosperity would eventually trickle down even to the lower working classes. Significantly, Erhard rejected any form of welfare state that would go beyond the provision of basic subsistence for those most in need.

Doc 48 Erhard's ideology

I should like to put at the beginning of these reflections a sentence which I have often repeated: the yardstick and criterion of what is good or bad in economic policy are not dogmas or the points of view of pressure groups, but exclusively the human being, the consumer, the people. Economic policy can only be regarded as good if and as long as it is regarded simply as useful and welcomed by the individual.

Whoever takes these reflections to their logical conclusion must agree with me that in every national economy vested interests exist. But these must not be allowed to determine economic policy, and no useful synthesis can be derived from a conflict between these interests. Any fragmentation of the national economy into vested interests cannot therefore be allowed ...

In this connection I have on a former occasion pointed to the role of the State as supreme judge ... I believe that, as the referee is not allowed to take part in the game, so the State must not participate. In a good game of football it is to be noted that the game follows definite rules; these are decided in advance. What I am aiming at with a market economy policy is – to continue with the same illustration – to lay down the order and the rules of the game ...

It is my firm conviction that we shall retain a free enterprise economy only for as long as the State protects freedom. If, on the other hand, free enterprise complains that that would be an unfair limitation of freedom by the State, then I can only reply that this is to misunderstand freedom, if in the name of freedom and with the dogma of freedom it is believed that freedom itself can be suppressed. As there is in the State, that is, in the political social structure, an order based on basic constitutional law which regulates the life of man and his relations with others, so there is for the economy. Here responsibilities are clearly divided. The businessman is responsible for his own business; there he can rightly demand that his activities should remain free from all State intervention, in fact, that he may enjoy and exercise real freedom of enterprise and freedom of manoeuvre. I am at the head of those supporting the businessman in this demand. But the State alone must carry responsibility for economic policy ...

The secret of market economy is just this, and herein lies its superiority over any kind of planning - that it enables processes of adaptation to take place almost daily and hourly, balancing supply and demand, national income and national product, both quantitatively and qualitatively. Whoever does not support competition and free market prices no longer has any argument available to oppose planning.

Some of my opponents may now ask whether the freedom of the entrepreneur, which I have so strongly stressed, is not circumscribed if the entrepreneur is no longer permitted to use his freedom in a way he considers proper - in other words, to use it in given circumstances to limit the free activity of the individual ... To ask and answer this question means that we have to demonstrate the great difference between the social market economy, which we have been trying to realize in West Germany since 1948, and the liberal economy of the old days.

In my conception the social market economy does not recognize the freedom of the entrepreneur to exclude competition through cartel agreements; it imposes far more the obligation to gain the favour of the consumer through one's own efforts in competition against rivals. The State must not decide who should be victorious in the market, nor should an industrial organization such as a cartel; it must be the consumer alone. Quality and price determine the form and direction of production, and it is only on the basis of these criteria that the selection is made ...

That is why, for example, it is contradictory to exclude from the market economic order private initiative, foresight and responsibility, even when the individual is not in a material position to exercise such virtues. Economic freedom and compulsory insurance are not compatible ...

In recent times I have frequently been alarmed by the powerful call for collective security in the social sphere. Where shall we get to and how are we to maintain progress if we increasingly adopt a way of life in which no one wants any longer to assume responsibility for himself and everyone seeks security in collectivism? I have drastically described this flight from responsibility when I said that if this mania increases we shall slide into a social order under which everyone has one hand in the pocket of another. The principle would be: I provide for someone else and someone else provides for me.

The blindness and the intellectual inertia which are pushing us towards a Welfare State can only bring disaster. This, more than any other tendency, will serve slowly but surely to kill the real human virtues – joy in assuming responsibility, love for one's fellow being, an urge to prove oneself, and a readiness to provide for oneself – and in the end there will probably ensue not a classless but a soulless mechanical society.

From: Ludwig Erhard, *Prosperity through Competition*, London 1959.

The economic recovery that took place in West Germany after 1948 was not a miracle but it was indeed very remarkable, both in terms of its speed, and more importantly because the benefits were eventually felt by the whole population. This stood in contrast to the Nazi economic recovery in the mid 1930s, for example, which created jobs, but not prosperity, nor a consumer society from which ordinary people could benefit. The development was not without interruptions, even crises – especially in the early years. Between 1949 and 1951 West Germany experienced deflation and high unemployment followed by a spell of inflation and an extreme balance of payment crisis. However, once the initial problems were overcome the boom seemed unstoppable. How far the Federal Republic progressed within a decade in economic terms, from the dependence on American economic aid in the late 1940s, to its position as Europe's economic powerhouse from the mid 1950s onward is demonstrated by a letter from President Eisenhower to Adenauer, in which he asked for West German financial contributions to Third World countries.

Doc 49 Eisenhower letter to Adenauer, 1960

Washington, October 7, 1960.
Dear Mr. Chancellor: I am writing to you on a personal and confidential basis not only as my good friend of long standing but also as the leader of a nation whose economic and financial power has grown to great dimensions in the community of the free nations. With that power has come an equal responsibility for the success of free nations and our free economies in critical and rapidly evolving era of the world's history. Upon us both rest great responsibilities that, I think, our two governments should consider together. In the financial and economic sphere, no less than in the political and strategic sphere, mutual understanding and co-operation between Europe and the United States are vital. In the United States, we recognized this when in 1948, we established the Marshall Plan ... After the Marshall Plan came the need for military assistance to fend off the Communist threat and the need lo give aid to less-developed countries ... Ever since, the American people have hoped that the burden of our foreign expenditures, economic and military, would eventually be lifted or at least substantially reduced by the co-operation of other nations.

Today the situation has substantially changed. The success of the Marshall Plan has led to the full recovery of Europe. The United States is now paying out to foreign countries more than we receive from our sales to them. This means that certain surplus countries, and notably the Federal Republic of Germany, are accumulating short-term dollar claims on the United States on a large scale. We meanwhile have lost, in the course of two and a half years, substantial amounts of gold while at the same time additional short-term dollar holdings have accumulated in other industrial countries. I believe that this burden upon our balance of payments should be reduced in a very substantial degree during the forthcoming year.

The Federal Republic is now the country which most nearly approaches the international financial and economic situation of the United States in 1948. It is consistently taking in from other countries far more than it is paying out. A continuation of this situation would stimulate demands for trade restrictions and threaten the future of economic development in the free world ... I now ask you to give your personal attention to the wider area of your nation's financial and economic relations with the United States on the one hand and the developing countries on the other.

The broad courses of action are clear. Long-term financing from Germany is needed for development in the less-developed areas. A way should be found also to finance the dollar cost of defense which now falls on the United States.

Finally, a larger market is needed in Germany for the goods of the United States and of the developing countries.

Action along these lines would conform to economic reality. Moreover, it is essential to maintain the political strength of the free world. And insofar as aid to less-developed countries is concerned, it commends itself both as a moral act and one in the self-interest of every industrialized nation.

Failure to make prompt, decisive and substantial progress in these directions may well set in motion cumulative events of a serious disruptive character, deleterious to world trade and prejudicial to the position and prestige of both our countries as leaders of the free world ...

I am sure that you will appreciate the strength of my conviction in this regard .... Many technical and detailed considerations need to be discussed between our two governments ... The two representatives I suggest have already had the opportunity to discuss these problems with Minister Erhard and President Blessing.

With warm regard,

Sincerely,

From: *FRUS*, 1958–1960, Volume IX.

4

Problems and challenges

The economic success of the Federal Republic, perhaps even more the speed with which it was achieved, helped to support the myth of the economic miracle which became the basis for a new West German identity. As a result, many of the problems and challenges the country faced were oversimplified or in some cases simply deleted from the public memory. In reality, the new state faced huge trials and trouble, because of some international issues, but mainly in the social and political field at home. Most problems brought with them a considerable financial burden, and in many instances the government initially had no idea how to tackle the problems or pay for them. First of all, four years after the war had ended, the country was physically still in ruins with infrastructure and housing particularly badly hit. Shortfalls in housing construction since the First World War and losses during the war meant that by 1949 there was a lack of some six million flats or houses. It was optimistically estimated that, if the Federal Republic were able to achieve and sustain the highest annual housing construction rate of the Weimar Republic, it would take 25 to 30 years to close this gap. Other than causing a lack of housing, the war had resulted in the destruction of schools, hospitals and municipal administrative buildings. Politically, not everyone trusted the new democratic system. On the left, the Communists wanted to establish a Soviet-style system and bring the Republic under Soviet control. On the right, some diehard former middle-ranking Nazis were trying to revive some form of National Socialism. The focal point of all the economic, political and, most importantly, social concerns were the refugees and expellees (for the sake of simplicity, here they will be referred to as simply one group, refugees). By 1950 almost one in five persons living in the Federal Republic had not lived in that territory before 1939. Most of them had fled to just west of the Iron Curtain to the rural areas of northern Bavaria, eastern Hesse, Lower Saxony and Schleswig-Holstein. Their living conditions were bad and unemployment was rampant, causing considerable burden for the welfare offices. In many parts of West Germany the influx of refugees shattered socio-cultural milieus that had existed for centuries, and this increased the tensions between the newcomers and the established locals. It was quite clear that if the refugees could not be integrated quickly into West German society they would become dissatisfied with the new state and turn to the political extremes of either the Left or the Right.

Doc 50 Report on refugees, 1949

'There is no escape from the refugees.'

For a very long time public opinion in the Western world has accepted the expulsion of 12 million Germans from their homeland as an automatic consequence of Hitler's crimes, as an action for which the National Socialists are to blame. Against the background of collective guilt, one argument suggested that the Germans had expelled themselves. Now a new understanding is dawning to the effect that revenge has made everything worse and not 'compensated for' anything [*wiedergutmacht*]. It is dawning that the share of responsibility in atrocities of revenge cannot be lied away by pointing towards the supposedly avenged atrocities ...

We can't excuse ourselves by declaring the [refugee] problem can't be solved as long as the injustice of the Oder-Neiße border exists. True: there is no real 'solution' for more than seven million people who have been squeezed into the already densely inhabited, and now destroyed and impoverished, area of the three Western zones which make up today's Federal Republic. If one includes those people who had already been evacuated from areas threatened by air raids during the war, as well as those who fled from the Soviet-occupied zone there will be 10 million uprooted people in the Federal Republic. Every fifth German is without a place to call home [*Heimat*]. And still the push from the Eastern zone continues, a remaining number of Germans still live under Polish or Czech rule, a reminder for whom the only issue to be addressed concerns their necessary liberation. Not only the refugees and the expellees, but equally all other Germans are unable to ever recognise the spurious border along the Oder and Neiße, to ever recognise the spurious *limes*. But the call for justice does not give anyone back their old home, as long as there are powers that trample high-handedly on justice. For the time being it is therefore necessary to create a substitute in the new homeland ...

Initially it was believed that the fate of the expellees was hopeless because they were made up of only the elderly and infirm, women and children. But the impression of the first transports of refugees was wrong. Today we know that the distribution of gender and age among the expellees is more favourable than the average make-up within the Federal Republic. The share of expellees able to work is relatively higher than among the old established population. Despite this, unemployment among refugees today is nearly three times as high as it is among the locals. A more clear-cut proof for the real social deprivation of their rights [*soziale Entrechtung*] is hard to find. Only 3 per cent of today's university students are expellees whereas it should be 15 per cent according to their share in the population as a whole. These figures speak volumes. Furthermore, one has to realise that an extraordinarily high percentage of working refugees are employed in positions unrelated to their trained occupation. The percentage of self-employed workers is only about four per cent compared to about 25 per cent in the old homeland. And hundreds of thousands still live in emergency housing. The social decline is unimaginable and the Emergency Aid bill [*Soforthilfegesetz*] will hardly change anything .... After all, the direct refugee costs have totalled four billion DM since the end of the war.

But the true task is to provide a humane existence for the expellees, to provide a workplace that is as close as possible to their previous one ... Freedom of movement [*Freizügigkeit*] has finally to become a prerogative for the refugees. But this does not change the fact that a vigorous improvement can only be achieved through a large scale and meticulously planned relief operation ...

Trans. from: Ernst Friedländer in *Die Zeit*, 22.9.1949.

Since many refugees had little more possessions than what they had carried in their suitcases, they were excluded from the black-market economy of the early post-war years, which had brought some relief to the established residents. Employment became an obvious and crucial means of integrating the refugees into West German society. However, with so many of them being stranded in rural areas with few job prospects they posed a threefold problem. They had insufficient housing; they had no work; and although the industrial centres needed workers, they often could not house them because of the large-scale destruction of housing stock. These factors and sometimes simply local prejudice against the newcomers meant that the proportion of refugees who were unemployed was well above the national average – which at its worst had been just above 12 per cent.

Doc 51 Refugee share of unemployed

Refugees' Share of the Population and Amongst the Unemployed, 1949–1957 (per cent)

Year	Share of Unemployed	Share of Population
1949	34.5	16.2
1950	31.4	16.6
1951	30.4	16.8
1952	29.6	16.9
1953	27.6	17.1
1954	26.1	17.2
1955	25.2	17.4
1956	23.1	17.7
1957	21.5	18.0

Trans. from source reprinted in: Abelshauser, *Die Langen fünfziger Jahre*.

By 1957 the situation had changed considerably. Although nearly half a million people were still living in more than 3,000 camps, they were no longer seen as part of the normal post-war life: now they had turned into an embarrassment for the 'economic miracle' society. While it was accepted that some of the camps' inhabitants lived there purely for economic reasons to save on rent, there was another group among the refugees that did not participate in the economic boom at all. The elderly and those disabled by the war but who did not receive the normal and fairly generous veterans' benefits made up the largest share of the continuing high number of unemployed refugees. The economic boom had passed them by and, since they were a relatively small group, much less attention was paid to them.

Doc 52 Refugees 1957

400,000 people still living in camps.
The most dwellings are dilapidated – but it is cheaper to live in a camp.
From the city centre we have to drive only 20 or 30 blocks to see the first Nissen huts. A short evening stroll away from the centre of a West German city in 1957 live people who do not participate in the often cited rising standard of living. There lives for example the man who was fished out of the Mediterranean five times during the last war and whom they could hardly patch up again the last time. In his right side, most of his ribs are missing, he is a total invalid. His wife and the children got bombed out in Hamburg. Some years ago a Nissen hut became vacant in Wandsbeck. The man moved in, finally securing a roof over his head again. He received 13 square metres of space – not enough for his nine children, seven of whom social services sent to a children's home. '… In the past, as a petty officer in the merchant navy I did not do badly', he says, 'together with my wife and all extras we made 700 RM. If I had been in the navy I would be entitled to large benefit. But now I'm getting only 185 DM. That's hardly enough to survive.'

3,000 camps in the area of the Federal Republic
For this man, West Germany's economic boom has not happened. In the approximately 3,000 camps in the Federal Republic some 372,000 people are living in similar circumstances. Add to this the 56 camps in West Berlin in which, according to the last inquiry, another 26,000 people live. That adds up to a total of 400,000 people. A dwelling [*Wohnung*] which fulfils basic standards currently costs between 16,000 and 20,000 DM. If we calculate one dwelling per family of four we will need 100,000 dwellings. A total of 2 billion DM would be necessary to build them. Government and Parliament have not yet found a way to set aside this amount from their total budget of 33 billion DM …

There are 16,000 huts, bunkers, sheds and barracks in the 3,000 camps. [Of these,] 6,600 are in a 'good' state – that is, they can be called inhabitable if modest standards are applied. But 9,400 are in a bad or very bad state … A hut has a lifetime of 10 years. It is therefore nearly a miracle that 10,000 wooden huts are still inhabited.

The majority of camps – 1,024 – are in Lower Saxony. In second place is North-Rhine Westphalia with 909. This is followed in third place by Schleswig-Holstein with 515 camps. While Lower Saxony and even more so North-Rhine Westphalia have employment opportunities, the greatest distress is to be found in Schleswig-Holstein. It is here where, after Lower Saxony's figure of 100,000, the second largest number of people – 80,000 – still live in camps … Schleswig-Holstein's state and municipal funds have to cover the costs for some 67,000 camp dwellers who fall under their jurisdiction. The heaviest burden has to be carried by the city of Lübeck, since with 14,000 camp occupants living in the city district, Lübeck accommodates one fifth of all the state's refugees. This means that even now, 12 years after the end of the war, every sixteenth Lübecker is living in a camp. This makes Lübeck the largest refugee town in West Germany, in relative terms. Only a few refugees in the Lübeck city district are doing at all well, such as the metal worker who could tell us: 'Despite the high strike support funding, the strike has cost me a full 1200 DM. And that right now, before we are moving house, when I need the money most.' The man has three children but he has found work in a shipyard. He belongs to those who have furniture in their small shed rooms, who were able to buy a radio or even a television set and who sometimes have a motorbike or even a small car. Except for the missing home these people, regardless of whether they are refugees, expellees or bombed out, have caught up. But not all of those who have a normal income are looking for housing. 'Why should I leave the camp?' asks a refugee who has now been living for 12 years in a shack. 'I'm living here together with my old friends, we all arrived with the same refugee trek. I am paying 10 DM rent per month. True, the accommodation is not luxurious. But a flat costs 80 to 100 DM and I would have to do without so much just to pay that amount of rent.'

During the years of cheap rent some have managed to save enough to think about building their own house. They will help with the construction work, the son is going to live with them. There will be subsidies from the equalisation of burden fund, and in their own house they won't have to do without the chicken they already kept in the camp. They might even keep a pig. Others have calculated that they have to stay only another three, five or ten years in the camp then they can achieve it as well. So, why move into a flat in the town and destroy all these plans? ...

Over the coming years, the active individuals among the camp population will move to other federal states or they will come to terms with their situation by getting a new job or by receiving aid provided under the Equalisation of Burden Act. But the camps will not disappear, not even after the end of the Schleswig-Holstein camp-clearing programme. The old, the disabled and those who have adapted to camp life will remain ... But even those who under their own strength are unable to earn their own share of the national product should be allowed to participate in the rising standard of living.

Trans. from source reprinted in Abelshauser, *Die Langen fünfziger Jahre*.

The images of refugee treks consisting of old men, women and children fleeing the advancing Red Army in January 1945 greatly contributed to the often held view that refugees were indeed predominantly elderly, female and small children. In fact, older people comprised only a small proportion of the refugees; most were young, flexible and willing to work when and wherever they could, thus they provided the reserve labour force necessary for the economic boom to continue in the second part of the 1950s. The government, not oblivious to their potential political power, enacted several important pieces of legislation in an attempt to integrate them into West Germany society. Of course, this was also done in order to accommodate and appease them so that they did not become a political threat. One of the more curious effects this approach caused was the 1953 Law on the Expellees, which made the legal distinction between three groups of refugees, but which also made the status of an expellee inheritable.

Doc 53 Federal Law Concerning Expellees *(Bundesvertriebenen- gesetz)*, 1953

Article 1

1) An Expellee is anyone who, as a German citizen or as an ethnic German, had his residence in the German eastern territories currently under foreign administration or in areas outside the borders of the German Reich as defined on 31 December 1937; and who had lost this residence in connection with events of the Second World War through expulsion, especially through deportation or flight.

2) As an Expellee is regarded a German citizen or an ethnic German who

a) after 30 January 1933 had to leave the areas mentioned in paragraph 1 because of threatened or actual violence by the National Socialists because of his political conviction, race, creed or world-view and who had to take residence outside the German Reich.

b) has been resettled from non-German areas because of international settlements concluded during the Second World War or who has been resettled from territories occupied by the German Wehrmacht because of measures by German authorities (this person is then classed as a re-settler).

c) after completion of the general expulsion measures has left or is going to leave the German eastern territories currently under foreign administration, namely Danzig, Estonia, Latvia, Lithuania, the

113

Soviet Union, Poland, Czechoslovakia, Hungary, Rumania, Bulgaria, Yugoslavia or Albania, ...

3) An expellee is also regarded as anyone who, without being a German citizen or an ethnic German, has lost his residence in the areas mentioned in paragraph 1 due to his status as the spouse of an expellee.

Article 4

1) A refugee from the Soviet Zone [*Sovietzonenflüchtling*] is a German citizen or ethnic German who has or had his residence in the Soviet zone of occupation or the Soviet-occupied sector of Berlin and who had to flee to escape a difficult predicament [*Zwangslage*] beyond his control, caused by the political situation and where through no fault of his own, his basic human or legal rights [*Grundsätze der Menschlichkeit und Reschtsstaatlichkeit*] had been violated. A severe predicament exists in particular if there was an immediate danger to life and limb or to personal freedom. Economic reasons alone do not justify the recognition as a refugee from the Soviet Zone.

Article 6

The meaning of the term Ethnic German in this law denotes a person who in his homeland [*Heimat*] had allied himself to German traditions [*Volkstum*] and that this declaration is confirmed by certain features such as ancestry, language, upbringing or culture.

Article 7

Children born after the expulsion gain the status [*Eigenschaft*] of Expellee or Refugee from the Soviet Zone from the parent who at the time of the child's birth or at the start of assumption of parental care [*Legitimation*] had or has the right to refugee or expellee status ...

Article 8

The status of Expellee or Refugee from the Soviet Zone can be neither acquired nor lost because of marriage or adoption after the expulsion.

Trans. from: *Bundesgesetzblatt*, 1953 (I), pp. 201 ff.

Making the expellee status inheritable was a sign of the strength of the refugee organisations at the time, as well as an attempt by the government to pre-empt political discontent by implicitly guaranteeing the continued existence of refugee organisations as political lobby groups. The move has also to be seen as a political signal that the government was not willing to abandon the Eastern territories. It was only in the 1970s, in the wake of Willy Brandt's Ostpolitik and East–West détente that the political influence of refugee organisations began to diminish.

The most significant, and at the same time most controversial legislation passed for the refugees by the Adenauer Government was the Law on the Equalisation of Burden, or *Lastenausgleich*. In 1948 the Americans had prevented the Germans from introducing any measures that could ease the social imbalances the currency reform would cause. From 1949 onward the Bizonal Economic Council and subsequently the Federal Government attempted through a series of different acts of legislation to ease some of the social inequality created by the currency reform; the most important of these would eventually be the 1952 Equalisation of Burden Act. Everyone who had assets on the day of the currency reform was levied on those assets, in order to compensate those who had lost their assets through expulsion – anything from big estates in the East to simple household goods. After 20 years, the various measures and acts of legislation, including the 1949 Bizonal Emergency Aid Act (*Sofort-hilfe Gesetz*), had redistributed some DM 75 billion.

Doc 54 Result of the *Lastenausgleich* (Equalisation of Burden), 31.12.1969

Income of the Equalisation of Burden Fund (in billions DM)

Equalisation levy including Emergency Aid levy and revenues from *Umstellungsgrundschuld**	40.4
Subsidiary by Federal and Land Governments	20.1
Returns from loans, other regular incomes	7.9
Proceeds from bonds	0.4
Funds from capital and money markets	6.2
Total	75.0

* Levy put on real-estate owners in the process of the currency reform

Spending of the Equalisation of Burden Fund (in millions DM):

Core Compensation	13,139
Compensation for Household Equipment	9,295
Currency Compensation	1,097
Saver Compensation (*Altsparer Entschädigung*)	2,998
Pensions for Victims of Nazi Persecution (*Entschädigungsrente*)	3,989
Housing Construction	12,456
Integration Subsidy Commercial Enterprises	2,473
Agriculture	2,188
Other Subsidies	1,265
Maintenance Support	20,269
Total*	72,254

* Possible discrepancies since not all subsidies listed

Trans. from source reprinted in: Abelshauser, *Die Langen fünfziger Jahre*.

Of course, the Equalisation of Burden Act was highly criticised by all sides. The refugees thought their compensation was not high enough and that only they had to pay the price for Hitler's war; the locals who had to pay broadly accepted the need for compensation but thought they had been taxed too heavily. With hindsight it is clear that the provision of the equalisation of burden funds, although at the time perceived by the refugees as a mere plaster on the wound, allowed the refugees to be integrated much more easily into the new state; and towards the end of the payment period most people had accepted the levy as being of the right amount.

Doc 55 *Die Zeit* editor Buccerius on the end of the Equalisation of Burden Act, 1979.

Sometimes farewell is not difficult. Since 1 April 1949 every quarter I had to pay DM 650 'Lastenausgleich' to the taxman [*Finanzamt*], DM 2,600 annually, DM 78,000 over 30 years. It is over now. I've just paid the last instalment (and cancelled the standing order with the bank).

DM 2,600 a year didn't hurt me much over the last years ... But during the 1950s business was bad; my outgoings were higher than my incomings; the future was unsure; and I had to run up high debts. Then the equalisation of burden was a tremendous burden. It had been imposed on me because on the currency reform's qualifying date – 30 June 1948 – I had assets. The fact that I had lost these assets in the meantime did not matter. I was not the only one in this situation: more than 3 million West Germans who had saved some property were supposed to pay. DM 37 billion were landed on them, which they had to pay off, with interests, over 30 years. 'The property levy amounts to 50 per cent of the assets liable to the levy (Art. 31, Equalisation of Burden Law). My assets were two slightly damaged but debt-free rental properties which had been run down during the war (both unsaleable at the qualifying date) and some shares that had yet to be listed again. The assets 'liable to the levy' were calculated according to the standardised value [*Einheitswert*]. For me, my assets amounted to DM 96,000. Half of it went to the equalisation of burden ... The annual payments were set at 6 per cent of the levied debt (rental properties only 5 per cent, for agriculture only 4 per cent). The duration for the payments was set at 30 years.

There had been a very long debate as to whether the standardised value was not too low a measure for the levy. Back then (with DM 48,000) I felt fairly fleeced – but every debtor feels this way. Certainly, my annuities were low. A bank would have charged me more. Thus I have estimated my 'real debt' to be one-third lower ... 37 billion of the new Deutsche Mark to be paid by 3 million citizens, that was the biggest property levy in the world's history ...

Trans from: Gerd Bucerius: 'Rechunung für Hitlers Krieg', in: *Die Zeit*, 13.4.1979.

The *Lastenausgleich* was not the only financial burden for the young state, and it could be seen simply as an internal redistribution of assets, similar to taxation. However, at around the same time, there were two other developments that caused a significant outflow of German assets and revenue. In 1952 the Federal Republic signed a compensation agreement with Israel (see ch. 14). Five months after that, in February 1953, West Germany signed the London Debt Agreement, in which the Federal Government acknowledged and agreed to repay Germany's pre-war debts and the liabilities that had arisen from post-war aid, in particular from the Marshall Plan. Although the total amount of debt had been reduced considerably, the treaty meant a significant burden on the state coffers and caused massive outrage when it was made public. It has to be kept in mind that West Germany's economic recovery was only beginning and that the annual federal budget at the time was less than DM 25 billion, so the debt settlement was seen as a very big burden.

Doc 56 London Debt Agreement 1953

... In regard to the United Kingdom's claim of £201 million, Her Majesty's Government is prepared to accept £150 million to settle its claim; to relinquish interest payments; and to accept repayment in 20 equal annual payments of £7.5 million. Concerning the French claim which, expressed in dollars, amounts to $15.7 million, so is the French Government prepared to accept $11.84 million for the settlement of its claim; to relinquish all claims for interest; and to accept the repayment in 20 equal annual payments of $592,000 in French Francs.

Concerning the United States' claim of $3200 million, the United States' Government is prepared to accept about $1,200 million to settle the claim. Annual interest of 2½ per cent is to be paid on the actual outstanding amount of this sum. During the first five years, only interest is to be paid; after this period the capital has to be repaid in 30 annual repayments ... the result of these payment negotiations constitutes a considerable success from the German point of view when measured against the full amount of pre-war debt that has been settled. The total pre-war debt, based on the loan agreement's gold basis, would have amounted to about DM 13.5 billion, or to DM 9.6 billion without the gold factor. The London agreement was concluded on the basis of DM 7.3 billion ... The difference between these amounts and the total annual repayment of DM 567 million (in the first five years) and DM 765 million (thereafter) is to be allocated for servicing the post-war economic aid. Thus the London debt settlement has achieved the reduction of the pre-war debts from DM 13.5 billion (including gold factor) or DM 9.6 billion (without gold factor) respectively to DM 7.3 billion ...

Trans. from: 'Denkschrift zu den deutschen Auslandsschulden' in: *Verhandlungen des Deutschen Bundestages, 1. Wahlperiode*, Anlagen, vol. 23.

With hindsight it is clear that the London Debt Agreement was a major success, since it restored Germany's international creditworthiness so that new funds from abroad could flow in, which in turn accelerated the reconstruction process, which then helped to pay off the debts.

Beyond the financial worries that arose from the international agreements and the social problems caused by the refugees, there were also significant political challenges for the new state. On the left of the political spectrum stood the Communist Party, the KPD. The party was heavily influenced by East Berlin and Moscow and wanted to overthrow democracy in favour of a Soviet-style regime. Although the KPD had suffered badly under the Nazis, and had lost many members in the concentration camps, and despite the huge anti-Soviet sentiments in the German public, nearly 1.4 million people – almost 6 per cent of the electorate – voted for the party in the 1949 general election. The KPD's extreme opposite on the right of the political spectrum was the Socialist Reichs Party, the SRP. It was made up of extreme nationalists and even diehard Nazis, with the party leadership coming from the NSDAP's middle ranks. They styled themselves on the Nazi party and were seen as a potential threat to the young democracy. In a 1950 opinion poll, a staggering 10 per cent of people named Adolf Hitler as the greatest German. For those people, the SRP could become the rallying point for a new extreme nationalistic movement. However, in contrast to circumstances in the Weimar Republic, the Basic Law contained safeguards against anti-democratic parties and in 1951 the government asked the Constitutional Court to ban those parties. The verdict on the SRP was passed in October 1952.

Doc 57 Constitutional Court ruling on the Socialist Reichs Party

The Sozialistische Reichspartei (SRP) had been founded on 2 October 1949. Prior to this, there had been several attempts to reorganize the members of the former right-wing parties politically. One of these attempts led to the foundation of the Deutsche Rechtspartei. During 1949 it suffered internal confrontations. This was the actual cause for the establishment of the SRP ... German constitutions after the First World War hardly mentioned political parties, although even at that time . . . democratic constitutional life was to a large extent determined by parties. The reasons for this omission are manifold, but in the final analysis, the cause lies in a democratic ideology that refused to recognize groups mediating between the free individual and the will of the entire people – composed of the sum of individual wills and represented in parliament by deputies as 'representatives of the entire people' ...

The Basic Law abandoned this viewpoint and, more realistically, expressly recognizes parties as agents – even if not the only ones –

forming the political will of the people ... In a free democratic state, as it corresponds to German constitutional development, freedom of political opinion and freedom of association, even for associations of a political kind, are guaranteed to individual citizens as basic rights. On the other hand, it is part of the nature of every democracy that the supreme power derived from the people is exercised in elections and voting. In the reality of the large modern democratic state, however, this popular will can emerge only through parties operating as political units. Both fundamental ideas lead to the basic conclusion that establishment and activity of political parties must not be restrained. The framer of the German Constitution was confronted with the question of whether he could fully implement this conclusion or whether he should not rather, enlightened by recent experiences, draw certain limits in this area ... In this connection the danger had to be taken into account that the Government might also be tempted to eliminate troublesome opposition parties.

Art. 21 of the Basic Law has tried to master these problems. On the one hand, it establishes the principle that formation of political parties shall be free. On the other hand, it offers a means of preventing activity by 'unconstitutional' parties. To avert the danger of an abuse of this means, Art. 21 authorises the Federal Constitutional Court to decide the question of unconstitutionality, and attempts to determine as far as possible the factual requirements for such a declaration ... The special importance of parties in a democratic state does not justify their elimination from the political scene if, by legal means, they wish to change individual provisions or even entire constitutional institutions, but only if they seek to topple supreme fundamental values of the free democratic order which are embodied in the Basic Law ...

According to the constitutional-political decision made by the Basic Law, the essential constitutional order is in the last analysis founded upon the idea that man has an independent value of his own and that freedom and equality are permanent, intrinsic values of national unity. Thus the basic order is an order heavily laden with values that oppose those of the totalitarian state which ... rejects human dignity, freedom and equality ...

Thus, the free democratic basic order can be defined as an order which excludes any form of tyranny or arbitrariness and represents a governmental system under a rule of law, based upon self-determination of the people as expressed by the will of the existing majority and upon freedom and equality. The fundamental principles of this order include at least: respect for the human rights given concrete form in the Basic Law, in particular for the right of a person to life and free development; popular sovereignty; separation of powers; responsibility of government; lawfulness of administration; independence of the judiciary; the multiparty principle; and equality of opportunities for all political parties ...

The SRP claims in its defence that other parties, too, have tried to enlist former National Socialists ...

This objection shows that the SRP misunderstands the situation. It is not reproached for having tried to enlist former National Socialists, but for collecting especially the hard core who have 'remained true to themselves', not in order to gain positive forces for democracy, but to preserve and propagate National Socialist ideas ...

The body of evidence on the SRP's personnel composition allows only one conclusion: Here gather the old and active Nazis in order to regain influence ... [T]hey are systematically sought out and enlisted ... They form the core of the SRP ... Former Nazis hold key positions in the party to such an extent as to determine its political and intellectual image, and no decision can be made against their will ... [The SRP's] organization is similar to that of the NSDAP ... That order does not follow democratic principles (Art 21, par. 1, sen. 3, of the Basic Law) ...

The SRP's rejection of a multi-party system is expressed even more strongly ...

The body of evidence leads to the following conclusions:

1. The SRP as a political party disregards ... basic human rights ...

4. The SRP in its programme, its ideology and its overall appearance is related in character to the former NSDAP ... That the SRP feels itself to be the successor organization of the NSDAP is visible in its leadership ... [Conclusion:]

The SRP is thus unconstitutional in the sense stipulated in Art. 21, par. 2, of the Basic Law ... The party, therefore, must be dissolved.

Trans. from: *Entscheidungen des Bundesverfassungsgerichts*, BVerfG 1BvB 1/51.

The case of the KPD was less clear cut and it took until 1956 for the party to be banned, although by this time it had lost its political significance. With the economic success of the Federal Republic – something that had eluded the Weimar Republic and contributed to its downfall – came its political stabilisation; with political stabilisation came a process of political concentration, with fewer and fewer parties elected into the Bundestag. This development reached its first high point in 1957 when the CDU/CSU gained the first and to date *only* absolute majority in the history of the Bundestag. The fate of the refugee party *Block der Heimatvertriebenen und Entrechteten / Gesamtdeutscher Block* (BHE/GB), which had been voted into the

second Bundestag in 1953 and was offered a place in the government by Adenauer for tactical reasons is a case in point. Although
the party's clientele was much larger than the votes cast for it, by
1957 it had failed to be re-elected. More and more of the smaller
parties merged with the two big 'people's parties' or *Volksparteien*,
the CDU/CSU and the SPD, a clear sign that a new form of political
stability had been achieved.

Doc 58 Federal election results, 1949–65

(Share of votes in per cent; Seats) (Governing Parties in bold)

Party	1949		1953		1957		1961		1965	
CDU	25.2	**115**	36.4	**191**	39.7	**215**	35.8	**192**	38.0	**196**
CSU	5.8	**24**	8.8	**52**	10.5	**55**	9.6	**50**	9.6	**49**
SPD	29.2	131	28.8	151	31.8	169	36.2	190	39.3	202
FDP/DVP	11.9	**52**	9.5	**48**	7.7	41	12.8	**67**	9.5	**49**
DP	4.0	**17**	3.3	**15**	3.4	**17**	–	–	–	–
BP	4.2	17	1.7	–	–	–	–	–	–	–
KPD	5.7	15	2.2	–	–	–	–	–	–	–
BHE/GB	–	–	5.9	27	4.7	–	2.8	–	–	–
WAV	2.9	12	–	–	–	–	–	–	–	–
ZP	3.1	10	0.8	3	–	–	–	–	–	–
DKP/DRP	1.8	5	–	–	–	–	–	–	–	–
DRP	–	–	1.2	–	1.0	–	0.8	–	–	–
GVP	–	–	0.2	–	–	–	–	–	–	–
SSW	0.3	1	0.2	–	–	–	–	–	–	–
Independ.	4.8	3	–	–	–	–	–	–	–	–
Others	1.1	–	0.3	–	1.5	–	2.2	–	3.6	–

Adapted and trans. from: G. Ritter and M. Niehaus, *Wahlen in Deutsch-land*.

A major reason for the process of political concentration and the
electoral successes of the CDU was the economic recovery. The
improving and then booming economy meant higher state revenue,
which in turn allowed for increased social benefits. The social
budget between 1950 and 1965 increased five fold, yet its share of
GDP rose only slightly, demonstrating the economic growth. By far

the biggest increase of the social budget appeared in the pensions sector, and it was the 1957 pension reform – announced just before the general elections that year – which brought the biggest increase in spending. The reform changed pensions from a system of fixed pension which reduced over time in real terms due to inflation to a 'dynamic' system where pensions rose in line with wages, thus banning the widespread fear of poverty in old age.

Doc 59 Social budget 1950–65

Social budget 1950–65 (in millions DM)

	1950	1955	1960	1965
Pensions	3,898	7,748	18,259	28,987
Farmers' Old Age Support	–	–	182	487
Health insurance and protection of nursing mothers	2,521	4,685	9,621	15,926
Accident Insurance	585	1,027	1,733	3,120
Unemployment Insurance	1,871	1,811	1,071	1,395
Child Benefit	–	463	916	2,820
Social Benefits	962	1,288	1,620	2,495
Youth Support	27	51	54	793
Housing Benefit	–	–	–	175
Public Health Service	123	218	342	667
(Civil Service) Pensions	2,479	5,094	6,859	10,410
Civil Service Child Supplement	441	760	1,031	1,634
War Victim Provision	2,087	3,206	3,678	5,801
Equalisation of Burden	718	980	1,345	1,990
Others	–	–	–	1,141
Social budget total	15,712	27,331	46,710	77,915
Social provisions as share of GDP	16.0	15.2	15.5	17.2

Trans. from: *Statistisches Jahrbuch für die Bundesrepublik Deutschland*, various years, reprinted in Abelshauser, *Die langen 50er Jahre.*

The biggest physical challenge that the Federal Republic faced in 1949 was the lack of housing. Even the most optimistic forecasts had predicted that many people, in particular the refugees or those living in the bombed-out cities and industrial centres, would have to live in crowded dwellings or in the squalor of emergency housing for decades to come. During the Marshall Plan programme the Americans had insisted that houses built with ERP money would provide higher standards than many German houses at the time did, with facilities such as indoor toilets and bathrooms. The German authorities and the government knew about the social and political significance of housing those who had been bombed out, and also understood the need to resettle the refugees into decent housing in areas where they could find work. Bad housing in the industrial centres contributed to poor labour productivity and diseases, in particular tuberculosis; and it was feared that it would encourage crime. Not housing the homeless risked their political radicalisation, either to the Right or to the Left. Huge sums of money were needed for the task. At a time when rents were still fixed, the incentive for large-scale construction could not be provided through rental profits. Instead they were achieved through most generous tax reductions on housing construction. The actual construction figures that were eventually achieved beat even the most optimistic forecasts, despite rising costs, which were in part caused by demands for larger and higher standard dwellings – another sign of economic prosperity.

Doc 60 Housing construction 1949–56

Costs and share of clients

	I new dwellings	II total costs in bn DM	III Social housing %	IV built by private[3]	V built by Gemein.[3]	share of col V over col. IV (%)
1949	200,000	3.0	69.1	n.n.	n.n	
1950	340,000	3.8	68.6	148,478	88,990	59.9
1951	350,000	4.7	69.5	n.n.	n.n	
1952	400,000	6.3	68.9	206,060	169,910	82.4
1953	475,000	7.8	56.4	250,060	194,650	77.8
1954	520,000	9.0	54[1]	304,896	172,032	56.4
1955	540,000	9.5	50.8[2]	323,226	154,024	47.6
1956	560,000	11.0	~50	340,047	160,597	47.0

[1] Plus another 17 % for miners, resettlers, refugees.
[2] Plus another 10 % for miners, resettlers, refugees.
[3] Figures from *Statistisches Jahrbuch*, Baufertigstellungen, Normalwoh-nungen. These figures do not add up to those in column 1 (KfW figures which are similar to *Statistisches Jahrbuch*, section 'Reinzugang an Wohnungen') since public construction is not mentioned, neither is the conversion of buildings.

From: Grünbacher, *Reconstruction and Cold War in Germany*

Housing construction is perhaps the biggest but also the most over-looked success in the early history of West Germany. By 1961, the six-millionth dwelling was officially handed over to its new occu-piers and the housing shortage declared over. Housing construction was a highly political affair in several ways. For one, construc-tion figures were used for Cold War propaganda against the East German state, demonstrating the superiority of the capitalist system. But it was also a domestic political battleground, between those who believed social housing could produce dwellings more quickly and in bigger numbers, and the Adenauer Government who saw in private homeownership a means of *Verbürgerlichung* or embour-geoisement of the working classes, as well as a cornerstone of their family policy. For this reason, in 1959 the government's Housing Minister announced a new approach to the housing market. He announced that the existing rental controls would be abolished, in particular for the older but usually larger flats in houses with multi-occupancy; and promised to provide better housing for large families. A further aim was to disperse the large urban conurbations through settlement policy: a move which had been the idealistic dream of conservative town planners for decades.

Doc 61 Lücke Plan, 1959

Lücke, Federal Minister for Housing
...
This bill aims to clear up one of the most difficult chapters of the last decades, the emergency housing legislation which had been implemented to perfection. The state-controlled housing market [*Wohnungszwangs-wirtschaft*] which had lasted now for more than 40 years had found ways into numerous bills and ordinances ...

Rents for rented accommodation have been kept artificially low and this, together with inflexible legislation to protect tenants [*Mieterschutz*], has led to a totally stagnant housing market. There is no movement on the housing market which is based on rents or incomes. This means that small households often remain in large flats because prices in the housing market have not regained their regulatory functions. Thus state-controlled housing has rendered housing conditions completely static.

Especially unsatisfactory is the fact that today a high proportion of larger flats remain blocked by single occupants who don't need these large flats and who would not keep them if a cost-covering rent could be charged. The 1956 housing census has shown that more than 700,000 singles inhabited larger flats in one of the 5 million old properties [*Altbauwohnung*] without subletting. It is obvious that many of these single persons are hoarding living space simply because it is cheap. Only when the rental price gradually regains its regulatory function and the end of state control becomes obvious to everybody will a large share of these flats become available to the housing market again and contribute to the reduction of the housing shortage ...

Just as we speak of a 'social market economy' in the economy, in the same way the reduction of state control in the housing market can only lead to a 'social rental law'. But this means that despite the expected self-initiative and self-responsibility the state cannot leave the people and the affair of the housing market completely to the free interplay of market forces. It is for this reason that the bill which has been passed by the Federal Government has an alternative name: the 'Bill for a Social Rental Law' ...

Because of this the regulations for allowance are of the utmost importance for the Federal Government because they guarantee economically and legally that every family – I emphasise: every family – has enough living space [*Wohnraum*]. There is also the fact that the Federal Government is striving to help as many families to acquire their own house and home in order to make them resistant against crisis and immunise them against the destructive poison of the ominous communist teachings. (*'Very good!' from the* CDU)

The significance of this thought becomes clear if one visualises that since the currency reform one million families have built or bought a family home and that 40 per cent of all savers with a building society are workers ...

In 1950, of the 15 million families in the Federal Republic, over one million had three or more children under the age of 15. It is the most noble task of the social renting and housing law to rid Germany of the undignified situation that still exists here and there which makes it difficult, sometimes even impossible, for large families to get the required minimal living space. And, when large families receive it, they must be able to maintain it economically and secure it legally. Shouts of children in a flat must not be a reason to terminate a rental contract ...

Linked to the end of state control in housing is another, very serious problem. Within the next years we have to achieve a dispersal of conurbations [*Ballungsräume*].

(*Applause from the CDU/CSU*)

...

It is possible and necessary to counteract the process of population concentration in big cities and conurbations by directing housing construction more and more towards the edges of towns and the surrounding countryside.

(*Applause from the CDU/CSU*)

I would regard a higher proportion of housing construction in large cities compared to all the other areas as a major mistake. Housing construction is not to support migration from the land but is supposed to counteract it ...

Trans. from: *Verhandlungen des Deutschen Bundestages, 3. Wahlperiode.*

5

Westintegration

Chancellor Adenauer had three overriding political aims during his time in office and these aims were closely interlinked. They were to regain full sovereignty for the FRG; to achieve reconciliation with France and last but not least to achieve *Westintegration*, integrating the country into the Western camp, even at the price of giving up on German unity. Not least for this reason, Adenauer's early foreign policy was highly contested, even despised, by critics on all sides of the political spectrum, even from within his own party. The other criticism that was levelled against him, again in particular during the first few years, was his perceived close co-operation, even collaboration, with the Western Allies and the aims they had for West Germany. Although by early 1950 he could present some small successes, the first real breakthrough of his policy was not of his own making. It came about because the Cold War had changed America's European priorities and made them rebuild West Germany as soon as possible. By early 1950, the French, who had opposed Germany's economic and political reconstruction, realised that they had to change their policy towards Germany from one of confrontation and blockade to one of co-operation. The French Schuman Plan proposal, which called for the pooling of the European coal and steel industry, and the subsequent creation of the European Coal and Steel Community (ECSC) was initially motivated out of fear of an American-sponsored German revival. The process of European integration that the ECSE kick-started developed further after the French and the other participating countries had realised that close European co-operation had huge economic benefits for them.

Adenauer on the other hand had seen the potential benefits since the inter-war years. In 1950 the ECSC benefited him further since it brought more international recognition for Germany and demonstrated its good will for closer European co-operation. Domestically his policy of European co-operation was heavily criticised, especially by the Social Democrats who saw the ECSC as a national sell-out. Furthermore, some of the more conservative representatives of heavy industry were opposed to the Coal and Steel Community for fear that they would be faced with increased state intervention and with losing some of their competitive advantage over the French economy. The outbreak of the war in Korea and the strategic consequences it brought made it easier for Adenauer to negotiate with the Western powers, not least because he was always able and willing to demonstrate German goodwill. Here, a good example was his acknowledgement of Germany's foreign debt that had arisen from pre-war loans and post-war aid and his readiness to settle it.

While Adenauer was trying to get the FRG integrated into the Western camp, the GDR and the Soviet Union tried to prevent this integration from happening by offering talks on German unification. Adenauer rejected all these attempts; first in 1950–51 when such an approach was made by the East German leadership (see Docs 132, 133), but most famously in 1952, when he was the strongest opponent of the so-called Stalin Note. Adenauer's policies were rewarded in November 1954 when the Three Powers signed a treaty that officially ended the occupation of West Germany. The political opposition to *Westintegration* by the Social Democrats ended in 1959/60 when they launched a new party manifesto and their parliamentary leader accepted the political realities that had been created by the Chancellor during the previous decade.

Adenauer's first step as Chancellor towards the West came in November 1949 when he signed the 'Petersberg Protocol'. Although the Allies conceded to a considerable reduction in the number of German industrial plants that were to be dismantled, the dismantling programme itself was not stopped. What enraged Adenauer's opponents in particular was his willingness to join international bodies such as the OEEC. However, even more upsetting was his acceptance of a seat in the International Ruhr Authority, the body that oversaw the dismantling process. In the eyes of the Protocol's critics, this amounted to a sell-out of German interests and an active participation in the dismantling process without any benefits for the Federal Republic whatsoever.

Doc 62 Petersberg Protocol

22 November 1949

Following upon the meeting of the three Foreign Ministers in Paris on 9th and 10th November the United Kingdom, French, and United States High Commissioners were authorised to discuss with the Federal Chancellor the letters which he had addressed to them on the subject of dismantling with a view to a final settlement of this problem. The instructions to the High Commissioners also covered a wider field and required them to examine with the Chancellor other points to be included in a general settlement. Discussions took place accordingly on 15th, 17th and 22nd November at Petersberg.

The discussions were animated throughout by the desire and the determination of both parties that their relations should develop progressively upon a basis of mutual confidence. Meanwhile, their primary objective is the incorporation of the Federal Republic as a peaceful member of the European community, and to this end German association with the countries of Western Europe in all fields should be diligently pursued by means of her entry into the appropriate international bodies and the exchange of commercial and consular representation with other countries. Both the High Commissioners and the Chancellor appreciate that progress towards this objective must depend upon the re-establishment of a true sense of security in Western Europe and they have addressed themselves particularly to this end. In all these matters they have been encouraged to find a wide community of ideas and intention, and they have in particular agreed upon the following:

I. The High Commission and the Federal Government are agreed to promote the participation of Germany in all those international organisations through which German experience and support can contribute to the general welfare. They record their satisfaction at the various steps already achieved in this direction, including German participation in the Organisation for European Economic Co-operation, the desire expressed on both sides that the Federal Republic should be promptly admitted to the Council of Europe as an associate member and the proposed signature of a bilateral agreement with the Government of the United States of America covering Economic Co-operation Administration assistance.

II. The Federal Government appreciating the desirability of the closest possible co-operation by Germany in the rehabilitation of Western European economy declares its intention of applying for membership of the International Authority for the Ruhr in which, at present, the Federal

Government is only represented by an observer, it being understood between both parties that German accession will not be subject to any special conditions under Article 31 of the Agreement for the establishment of the Authority.

IV. It is further agreed between them that the Federal Government shall now initiate the gradual re-establishment of consular and commercial relations with those countries where such relations appear advantageous.

V. The Federal Government affirms its resolve as a freely-elected democratic body to pursue unreservedly the principles of freedom, tolerance and humanity which unite the nations of Western Europe and to conduct its affairs according to those principles. The Federal Government is firmly determined to eradicate all traces of Nazism from German life and institutions and to prevent the revival of totalitarianism in this or any form. It will seek to liberalise the structure of Government and to exclude authoritarianism.

VI. In the field of decartelisation and monopolistic practices the Federal Government will take legislative action corresponding to decisions taken by the High Commission in accordance with Article 2 (b) of the Occupation Statute.

VII. The High Commission has communicated to the Chancellor the terms of an agreement reached by the three Powers for the relaxation of the present restrictions on German shipbuilding ...

VIII. On the question of dismantling, the High Commission has reviewed the present position in the light of the assurances given by the Federal Government and has agreed to the following modification of the programme. The following plants will be removed from the reparations list and dismantling of their equipment will cease forthwith.
A. *Synthetic Oil and Rubber Plants*
   Farbenfabriken Bayer, Leverkusen.
   Chemische Werke, Hüls.
   Except for certain research equipment at these plants involving an important security element.
   Gelsenberg Benzin AG., Gelsenkirchen-Horst.
   Hydrierwerke Scholven AG. Gelsenkirchen-Buer.
   Ruhroel G.m.b.H., Bottrop.
   Ruhrchemie A.G., Oberhausen-Holten.
   Gewerkschaft Victor, Castrop-Rauxel.
   Krupp Treibstoff G.m.b.H., Wanne-Eickel.
   Steinkohlenbergwerke, Rheinpreussen, Moens.

131

Dortmund Paraffinwerke G.m.b.H., Dortmund.
Chemische Werke Essener Steinkohle AG., Bergkamen.
B. *Steel plants*
 August Thyssen Hütte, Duisburg-Hamborn.
 Hüttenwerke Siegerland AG., Charlottenhütte, Niederschelden.
 Deutsche Edelstahlwerke, Krefeld.
 Hüttenwerk Niederrhein AG., Duisburg-Hochfeld.
 Klöckner-Werke AG. Düsseldorf.
 Ruhrstahl AG., Heinrichshütte, Hattingen.
 Bochumer Verein Gussstahlwerke, Bochum.
 Except that electric furnaces not essential to the functioning of the works will continue to be dismantled or destroyed.
C. Further dismantling at the I.G. Farben plant at Ludwigshafen will not take place except for the removal of the equipment for the production of synthetic ammonia and methanol to the extent provided for in the reparations programme.
D. All dismantling in Berlin will cease and work in the affected plants will be again rendered possible.
It is understood that equipment already dismantled will be made available to the Inter-Allied Reparations Agency except in the case of Berlin. The present modification of the reparations list will not affect the existing prohibitions and restrictions upon the production of certain materials. Dismantled plants may be reconstructed or re-equipped only as permitted by the Military Security Board and those plants at which dismantling has been stopped will be subject to suitable control to ensure that the limitation on the production of steel (11.1 million tons per annum) is not exceeded.

IX. The question of the termination of the State of War was discussed. Although such termination may be regarded as consistent with the spirit of this Protocol, it presents considerable legal and practical difficulties which need to be examined.

X. The High Commissioners and the Federal Chancellor have signed this Protocol with the joint determination to carry into effect the purposes stated in the preamble hereof and with the hope that their understandings will constitute a notable contribution to the incorporation of Germany into a peaceful and stable European community of nations.
 B.H. Robertson
 A. François-Poncet   K. Adenauer
 J.J. McCloy

From: US Department of State (ed.), *Documents on Germany, 1944–85.*

When Adenauer made a statement on government policy (*Regierungserklärung*) about the Protocol to Parliament, he faced fierce opposition. The debate, which went down in West German parliamentary history, reached its climax after Adenauer defended his entry into the Ruhr Authority when the leader of the Social Democrats, Kurt Schumacher, accused Adenauer of being the 'Allies' Chancellor' (*Kanzler der Alliierten*). Such a claim was tantamount to accusing the head of the government of high treason and Schumacher, who refused to retract the statement, was barred for 20 days from parliamentary proceedings for damaging the reputation of Parliament.

Doc 63 'The Allies' Chancellor'

President Dr. Köhler: Ladies and gentlemen, once again I open the discussion to the interrupted 18th session of the German Bundestag. Only point on the Agenda is the discussion of the Government's Policy Statement. ...

Dr. Adenauer, Federal Chancellor: ... When my colleague Herr Baade cites my statements before the North Rhine Westphalian Parliament [*Landtag*], I'd ask him to also cite what I said last December on the Ruhr agreement. At the time I said: 'It will depend on the spirit with which the Ruhr agreement is being carried out.' I hope that we can make sure that it is carried out in the right spirit ... But, ladies and gentlemen, it remains that I've been accused of paying too high a price for these concessions. Let me state categorically that a single concession has been made when it was declared: we are prepared to co-operate with the Military Security Board ... It has further been declared that we are determined to take the German votes in the Ruhr authority so that it can work in the right spirit ... I have just received the following telegram from Düsseldorf, a statement by the German Trade Union Federation on the German-Allied agreement. It reads: 'In the newly published German-Allied protocol a serious endeavour by the Allies can be recognised to accommodate German wishes, according to an initial statement by the German Trade Union Federation ... Unfortunately, a number of problems still remain. Therefore it would be the most noble task of all relevant authorities [*berufene Stellen*] to allay the fears of the working people still threatened with the loss of their livelihoods by dismantling ... Although the German-Allied agreement is not completely satisfactory in all its aspects, the Federal Government's co-operation with the International Ruhr Authority is correct according to the Trade Unions.' ...

(*Deputy Schumacher*: Who has signed for the telegram? – *Shout from the Left*: Signed: 'Adenauer'! ...

This telegram is a report from 'United Press' in Düsseldorf.
(*Laughs from the Left – shouts from the Left*: Aha! – Ordered! – By Adenauer!) ...
You are well aware that the General Secretariat exists and you know that the bureaucratic apparatus is already well above 100 strong. You know all of this! And you are well aware, as is everyone else in this House, that the only question to be addressed is: should we send a German representative who casts the three German votes or should we simply let dismantling continue unhindered to its end regardless? ...
And, ladies and gentlemen, I declare – and after the last speech by the Deputy Ollenhauer I'm afraid that I have to declare – that the Social Democratic group [*Fraktion*] is prepared to let dismantling happen to its end ...
This question has to be answered by the opposition (*Lively agreement by the government parties; shouts from the Left*)
– this is the question that needs to be answered and no other: are they prepared to send a representative to the Ruhr Authority or are they not? And if they declare: No – then they know, based on the declaration given to me by General Robertson, that the dismantling will be implemented to its end.
(*Deputy Schumacher*: That is not true! – Hear, hear! *And opposing shouts by the government parties. – Further excited shouts from SPD and KPD. Presidential bell. Deputy Renner*: Where is that written? – *Shouts from the Left*: Are you still German? – Do you speak as German Chancellor? – *Deputy Schumacher*: The Allies' Chancellor!)
President Dr Köhler: Herr Deputy Schumacher – (*Rousing shouts of protest in the Middle and from the Right. Massive noise and clapping of desk covers. – MPs from SPD and CDU/CSU rise from their seats and have excited altercations. – Continuing ringing of the presidential bell. – Continuing noise*).
...
President Dr Köhler: ... In the discussion with the Parliamentary groups I have found out that this House's overwhelming majority believes the interruption of Herr Dr Schumacher against the Federal Chancellor constitutes ... a deliberate violation of rules. I do regret that all attempts to make Herr Dr Schumacher to withdraw this remark have been in vain. I therefore now execute my right and my obligation towards the Federal Chancellor ... and towards the House by excluding the Deputy Dr Schumacher for 20 days from *Bundestags* proceedings on the grounds of deliberate violation of rules.

Trans. from: *Verhandlungen des Deutschen Bundestages, 1. Wahl-periode.*

Kurt Schumacher was in many respects a more 'traditional' patriot than Adenauer. Unlike the Chancellor, he had spent time in prisons and concentration camps during the Nazi years and because of his experience he believed that there were Germans who could and should lead a united Germany into a democratic future, without Allied interference, tutelage or control. Because of his inflexible and often dogmatic style, which caused a lot of irritation among the Allies and stood in sharp contrast to Adenauer's approach, the Allies never fully trusted Schumacher's political aims. Eventually it caused some opposition from within his own party, although his position as SPD leader was never challenged. The day after Schumacher's outburst, another Social Democrat, Heinrich Troeger, former Secretary General of the *Länderrat* and future Finance Minister of Hesse, made the following comments in his diary.

Doc 64 Troeger diary

26 November 1949

The hatred between Adenauer and Schumacher led to a first explosion: yesterday Schumacher called his opponent 'the Allies' Chancellor'. Result: Schumacher will be suspended for 20 days from the Bundestag. All the deputies I spoke to yesterday and today were outraged by Schumacher's behaviour which will certainly greatly damage the SPD's opposition. Schumacher will have to accept that the government can harvest a number of successes in foreign policy as well as in the economic field. Thus it would be more sensible if the opposition would concentrate on those political fields in which it would be difficult for the government, with its conservative-capitalist attitudes, to counter with a satisfactory solution. Social policy, pricing policy and wage policy, work creation and the simplification of administration etc. are the areas that come to mind. Let's see how things continue. Some SPD deputies said: 'Unfortunately, Schumacher can't be suspended from the Bundestag permanently – the CDU wouldn't be that silly'. Today Schumacher attended a meeting of the SPD's Economic Policy Committee where he made some statements of principle. I have to admit they were the most significant of all statements made. Schumacher once more displayed his outstanding attitudes to the basic sociological questions.

Trans. from: Benz and Goschler (eds) *Heinrich Troeger, Interregnum.*

It was France that would make a decisive move towards West Germany's integration into the Western camp. Considering the French experiences of the previous 75 years, it is not surprising that since the end of the war, the French government had done whatever they could to prevent the re-establishment of a central German government. However, two developments caused a major rethink of their policy. For one, the Cold War situation had fundamentally changed American attitudes towards West Germany, and since at least 1948 the US had began to systematically rebuild the country. In this process, they had increasingly outflanked and outmanoeuvred French attempts to prevent West German reconstruction. By late 1949 it had become clear to French officials that, thanks to American insistence on the subject, it would be only a matter of time before any remaining Allied restrictions on German industry would be lifted. The other development was the stagnation of the so-called Monnet Plan, a scheme which had envisaged the modernisation of the entire French economy, from agriculture to steel production and manufacturing. It had been hoped that a modernised French industry could take the place of Germany as the predominant economic power in continental Europe. Had the plan been successful, France could have prevented Germany's return as the strongest economic player and therefore thwarted the resurrection of a sizeable German steel industry that would have been necessary for any rearmament. But despite massive investments and considerable successes, the Monnet Plan missed its target, in part, ironically, because the French steel industry depended on German coal of which it could not receive enough. It is not the French analysis of the dilemma that deserves attention, but the solution they proposed to their problem. The memorandum Jean Monnet wrote in response to the situation suggested a radical new approach, the creation of a supra-national body to oversee European coal and steel industries. There can be no doubt that he came to this conclusion not because he was a European idealist, but because he believed in traditional national power politics.

Doc 65 Monnet Memorandum

3 May 1950

II.

The situation in Germany is developing quickly into a dangerous cancerous disease for peace in the near future, and for France very soon, if this development cannot be directed in a way that the Germans can find hope and co-operate with the free nations. This situation cannot be settled by the unification of Germany, since for that an agreement between the USA and the Soviet Union is necessary, and this is currently unthinkable. The situation cannot be solved either by West Germany's integration into the West because:

– then the West Germans would have to admit to the East that they are accepting the division when inevitably unity has to be their permanent aim;

– the prospect of integration raises the question of German rearmament and will lead, because it will be seen as a provocation by the Russians, to war.

– there are political questions that cannot be solved.

Despite this, the Americans will insist that this integration into the West is to proceed

– because they want something to happen but they have no other obvious ideas;

– because they doubt French reliability and dynamics. Some believe that it is time to look for a substitute for France.

...

III.

The resurrection of France will not continue if the question of German industrial production and competitive capacity is not solved quickly. The basis for the superiority which French industrialists traditionally grant to Germany lies in the fact that it can produce steel at a price France can't compete against. From this they conclude that the whole French production has to suffer. Already Germany is demanding to raise its production limit from 11 to 14 million tons. We will reject this demand, but the Americans will insist on it. Then we will make reservations and in the end we will give in. At the same time, French production is stagnant; it is even in decline ...

The question of the dominance of German industry which would cause fear in Europe, which would be the reason for continuing unrest and would ultimately prevent the unification of Europe, and which would push Germany into the abyss once more would disappear with our proposed solution. In contrast, this solution creates conditions, in both Germany and France, for common industrial competitive expansion in which any form of domination would disappear ...

V.
At the current point in time, Europe can only be born out of France. Only France can speak and act. But what will happen if France does not speak and act now?

Others will rally round the United States with the clear aim of conduction the Cold War with greater strength. The obvious reason for this is that the European countries are afraid and are looking for help. England will get closer and closer to the United States; Germany will quickly develop, we can't stop its rearmament ...

Trans. from: *Le Monde*, 9.5.1970.

Because the proposal and the invitation to join the scheme were sent by the French Foreign Minister, Robert Schuman, it became known simply as the Schuman Plan. When the note reached Adenauer, he grabbed the opportunity at once. Writing about the event some 14 years later in his memoirs when the idea had long since turned into a success story, he mentions the political nature of the plan but emphasises the magnitude and significance of the proposals, and how much the ideas corresponded with his own long-held vision. To him the plan was a chance to alleviate some French fears, so that the two countries could eventually start their process of reconciliation. It also represented an opportunity in the upcoming negotiations to regain some international credibility for Germany – and most certainly more sovereignty, as well.

Doc 66 Adenauer on Schuman's proposal

On Tuesday 9 May 1950 we held the cabinet meeting on entry into the Council of Europe ... I regarded the cabinet decision of 9 May as of great importance and had therefore called a press conference for 8 p.m. in order to announce it to the German and international public; in the morning I did not know that the day was to bring a significant turn in the fortunes of Europe.

While the cabinet was conferring I was informed that an emissary of the French Foreign Minister Schuman had an urgent communication for me ...

Blankenhorn handed me the letters in the cabinet room. One was a handwritten, personal letter by Robert Schuman. The other was an official covering letter for the project laid down in a memorandum which later became known as the Schuman Plan.

In essence Robert Schuman proposed to place the entire French and German production of coal and steel under a common High Authority within the framework of an organization that should be open to other European countries as well. Schuman explained that the pooling of coal and steel production would immediately provide for the first stage of a European federation, the immediate creation of a common basis for economic development, and for a comprehensive change in their development. The merger of the basic production of coal and steel and the establishment of an authority whose decisions would be binding for France, Germany, and the other member countries, would create the first firm foundations for the European federation which was indispensable for the preservation of peace.

In his personal letter to me Schuman wrote that the purpose of his proposal was not economic, but eminently political. In France there was a fear that once Germany had recovered, she would attack France. He could imagine that the corresponding fears might be present in Germany. Rearmament always showed first in an increased production of coal, iron, and steel. If an organization such as he was proposing were to be set up, it would enable each country to detect the first signs of rearmament, and would have an extraordinarily calming effect in France.

Schuman's plan corresponded entirely with the ideas I had been advocating for a long time concerning the integration of the key industries of Europe. I informed Robert Schuman at once that I accepted his proposal wholeheartedly ...

At the evening's press conference I commented on the Schuman Plan and on the Federal Government's decision to join the Council of Europe. I had asked all members of the cabinet to be present because I wanted to underline the great importance of what I had to say. I explained that the two decisions, that of the French cabinet on the Schuman Plan and that of the German cabinet on entry into the Council of Europe, coincided in time quite accidentally. There had been no prior negotiations ...

I then spoke about the decision of the French Council of Ministers of this morning, 9 May 1950. I stated very emphatically that I regarded it as a magnanimous step toward Germany and Europe on the part of France and [its] Foreign Minister Schuman. It was undoubtedly of the greatest imaginable importance for relations between Germany and France and for the entire future development of Europe. The decision was not a matter of fine phrases but of concrete and precise proposals for a pooling of French and German production of coal, iron, and steel, with the explicit provision that all other countries could join the agreement. I stressed that the French proposal was based on the principle of equality … I regarded Schuman's proposal as a very important step forward in Franco-German relations, a step whose significance could not be underlined emphatically enough …

Foreign Minister Schuman's proposal which, as McCloy put it, had had the effect of a little atom bomb, had also been discussed in detail. McCloy observed that all had welcomed the speed with which I had taken up the plan of Foreign Minister Schuman and declared that I was in agreement with the plan and its underlying principles.

From: Konrad Adenauer, *Memoirs*, Weidenfeld & Nicolson, 1966.

Although the invitation to join the Schuman Plan went out to all Western European countries, only six, France, Germany, Italy and the Benelux countries would join. Great Britain declined the offer, partly because of imperial grandeur and partly due to concerns about the just nationalised coal and steel industries. The negotiations on, and ratification of, what would become the treaty on the European Coal and Steel Community (ECSC) were carried out with amazing speed. On 18 April 1951 the six countries were able to sign the treaty. Once again, it was the SPD and Schumacher who voiced concern about the treaty, and demanded changes before the SPD would support it in the Bundestag. Some of these demands concerned traditional nationalist issues; others addressed the form and size of the new Europe or matters that were traditionally closer to Social Democratic politics.

Doc 67 SPD pre-conditions for ECSC membership

SPD Press Statement 20 April 1951: Seven preconditions for the Agreement to the European Coal and Steel Community
1. General political, legal and factual equality as the basis and requirement of all specific plans.
2. Union of all democratic Europe including Scandinavia and Great Britain and exclusion of the Small Europe of clerical, conservative and cartelistic groups.
3. European planning based on the rules and planning in the individual national economies under rejection of all attempts to hand over the German basic industries to the egoisms of individual groups of capital and countries.

4. Representation in all international institutions according to significance and capacity of the individual countries without privileges and without discrimination.

5. A international democratic parliament as the source and architect of all economic policy which elects an executive and directing authority which is solely dependent on it and over which it has sole control.

6. Maintenance and development of the existing economic power sources including the organisational conditions in the individual countries' economies without preference or discrimination by means of power politics.

7. Equal participation of working people in social affairs and in the rules and guidance of the economy.

Trans. from: *Kurt Schumacher, Redern – Schriften – Korrespondenzen 1945–1952.*

The significance of Adenauer's next step of *Westintegration* is often not recognised fully. His acknowledgement of Germany's foreign debt and his willingness to find a mutually acceptable way of repayment during the subsequent London Debt Conference (see Doc 56) eventually brought in foreign investment that was desperately needed for the reconstruction. But beyond the simple economic motivation lay as well two political motives. When Adenauer made the offer, the Federal Republic was just beginning to recover from a major balance of payment crisis which had seriously threatened the whole experiment of the social market economy. The timing of his démarche would have convinced the Allies a little more of his sincere intentions. Secondly, by also accepting responsibility for the foreign debt of pre-war Germany, Adenauer strengthened his government's claim of being the only rightful successor of the German Reich and thus being the only government that could legally speak for all Germans. In other words, the acceptance of the Reich's debts strengthened his claim for the sole representation of Germany against the East German government.

Doc 68 Adenauer acknowledges German foreign debt

Federal Republic of Germany   6 March 1951
The Federal Chancellor

His Excellency, The Chairman of the Allied High Commission
Ambassador André François-Poncet
Mr High Commissioner,
... I have the honour to inform you as follows:

I. The Federal Republic hereby confirms that it is liable for the pre-war external debt of the German Reich, including the debts of other corporate bodies subsequently declared liabilities of the Reich, as well as for interest and other charges on securities of the Government of Austria to the extent that such interest and charges became due after 12 March 1938 and before 8 May 1945.

The Federal Government understands that in the determination of the manner in which and the extent to which the Federal Republic will fulfil this liability, account will be taken of the general situation of the Federal Republic including, in particular, the effects of the limitations on its territorial jurisdiction and its capacity to pay.

II. The Federal Government acknowledges hereby in principle the debt arising from the economic assistance furnished to Germany since 8 May 1945, to the extent to which liability for such debt has not previously been acknowledged in the Agreement on Economic Co-operation concluded on 15 December 1949 between the Federal Republic and the United States of America, or for which the Federal Republic has not already taken over responsibility under Article 133 of the Basic Law. The Federal Government is ready to accord the obligations arising from the economic assistance priority over all other foreign claims against Germany or German nationals.

The Federal Government regards it as appropriate to regulate any question connected with the recognition and settlement of these debts by bilateral agreements with the Governments of the countries which have rendered economic assistance, patterned on the Agreement concluded with the United States of America on 15 December 1949.

The Federal Government takes for granted that these agreements will contain an arbitration clause for cases of dispute. The Federal Government is prepared at once to enter into negotiations for the conclusion of such agreements with the Governments concerned.

III. The Federal Government hereby expresses its desire to resume payments on the German external debt. It understands that there is agree-

142

ment between it and the Governments of France, the United Kingdom of Great Britain and Northern Ireland and of the United States of America on the following:

It is in the interest of re-establishment of normal economic relations between the Federal Republic and other countries to work out as soon as possible a settlement plan which will govern the settlement of public and private claims against Germany and German nationals. Interested Governments including the Federal Republic, creditors and debtors, shall participate in working out this plan.

The settlement plan shall in particular deal with these claims, the settlement of which would achieve the objective of normalising economic and financial relations of the Federal Republic with other countries. It will take into account the general economic position of the Federal Republic, notably the increase of its burdens and the reduction in its economic wealth. The general effect of this plan shall neither dislocate the German economy through undesirable effects on the internal financial situation nor unduly drain existing or potential German foreign-exchange resources. It shall also not add appreciably to the financial burden of any Occupation Power.

...

From: NA PRO FO 371 93728.

There were, of course, attempts made by the East to prevent West Germany's accelerating integration into the Western camp by suggesting ways forward to all-German elections and to the re-unification of the zones of occupation. But since neither side really believed in the possibility of unification any longer, those attempts have to be seen more as a direct appeal to the West German people in the faint hope that they would object against further *Westintegration*. An early attempt at this was the letter by GDR Minister President Otto Grotewohl to Chancellor Adenauer in November 1950 (see Doc 134) but this was easily rejected because the Bonn government did not recognise the GDR's legitimacy. Potentially the most serious offer for a solution to the 'German problem' came in 1952, when Stalin himself made a proposal to end the country's division. For the first time, the Soviet leader himself suggested the neutralisation of a unified country. In other words, Germany would become a united country but would be a political, economic and militarily neutral state between both power blocks.

Doc 69 Stalin note

Draft for a German Peace Treaty, March 10 1952
The Soviet Government considers it necessary to direct the attention of the Government of the United States of America to the fact that although about seven years have passed since the end of the war in Europe a peace treaty with Germany is not yet concluded.

With the aim of eliminating such an abnormal situation the Soviet Government, supporting the communication of the Government of the German Democratic Republic to the Four Powers requesting that conclusion of a peace treaty with Germany be expedited, on its part addresses itself to the Government of the United States and also to the Governments of Great Britain and France with the proposal to urgently discuss the question of a peace treaty with Germany with a view to preparing in the nearest future an agreed draft peace treaty and present it for examination by an appropriate international conference with the participation of all interested governments. It is understood that such a peace treaty must be worked out with the direct participation of Germany in the form of an all-German Government. From this it follows that the U.S.S.R., U.S.A., England, and France who are fulfilling control functions in Germany must also consider the question of conditions favouring the earliest formation of an all-German Government expressing the will of the German people.

With the aim of facilitating the preparation of a draft peace treaty the Soviet Government on its part proposes for the consideration of the Governments of the U.S.A., Great Britain and France the attached draft as a basis of a peace treaty with Germany.

In proposing consideration of this draft the Soviet Government at the same time expressed its readiness also to consider other possible proposals on this question ...

Draft of Soviet Government of Peace Treaty With Germany
... Conclusion of peace treaty with Germany has an important significance for the strengthening of peace in Europe. A peace treaty with Germany will permit final decision of questions which have arisen as a consequence of the second world war. The European states which have suffered from German aggression, particularly the neighbours of Germany, have a vital interest in the solution of these questions. Conclusion of a peace treaty with Germany will aid improvement of the international situation as a whole and at the same time aid the establishment of a lasting peace.

The necessity of hastening the conclusion of a peace treaty with Germany is required by the fact that the danger of re-establishment of German militarism which has twice unleashed world wars has not been eliminated in as much as appropriate provisions of the Potsdam conference still remain unfilled. A peace treaty with Germany must guarantee elimination of the possibility of a rebirth of German militarism and German aggression ...

The Governments of the Union of Soviet Socialist Republics, United States of America, Great Britain and France consider that preparations of the peace treaty should be accomplished with the participation of Germany in the form of an all-German Government and that the peace treaty with Germany should be formed on the following basis:
Basis of Peace Treaty with Germany

Participants
Great Britain, the Soviet Union, the United States of America, France, Poland, Czechoslovakia, Belgium, Holland and other governments which participated with their armed forces in the war against Germany.

Political Provisions
(1) Germany is re-established as a unified state, thereby an end is put to the division of Germany and a unified Germany has a possibility of development as an independent democratic peace-loving state.
(2) All armed forces of the occupying powers must be withdrawn from Germany not later than one year from the date of entry into force of the peace treaty. Simultaneously all foreign military bases on the territory of Germany must be liquidated.
(3) Democratic rights must be guaranteed to the German people to the end that all persons under German jurisdiction without regard to race, sex, language or religion enjoy the rights of man and basic freedoms including freedom of speech, press, religious persuasion, political conviction and assembly.
(4) Free activity of democratic parties and organisations must be guaranteed in Germany with the right of freedom to decide their own internal affairs, to conduct meetings and assembly, to enjoy freedom of press and publication.
(5) The existence of organizations inimical to democracy and to the maintenance of peace must not be permitted on the territory of Germany.
(6) Civil and political rights equal to all other German citizens for participation in the building of peace-loving democratic Germany must be made available to all former members of the German army, including officers and generals, all former Nazis, excluding those who are serving court sentences for commissions of crimes.
(7) Germany obligates itself not to enter into any kind of coalition or military alliance directed against any power which took part with its armed forces in the war against Germany.

Territory
The territory of Germany is defined by the borders established by the provisions of the Potsdam Conference of the Great Powers.

Economic Provisions
No kind of limitations are imposed on Germany as to development of its peaceful economy, which must contribute to the growth of the welfare of the German people.
Likewise, Germany will have no kind of limitation as regards trade with other countries, navigation and access to world markets.

Military Provisions
(1) Germany will be permitted to have its own national armed forces (land, air, and sea) which are necessary for the defence of the country.
(2) Germany is permitted to produce war materials and equipment, the quantity and type of which must not exceed the limitations required for the armed forces established for Germany by the peace treaty.

Germany and the United Nations Organisation
The governments concluding a peace treaty with Germany will support the application of Germany for acceptance as a member of the United Nations Organization.

From: US Department of State (ed.), *Documents on Germany 1944–61.*

It is not surprising that both the three Western Allies and Adenauer rejected the proposal as a Soviet ruse. A united but neutralised Germany in the middle of Europe would have been a much greater benefit to the Soviet Union than to the West. For the next 40 years or so after the rejection of the note, a sometimes fierce debate raged in Germany as to whether or not Stalin's offer was genuine and whether or not the West's refusal to seriously negotiate it constituted 'a missed opportunity' for German unity. Based on the latest research, it appears that Stalin did indeed only try to test Western response. However, what has often been forgotten in this debate is to consider Western and German reactions if the proposal had been genuine. It is quite clear that in 1952 the United States were not prepared to give up the Federal Republic, with its economic and military potential, for the sake of a united but neutralised Germany in the middle of the continent. By this time, the political preparations for the integration of the Federal Republic into the planned

146

European Defence Community were nearly completed. Two months after the West's rejection of the Stalin Note, on 26 May 1952, the three Western powers and the FRG signed the 'General Treaty', which turned the Allied occupying forces in West Germany into protecting forces. More importantly for Adenauer, the treaty gave wider-ranging powers to the German government, though they still fell short of full sovereignty.

Doc 70 'General Treaty'

Bonn May 26, 1952.

The United States of America, The United Kingdom Of Great Britain And Northern Ireland and The French Republic, of the one part, and The Federal Republic Of Germany, of the other part:
...
Whereas it is the common aim of the Signatory States to integrate the Federal Republic on the basis of equality within the European Community itself included in a developing Atlantic Community;
...
Whereas the retention of the Occupation Statute with its powers of intervention in the domestic affairs of the Federal Republic is inconsistent with the purpose of integrating the Federal Republic within the European Community; ...
Whereas the Three Powers and the Federal Republic recognize that both the new relationship to be established between them by the present Convention and its related Conventions and the Treaties for the creation of an integrated European Community, ... and the Treaty on the Establishment of the European Defence Community, are essential steps to the achievement of their common aim for a unified Germany integrated within the European Community;
Have entered into the following Convention setting forth the basis for their new relationship:

ARTICLE 1
1. The Federal Republic shall have full authority over its internal and external affairs, except as provided in the present Convention.
2. The Three Powers will revoke the Occupation Statute and abolish the Allied High Commission and the Offices of the Land Commissioners upon the entry into force of the present Convention and the Conventions listed in Article 8 ...

ARTICLE 2
1. The Three Powers retain, in view of the international situation, the rights, heretofore exercised or held by them, relating to (a) the stationing of armed forces in Germany and the protection of their security, (b) Berlin, and (c) Germany as a whole, including the unification of Germany and a peace settlement ...

ARTICLE 4
1. The mission of the armed forces stationed by the Three Powers in the Federal territory will be the defence of the free world, of which the Federal Republic and Berlin form part ...
4. The Federal Republic will participate in the European Defence Community in order to contribute to the common defence of the free world,

ARTICLE 5
2. In case the Federal Republic and the European Defence Community are unable to deal with a situation which is created by
    an attack on the Federal Republic or Berlin,
    subversion of the liberal democratic basic order,
    a serious disturbance of public order or
    a grave threat of any of these events,
and which in the opinion of the Three Powers endangers the security of their forces, the Three Powers may, after consultation to the fullest extent possible with the Federal Government, proclaim a state of emergency in the whole or any part of the Federal Republic ...

ARTICLE 6
2. The Federal Republic, on its part, will co-operate with the Three Powers in order to facilitate the discharge of their responsibilities with regard to Berlin. The Federal Republic will continue its aid to the polit-ical, cultural, economic and financial reconstruction of Berlin and, in particular, will grant it such aid as is set out in the annexed Declaration of the Federal Republic ...

Done at Bonn this twenty-sixth day of May 1952 in three texts, in the English, French and German languages, all being equally authentic.

From: *FRUS 1952–54*, Vol. VII.

Very much to Adenauer's disappointment (see Doc 80), the European Defence Community did not become a reality but the improvements the General Treaty had brought for the Federal Republic were not revoked, and the process of integration continued. In October 1954 the occupation regime was eventually terminated. The Adenauer Government in turn portrayed the termination as the Federal Republic's return to sovereignty, which is not entirely true since the Allies retained certain rights and powers. Only in 1990, in the wake of the German reunification, did the Allies abandon those remaining rights, thus finally bringing to an end the last remnants of the post-war occupation.

Doc 71 Termination of occupation regime

Paris, 23 October 1954

The United States of America, the United Kingdom of Great Britain and Northern Ireland, the French Republic and the Federal Republic of Germany agree as follows:

Article 1. The Convention on Relations between the Three Powers and the Federal Republic of Germany, the Convention on the Rights and Obligations of Foreign Forces and their Members in the Federal Republic of Germany, the Finance Convention, the Convention on the Settlement of Matters arising out of the War and the Occupation, signed at Bonn on 26 May 1952, the Protocol signed at Bonn on 27 June 1952 to correct certain textual errors in the aforementioned Conventions and the Agreement on the Tax Treatment of the Forces and their Members signed at Bonn on 26 May 1952, as amended by the Protocol signed at Bonn on 26 July 1952, shall be amended in accordance with the five Schedules to the present Protocol and as so amended shall enter into force (together with subsidiary documents agreed by the signatory States relating to any of the aforementioned instruments) simultaneously with it.

Article 2. Pending the entry into force of the arrangements for the German Defence Contribution, the following provisions shall apply;
1. The rights heretofore held or exercised by the United States of America, the United Kingdom of Great Britain and Northern Ireland and the French Republic relating to the fields of disarmament and demilitarisation shall be retained and exercised by them, and nothing in any of the instruments mentioned in Article 1 of the present Protocol shall authorize the enactment, amendment, repeal or deprivation of effect of legislation or, subject to the provisions of paragraph 2 of this Article, executive action in those fields by any other authority.

2. On the entry into force of the present Protocol, the Military Security Board shall be abolished (without prejudice to the validity of any action or decisions taken by it) and the controls in the fields of disarmament and demilitarisation shall thereafter be applied by a Joint Four-Power Commission to which each of the signatory States shall appoint one representative and which shall take its decisions by majority vote of the four members.

3. The Governments of the signatory States will conclude an administrative agreement which shall provide, in conformity with the provisions of this Article, for the establishment of the Joint Four-Power Commission and its staff and for the organization of its work.

Article 3. 1. The present Protocol shall be ratified or approved by the signatory States in accordance with their respective constitutional procedures. The Instruments of Ratification or Approval shall be deposited by the signatory States with the Government of the Federal Republic of Germany.

2. The present Protocol and subsidiary documents relating to it agreed between the signatory States shall enter into force upon the deposit by all the signatory States of the instruments of ratification or approval as provided in paragraph 1 of this Article.

3. The present Protocol shall be deposited in the Archives of the Government of the Federal Republic of Germany, which will furnish each signatory State with certified copies thereof and notify each State of the date of entry into force of the present Protocol.

[Signed] Dulles, Eden, Mendès-France
Adenauer

Reprinted in: J.A.S. Grenvill and B. Wasserstein, *The Major International Treaties*.

In 1959 and 1960 the Social Democratic Party finally acknowledged and accepted Adenauer's defence and foreign policy towards the West, thus completing the developments of the last decade and the Federal Republic's integration into the Western world. The first step was the party abandoning their official Socialist manifesto in their landmark 'Godesberg Programme'; in practice the party had long accepted the market economy.

Doc 72 SPD Godesberg Programme

...

National defence

The German Social Democratic Party declare their support for the defence of the liberal-democratic basic order [*freiheitlich-demokratische Grundordnung*] and approve national defence.

National defence has to be in accordance with Germany's political and geographic situation and thus has to keep limits which are necessary for the creation of requirements for international détente, for an effective controllable disarmament and for Germany's reunification. The protection of the civilian population is a significant part of the country's defence. The Social Democratic Party calls for the worldwide outlawing of weapons of mass destruction under international law.

...

Economic and social order

Aim of social-democratic economic order is a continuous growing prosperity and a just participation of all in the national economy's yield, a life in freedom without degrading dependence and without exploitation.

Steady economic growth [*Wirtschaftsaufschwung*]

The second industrial revolution created the prerequisite to raise the general standard of living further than before and to eliminate the poverty and misery which still depresses many people.

Economic policy, on the basis of a stable currency, has to guarantee full employment, to increase the national economy's productivity and to increase the general prosperity.

In order to allow all to participate in the rising prosperity, the economy has to be adapted methodically to the continuing structural changes so that a balanced economic development can be achieved. Such a policy needs the calculation of the Gross Domestic Product [*volkswirtschaftliche Gesamtrechnung*] (GDP) and the national budget. The national budget will be passed by Parliament. It is binding for government policy, is an important basis for an independent central bank policy and provides guiding points for the economy which keeps the right to independent decisions.

The modern state constantly influences the economy through its decisions on tax and finances, on monetary and borrowing matters, its customs, trade, social and pricing policies, its public orders as well as agricultural and housing construction policies. More than a third of the GDP constitutes public spending of this kind. It is therefore not a question of whether arrangements and planning are useful in the economy but a matter of who makes these arrangements and in whose favour they work. The state cannot withdraw from this responsibility for economic developments. It is responsible for a far-sighted economic policy [*Konjunkturpolitik*] and is basically supposed to limit itself to indirect methods of influencing the economy.

Free choice of consumption [*freie Konsumwahl*] and free choice of workplace are decisive bases; free competition and free entrepreneurial initiative are important elements of social democratic economic policy. The autonomy of employees and employer organisation in concluding collective bargaining agreements is an essential part of the liberal order. Totalitarian economic planning destroys freedom. For this reason the Social Democratic Party approves of the free market wherever there is free competition. But wherever the markets are falling under the predominance of individuals or groups, a wide variety of measures is to be taken to retain the freedom in the economy. Competition as far as possible, planning so far as necessary!

[...]

Private ownership of the means of production is entitled to receive protection and support as long as it does not hinder the creation of a just social order. Efficient medium-sized and small enterprises are to be strengthened so that they can stand up in the economic clash with big business ...

Trans. from: *Grundsatzprogramm der Sozialdemokratischen Partei Deutschlands. Beschlossen vom Außerordentlichen Parteitag der Sozialdemokratischen Partei Deutschlands in Bad Godesberg vom 13. bis 15. November 1959.*

With the Godesberg Programme, Keynesianism became the official economic-policy doctrine of a major party in Germany for the first time. Then, in 1960 in a speech before Parliament on behalf of the party, the SPD's deputy chairman Herbert Wehner accepted West Germany's participation in the European institutions and in NATO. In doing so, the second biggest party in the Federal Republic acknowledged the political realities. Accepting the international status quo and giving up on an outdated idealistic dream of a united and neutral Germany would greatly improve the party's political fortunes in the near future.

Doc 73 Wehner speech, 1960

A couple of days ago the Governing Mayor of Berlin, Willy Brandt, indicated the points of contact in the views of the democratic parties, over which, as he put it – and I am of the same opinion – there needed to be no disagreement within the Federal Republic. I suppose these points of contact can, when one thinks it through, be brought in from all sides as assets in the appraisal of foreign policy meassures.

These are:

First: Berlin has to remain with the Federal Republic. Germany's division into two cannot become a division into three.

Secondly: The German people and the Federal Republic have decided against any form of dictatorship and in favour of the Western community, i.e. for a close co-operation with the Western neighbours and the free world.

Thirdly: Germany's responsible groups (*verantwortungsbewussten Kräfte*) decided against Communism and against Soviet politics in Germany.

Fourthly: Everything has to be done to improve the life and the fate of 17 million fellow Germans in the Soviet-occupied part of Germany. We cannot allow the desire for self-determination to become weary in our people and we have to constantly look for new approaches to the solution of the German question.

Fifthly: Since Europe has already been divided by the Communists, no further contribution is to be made towards a further division. Rather, as far as we can contribute, everything has to be brought on track so that Europe can work together in a broad community.

Sixthly: Despite the necessity to do justice to questions of military security, the Federal Republic has to make every effort to contribute towards peace in the world.

...

A few days ago in Schleswig the Federal Minister for Defence, Herr Strauß, said that striving for a common foreign policy by government and opposition is a matter of great political significance since it would not only guarantee the current government's political friendship from the Allies, but also the friendship for any future government. Shortly afterwards at Erlangen he spoke of four preconditions for a common foreign policy ... The four preconditions ... are:

a) The Social Democrats have to recognise together with the CDU that European unity and the Atlantic Alliance are the preconditions for maintaining freedom and for the achievement of German reunification. [*Very true* from the CDU/CSU].

b) The Social Democratic party has to distance itself from the old theory that reunification is only possible if the Federal Republic leaves NATO and the European Alliance.

c) The Social Democrats would have to be prepared to carry the burdens of national defence with the Union parties with deeds and not only with words, regardless of who has governmental responsibility and who is in opposition ...

d) The Social Democrats would have to recognise unequivocally the term 'self-determination', i.e. after free elections for reunification, for the whole of Germany.

These are ... the four preconditions of which Herr Strauß has spoken. Now something in advance. Before a stock-take and discussion where one can look at the facts in detail I would like to say today:

Re a) The Social Democratic Party of Germany takes the view that the European and Atlantic system of alliance – of which the Federal Republic is part – forms the basis and framework of all efforts of German foreign policy and reunification policy.

Re b) The Social Democratic Party of Germany has not demanded and is not intending to push ahead with the policy of the Federal Republic abandoning treaty and alliance obligations. It is of the opinion that a European security system would be the suitable form to enable a reunited Germany to make its contribution to achieving security in Europe and the world. [*Very true!* from the SPD].

Re c) The Social Democratic Party of Germany declares itself in word and deed in support of the defence of the liberal democratic basic rights and the basic order and agrees to national defence. [Agitation from the CDU/CSU].

– Ladies and gentlemen, different views on the expediency and fitness for purpose in this area, which are legitimate in a democratic state and which are dealt with democratic- parliamentarily, do not mean that the parliamentary opposition [*parlamentarische Opposition*] is less keen on responsibility than the Government ...

Re d) I refer verbatim to the resolution which the Bundestag had passed unanimously with the votes of the Social Democrats on 1 October 1958 in Berlin. It reads: 'The German Bundestag expects the reestablishment of Germany's national unity through a direct decision of free will by the whole of the German people in all the parts that are still separated today; this will be brought about after the removal of the obstacles outside of German jurisdiction. The German Bundestag declares its willingness to support any negotiation that will pave the way to the wilful decision by the German people as soon as an agreement by the Four Powers has opened up this possibility.'

So much for the four preconditions or questions ...

Translated from: *Verhandlungen des Deutschen Bundestages, 3. Wahlperiode.*

Wehner's speech was a continuation of what had begun with the Godesberg Programme. It meant that for the first time the SPD officially committed itself to the defence of the West within the framework of NATO. Now the CDU could no longer claim that the SPD was unfit for government because it would abandon defence commitments. With Wehner's speech, the SPD had again become a serious contender for participation in government.

6

Rearmament

Westintegration and West German rearmament were closely linked and intertwined, both with each other and the wider Cold War developments. When the Allies defeated Germany in 1945, one of their aims was to end German militarism forever. The events and policies which led within ten years to an U-turn on German demilitarisation and to the establishment of West German armed forces is indicative of wider attitudes that were prevalent in the West. Adenauer, for one, believed that armed forces were an essential aspect of a state's sovereignty; and long before the Americans picked up the topic, there were strong voices in Great Britain, most notably the voice of Winston Churchill, which called for a re-arming of German forces so that they could be used against further Soviet aggression. The Americans needed slightly longer to become accustomed to this idea, however. The Berlin Blockade by the Soviets in 1948/9, and the subsequent American-led airlift to the city helped to change attitudes quickly. The outbreak of the war in Korea on 25 June 1950 made it clear that the West was utterly unprepared for a possible attack by the Soviet Union. Even one year after its foundation in April 1949 NATO had neither the personnel nor the equipment nor the infrastructure in place to withstand a potential Soviet attack. Adenauer seized this opportunity to offer a German contribution to the defence of Western Europe.

While the American and British political leaders were in principle in favour of such a move, the French perspective was quite different. Having suffered German invasion three times in 70 years, resulting in massive destruction in the First World War and a four-year occupation in the Second World War, the French were to say the least not happy about the idea of a new German army. The solution eventually thought to be acceptable for all sides was the European Defence Community (EDC). In the newly discovered spirit of European unity, the EDC was supposed to create, under French command, a European Army made up of contingents from the various participating nations. Although the preparations for the EDC led to the signing in 1952 of the 'General Treaty', which reduced Allied control over the FRG, in 1954 the French Parliament voted against the ratification of the EDC treaty and thus killed off the project. By this time, however, preparations for West German armed forces had moved far ahead. With the Americans insisting on a German military contribution, the rearmament of the FRG could no longer be prevented. Instead of becoming part of a European army, German troops became a national contingent in their own right as part of NATO in 1955.

It was not all plain sailing for Adenauer. The political preparations for German rearmament prior to 1955 were accompanied by a wide domestic debate and considerable hostility towards a new German army. The anti-militarist and pacifist '*Ohne Mich*' (Without me) movement, pointing to the war experience, was opposed to any remilitarisation of Germany and had widespread public support.

The shock in the Western world caused by the North Korean invasion of the southern part of the country was immense, and nowhere more so than in the Federal Republic. Politicians and the general public alike were painfully aware of the similarities between Korea and Germany, i.e. the split of each country into a Communist and a non-Communist part. Although there had been some tentative planning under way for West German remilitarisation since at least May 1950, Adenauer wrote to American High Commissioner John McCloy after the outbreak of the Korean War to outline the threat faced by the FRG. Adenauer warned not only against the Soviet forces stationed in Eastern Europe but also against the accelerated build up of paramilitary police forces within the GDR. In view of the weak and insufficient Allied units stationed in West Germany at this time, he offered to provide German troops within the framework of a European defence force. The potential appeal of such a move for the Allies was obvious. It could help to bolster European defence, while at the same time, as Adenauer pointed out, it would prevent the resurgence of German militarism. The Chancellor also suggested the establishment of a federal police force and asked for Allied orders to the German government to initiate proceedings to its build-up. The call for the establishment of a federal police force that could match the East German *Volkspolizei* was a particu-

157

larly shrewd move. Police matters in the FRG were, and still are, a concern of the individual *Länder*; thus the federal police force would increase the muscle of the Federal Government. And as it turned out, the new *Bundesgrenzschutz*, or Federal Border Police, became the founding cell of the future German army in which many ex-soldiers waited their time before the establishment of the new armed forces in 1955.

Doc 74 Adenauer on the defence of the FRG

I.

The developments in the Far East have caused agitation and insecurity among the German population. The confidence that the Western world would be able to encounter assaults on Western Europe quickly and effectively is deteriorating at an alarming rate and has caused a dangerous lethargy within the German population.

II.

The seriousness of the whole situation is obvious by looking at the Soviet forces gathered in the Eastern zone and the accelerated build-up of the people's police force.

According to confirmed information there are Soviet troops within the territory of the Eastern zone currently comprising two armies of fast columns [*schnelle Truppen*], with nine mechanised divisions, four *Panzer* armies with 13 divisions, 22 mechanised and armoured divisions in total ... The number of operational tanks has to be presumed to be 5,000 to 6,000. The fighter wing of the Soviet air force is implementing a greatly accelerated re-equipping to turbo fighter (jet fighter) of the most modern production. At constant speed of re-equipment one can assume that there are currently some 3,000 turbo fighters and some 5,000 by the end of September ...

Apart from these extraordinarily strong Soviet-Russian forces there is a particular advancement in the build-up of the Eastern zone's people's police. In particular its development from police force to paramilitary army has to be noted. Over the last few months some 70,000 men have been extracted out of the Eastern zone's general police; transferred into military-like formations and trained in military procedures ...

So far, the armaments of the people's police squads [*Volkspolizei-bereitschaften*] consists only of light infantry weapons. According to the latest, yet unconfirmed reports, there are people's police divisions in Lower Silesia and near Stettin, i.e. on Polish-occupied territory, which are already equipped with tanks ... It has to be expected that in the near future the people's police will include some 150,000 men and will be expanded to 300,000 according to the general plan.

III.

The counterweight in Western Germany to these enemy forces consist of two American and two British divisions and a couple of French units ...

IV.

The problem of the Federal Republic's [*des Bundes*] security has first to be addressed from the foreign-policy point of view. The external defence of the Federal Republic lies in the first instance with the occupation troops. The Federal Chancellor has repeatedly requested the reinforcement of these occupation troops and renews this request in the most urgent way possible. For only the reinforcement of the Allied occupation troops in Western Europe can show to the population the Western powers' will to defend West Germany in case of war [*im Ernstfall*]. Such a reinforcement of Allied troops is also necessary because the defence measures currently implemented in Western Europe can only be carried out under the protection of a sufficient number of well-equipped Allied divisions.

The Federal Chancellor has repeatedly declared his willingness to provide a contribution in the form of a German contingent if an international Western European army were to be established. This is the unambiguous expression of the Federal Chancellor's opposition to Germany's remilitarisation through the establishment of an independent national military force.

V.

...

The Federal Government therefore proposes the immediate establishment on the Federal level of a police force in such strength that it can guarantee the interior security [of the federal territory].

The Federal Government is aware of the fact that such a police force can only be established through a law which would require amendments to be made to the constitution. The Government is prepared to immediately send a draft bill to the legislative bodies, but it has to point out that several months will go by before such a bill will be passed. Since the preparations have to start immediately it is necessary for the Allied High Commission to instructing the Federal Government to take the necessary steps for the creation of this police force ...

Trans. from source reprinted in: K. v. Schubert (ed.), *Sicherheitspolitik in der Bundesrepublik Deutschland 1945–1977.*

Whether or not the anxiety Adenauer displayed in his memo was real, or whether he used it to achieve his own objectives, is still debated today. When McCloy reported back to his superiors in Washington, he was certainly not too impressed by the horror scenario Adenauer had painted in his memo and during their meeting. Not without reason he accused the Chancellor of applying pressure tactics and viewing the whole situation only from a German perspective, without considering wider Soviet objectives or possible further responses.

Doc 75 McCloy on meeting with Adenauer

Frankfurt, August 18, 1950

Adenauer's first visit with Commission since his return from vacation dealt only with matter of security. He said that time had come for comprehensive statement of international situation from German point of view. He found state of great demoralization in Germany on his return from Switzerland and felt that Allied Governments should face facts as he saw them.

He read from comprehensive intelligence report ...

Chancellor estimates German population's reaction to *Volkspolizei* attack under present circumstances would not be one of resistance.

They would be quite neutral. Confidence of average German in US military strength has been greatly shaken by Korean developments. Morale generally is low. Inner will to resist has been substantially reduced. They have not become Communists, but they have lost their belief in resistance, belief they once had largely because of assured strength of US. Chancellor referred to some demonstrations in Esslingen and Munich which he felt showed communist strength in contra-distinction to police weakness and again repeated his lack of confidence in police as they are now formed.

Although Soviet forces are definitely marshalled in East Germany in offensive form as could be shown by a location map he gave us, he felt Soviets themselves would not attack although their divisions in East Germany are at war strength with full supplies ammunition and fuel. He was confident that Stalin's chief purpose was to get Germany with as little damage as possible and consolidate it with Russian strength to oppose US and a destroyed Germany would be of less use to his purpose ....

He feels that immediate danger is an attack by *Volkspolizei* and doubts whether the US would drop bomb on Moscow if all that were involved was situation similar to that in Korea. He made strong appeal for Allied Governments to display greater strength in Germany to increase the number of divisions immediately and to show their strength throughout

Germany more than is now being done. More troops, more planes flying, and more troops and equipment should be in evidence to be observed by population. In addition immediate permission for Federal Government to build up a force adequate to meet the *Volkspolizei*. He has in mind 150,000 men, volunteers adequately armed. Call them police or what you will, but they must be a counter to *Volkspolizei* ... He concluded by saying he hated thought of re-arming Germany in any form but that temptation must be removed promptly from the Soviets to get Germany with out risking World War ... As for European army he said that he felt it was only eventual hope and that he would strongly support German participation in any such force, but as he put it 'when will we get it?' He kept reiterating that any propaganda effort to be of any account depends upon a manifestation of strength. Chancellor was obviously suffering from real anxiety but was also engaging in his usual pressure tactics in my judgment ...

... my offhand estimates of Adenauer's appraisal of *Volkspolizei* strength and capacity is that he is rather building up their potentials, [as to both] objectives and timing. As usual he is taking the whole thing purely from German point of view, without any consideration of other Soviet objectives or timing ...

From: *FRUS 1950*, vol. IV.

McCloy's reluctant comment most likely resulted from his previous experiences with Adenauer and from the Chancellor's general attitude. The Americans nevertheless strongly welcomed a West German defence contribution and were looking for a way to sell it to the French. Adenauer seemed to have sensed the turning tide even before the outbreak of the Korean War. In May 1950 he had appointed an 'Advisor for Military and Security Matters' within the *Zentrale für Heimatdienst* or 'Office for *Heimat* Service'. Despite its fairly innocent name the office was in reality a think tank staffed with former Wehrmacht officers that provided the intellectual basis for German rearmament. On 9 October, after a four day conference at the monastery of Himmerod, they produced a memorandum about the military, political and psychological preconditions for West German rearmament. The memorandum produced at the meeting, the so-called *Himmeroder Denkschrift*, became one of the intellectual blueprints for the reestablishment of West German armed forces, and displayed some of the implicit thinking of the traditional German officer class about Germany's recent past and their role in it.

Doc 76 *Himmeroder Denkschrift*

I. Military political basis and requirements

Germany's military political position is more unfavourable now than in any time in history ...
From a political, military and psychological perspective, the following requirements are regarded as necessary:

1. From the Western Powers:
Politically:
> To strive for full sovereignty of the West German Federal Republic after its government has been recognised in New York as the only German government for the whole of Germany [*einzige Regierung Gesamtdeutschlands*] (in its 1937 borders).
> The lifting of the Control Council Laws and other regulations on demilitarisation as far as they concern national defence.
> The inclusion of representatives of the West German Government into the Council of Ministers in Strasbourg.

Militarily:
> The military equality of the West German Federal Republic within the framework of the European-Atlantic community. Even if full sovereignty in the political and economic fields cannot be achieved yet, immediate military equality is indispensable nevertheless. A 'second-class-soldier' will never commit himself with the necessary moral vigour.
> By land Germany is not to be seen as the advanced territory of an intended main line of defence on the river Rhine.
> The raising of modern units capable of their own operations, similar to those of other states, up to at least corps size, including their own tactical air force and forces for advanced coastal defence [*Küstenvor-feld-Streitkräfte*].
> Equal place within the European-Atlantic supreme command ...
> Rejection of any and every solution which would incorporate the German man, individually or in small units, into western military units in the way of the Russian 'Hiwi' of the last war.
> The possibility of a security contribution by preparing for partisan warfare is to be ruled out. The German people, the German terrain and vegetation are unsuitable for this kind of warfare ...

Psychologically:
> Rehabilitation of the German soldier through a declaration by government representatives of the Western powers (revocation of the past defamation by Control Council and other laws).

Release of Germans sentenced as 'war criminals' as long as they only acted under orders and did not commit offences under old German law. The cessation of all pending trials. This aim can only be reached gradually; but an apparent start has to be made before the raising of troops. The question of the convicted in Spandau (especially the two soldiers) has to be addressed.

Termination of any kind of defamation of the German soldier (including those of the Waffen-SS who then operated under the Wehrmacht) and actions for the transformation of public opinion at home and abroad ...

2. Proposals for the West German Federal Government

Politically:

Swearing in [*Verpflichtung*] of the German soldier in the name of the German people – represented through the Federal President – with emphasis on the all-European idea as long as the Western European Federation has not found a supra-national form ...

The deployment of the German contingent only within Europe ...

The agreement of the opposition and of the Trade Unions for the build-up of a German contingent is an obvious precondition; the ethos of national defence has to take hold in the whole nation.

A forceful fight against all elements which subvert the democracy, internal protection of the beginning military build-up, methodical start to the instructional work within the German people.

Militarily:

Clear structural division between the Wehrmacht (external security) and the police (internal security).

Psychologically:

Declaration in defence of the honour of the German soldier by the Federal Government and the peoples' representatives [*Volksvertreter*].

Fair arrangements for the care of past and future soldiers and their surviving dependents. Equal right for all public servants [*Staatsdiener*].

From: Bundesarchiv Koblenz BW9/3119.

The former officers had realised that a new German army had to be accepted by the large majority of the German people if it was to be successful. For this reason they asked for explicit acceptance of the new forces from the opposition parties and especially the trade unions, due to their reputation as staunch opponents of militarism.

For obvious reasons the new army should take an oath in the name of the German people and in the spirit of a common European identity. At the same time, the deployment of the new force was to be restricted to Europe only. This was to avoid the possibility of Germany being drawn into the colonial conflicts that were going on at the time, especially in French Indochina. Concerning the reputation of German soldiers, the memorandum achieved a very quick success. It was no lesser man than General Eisenhower, the Allied wartime Supreme Commander, who had to speak out for them. In his memoirs he had equated all German officers to the evil of the Nazi regime, and had refused German generals the traditional gestures of military honour. In January 1951, as newly appointed Supreme Commander of NATO, he visited NATO troops in Germany. During this visit, a meeting with Adenauer and some of his military advisors was arranged and the following day Eisenhower gave the following press statement.

Doc 77 Eisenhower rehabilitates German soldiers

General Eisenhower arrived at Frankfurt, this being his first visit to Germany since the end of the war in 1945; it was stated that his mission was primarily to consult American, British and French commanders and to inspect occupation troops and that he would have no official conferences with German political leaders in view of the fact that Germany was not at the present a member of the NATO. In a press statement on his arrival he ... added: 'For my part bygones are bygones. I bear no resentment against the Germans as a nation and surely not against the German people. I would be a liar if I were to say that at the time of the conflict I did not bear in my heart a very definite antagonism towards Germany and a hatred for all the Nazis stood for. I fought as hard as I knew to destroy it. But from today I would like to see the German people – all people – saying to themselves "We want to be free, we want to live with friends to everyone".' ...

On 22 Jan. [he] attended a reception given in his honour at Bad Homburg by Mr McCloy, at which the guests included Dr. Adenauer, the Länder Premiers and the former Generals Heusinger and Speidel, both of whom were members of the German expert committee negotiating with the Allied authorities on a possible German contribution to a collective defence of Western Europe [11169A]. During the reception General Eisenhower had informal conversations with Dr. Adenauer and ex-generals Heusinger and Speidel. Prior to leaving Frankfurt for Paris on Jan. 23, General Eisenhower made the following statement: 'I have come to know that there is a real difference between the regular German soldier and officer and Hitler and his criminal group. For my part, I do not believe that the German soldier as such lost his honour. The fact that certain individuals committed dishonourable and despicable acts during the war, reflect on the individuals concerned and not on the great majority of German soldiers and officers.'

From: *Keesings Contemporary Archives*, 1950–52, February 3–10, 1951.

Unbeknown to the press, Eisenhower had gone a step further in his informal meeting with Adenauer and the former German generals: he actually apologised to them for his earlier statements. This apology, even though it was made behind closed doors and did not become public until several years later, was a precondition for the willingness of many former German officers to join the intended forces once they were to be set up. Eisenhower, who would soon give up his military command to become US President, had been realistic enough to recognise that he had to make both the public and the off-the-record statements if the West wanted to draw on the military knowledge of the former German officers. Faced with an increased threat of a Soviet invasion of Western Europe, Eisenhower had to reverse his previous opinions to get that know-how. One long-term result of his statement, and a similar one made by Adenauer to the German parliament, was a massive boost for the myth of the 'clean' Wehrmacht, i.e. the claim that Wehrmacht units were not involved in war crimes or the Holocaust, but that those crimes had all been committed by the SS and other special units. The political situation of the Cold War helped to cement this myth. Although some academics investigated and wrote about Wehrmacht involvement in war crimes from at least the 1970s, it took until the 1990s for the general public to accept the army's connection to the crimes.

General Eisenhower's statement did not come unexpectedly. US State Department officials came to a similar conclusion about the importance of West Germany, not only because of its potential military prowess but perhaps even more so because of its economic potential which under no circumstances could be allowed to fall under Soviet influence.

Doc 78 US State Department on Germany's military importance, 1951

Washington, February 8, 1951

General Considerations with Respect to Allies of the United States
Comparative Strength
...
2. The non-Soviet world still has far greater resources and a far larger military potential than the Soviet empire. Much of the strength of the non-Soviet world, however, lies in Western Europe, the Middle East and Southeast Asia, all of which are experiencing increased Soviet pressure.
3. The Soviet Union is aware of the fact that the resources and potential of the non-Soviet world would probably result in the ultimate defeat of the Soviet Union unless a significant part of such resources and potential can be utilized by the Soviet Union or at least denied to the free world.
4. There would be a critical shift in the ability of the United States to achieve ultimate victory if the Soviet Union succeeded in utilizing or denying to the West all or even a substantial part of the resources and potential outside of the Western Hemisphere.

The Relative Importance to the United States of Various Parts of the Non-Soviet World
...
5. Germany and Japan
In the last war the strength which Germany and Japan were able to develop brought much of Eurasia, the Pacific and Africa under their domination. The potential strength of these two areas in the hands of the Soviet Union would greatly affect the power balance between the U.S.S.R. and U.S. Our problem with respect to these two former enemies is two-fold, since [not only must we deny] them to the U.S.S.R. but also we must seek to utilize their potential in our own behalf. Their neutralization would be an invitation to their absorption into the Soviet Union and therefore their orientation toward the West must be accomplished and must carry with it the will to develop their strength for the common purpose of the non-Soviet world rather than their own aggrandizement.
...

From: *FRUS 1951* vol. I, pp. 44 ff.

Economic concerns played an important role in 'the defence of the West' on both sides of the Atlantic in early 1951. The war in the Far East had quickly caused an economic 'Korean Crisis' once the Americans had put their national economy on a war footing again. This shift caused a huge and worldwide American demand for strategic raw materials, with the result that raw material prices on the world market rose by up to 30 per cent. The Americans reintroduced strict controls on their economy and expected their allies to do likewise (see Doc 43). This idea was complete anathema to Erhard and to most German industrialists who were already suffering from the higher raw-material prices. In West Germany, the surge in economic activity meant that the basic industries, in particular coal production, could not satisfy demand. To avoid economic restrictions similar to those in the USA, or worse, a reduction in raw-material deliveries under the Marshall Plan, the *Bundesverband der deutschen Industrie* (BDI, Federation of German Industry), the influential and powerful association of German industry, had set up a committee that was tasked with countering such a threat. In February 1951 the committee published a report in which it outlined the way West German industry should react to the crisis in Far East.

Doc 79 BDI guidelines for supplying armaments to the Allies

1) Task:
As a result of the declaration of a national emergency in the United States, effects have appeared that will soon show up in the German economy as well. It is therefore imperative – for political reasons as well – to make it clear to the Western world that West Germany has the firm will to contribute in any form, as an equal partner, to the defence of Western cultural values [*des westlichen Kulturgutes*].

Therefore, a 'practical contribution for the maintenance of peace' is to be provided but one which does not intend to provide any equipment for explicit military purposes [*ausgesprochenes Rüstungsmaterial*] ...

5) Participation of the whole of West German industry
All companies of West German industry are to be informed by their associations on the intended supplies offered according to the directives by the subcommittees' chairmen; the companies should have the opportunity to submit their offers.

6) Scope of the offers:
Offers include:

Consumer goods
Means of production (machine tools etc.)
Supplemental material [*Hilfsmittel*]
Equipment
It is left to the individual companies' initiative to offer articles that fit their product range and from which they expect, based on their knowledge of the market, will be needed by the purchasing countries. The offers do not include equipment for explicit military use [*ausgesprochenes Rüstungsmaterial*]. Instead it is intended to provide relieve for those industries in Western countries that have, on the commission of their governments, switched from producing consumer goods to armaments. The German consumer-goods industry will step into those gaps in the production of consumer goods but at the same time also commits itself to the delivery of means of production, supplementary and armaments material [*Aufrüstungsmittel*].
The following items are not regarded as armaments:
Individual military equipment [*militärisches Einzelgeräte*]
Optical equipment
Uniforms
Engines
Caterpillar tracks
Lorries etc.
...

Trans. from: NA PRO FO 371 93727.

It was hardly surprising that German industrialists wanted to help defend 'Western cultural values'; what was slightly more surprising was how narrowly they defined the term 'military equipment' so that they could support the war effort in Korea even at a time when there were still considerable Allied production limits and even production bans in place. This apparent willingness to produce for the Allied military stands in sharp contrast to the considerable hesitation many companies were to display in the second half of the 1950s when they were asked to produce armaments for the new *Bundeswehr*. The difference was that in 1951 unemployment was still very high and Allied contracts meant both continuing supply of raw materials and export revenue in hard currencies which was most welcomed; in contrast, in the mid-1950s the German economy was booming, so many companies shied from taking on the often unsteady but certainly disreputable armament contracts.

In the political realm, considerable progress was made towards German rearmament during 1951. The negotiations on, and eventual signing of, the Coal and Steel Community treaty had provided a blueprint on which a European Defence Community was to be built. On 27 May 1952 government representatives of the participating countries signed the EDC treaty in Paris. The West German government faced severe criticism and had to mount a strong defence of the treaty in the Bundestag. Despite widespread fears of Communism in the Federal Republic, the initial near panic of 1950 had eased, and many Germans – particularly the SPD opposition – feared that the treaty and the subsequent rearmament of the FRG would only lead to the permanent division of Germany, and were therefore totally opposed to the signing. The government in its defence of the signing played the 'European' card.

Doc 80 Government defence of the EDC treaty

The negotiations that led to the conclusion of the treaty on the Defence Community go back to two considerations, one military-political, and one general political [*allgemein-politische*]. The military-political consideration was the observation that it was necessary to secure the defence of the Western world and to include German defence powers as well. The general political consideration arose from the efforts of European integration that suggested the inclusion of defence efforts as an element of such an integration attempt ...

The European Defence Community is, like the European Coal and Steel Community, a supra-national community provided with its own sovereignty rights [*Hoheitsbefugnisse*] ... The treaty does not regulate, like previous military alliances, the rights and obligations of the states' military assistance and co-operation. Instead it creates in the area of defence, in a similar way as the European Coal and Steel Community has done for the basic industries, a European structure with its own instruments, its own armed forces and its own budget. The armed forces in particular are European, not national. Thus the Defence Community stands in contrast to the coalition armies of old. In the latter the troops remain national in status, they remain troops of individual states, only under a supreme command ...

The European Defence Community ... is built on the unreserved equality of all participating states, and its norms not only bind the participating states but also principally the states' citizens. Thus the Defence Community intervenes much more into national sovereignty than the

Coal and Steel Community. One of the fundamental sovereignty rights, the right to self-defence, will be transferred to the Community as soon as it is established. This has implications far beyond military matters as it also affects fiscal and economic policies. Thus the Defence Community is pressing towards the overall political federalisation of Europe. The Defence Community is not only the preparation of such a Federation but is a decisive part in it ...

The Community will face organisations such as the North Atlantic Treaty Organisation as a unit, as well. It places itself, as far as operational matters are concerned, as a member into the framework of that organisation.

Trans. from: *Verhandlungen des Deutschen Bundestages, 1. Wahlperiode*, Anlage 2 zu DrS. 3501.

Ten months later, on 19 March 1953, the Bundestag ratified the EDC treaty with the government's majority, and the Federal Republic seemed well on its way to providing its share of soldiers for the new European army. However, events took a different turn. On 30 August 1954 the French National Assembly rejected the ratification of the treaty and thus killed off the project. At the time, and for many years to come, the general perception was that the French Parliament rejected the treaty out of fear of renewed German militarism. However, this explanation hides other significant aspects. It was a weak French government that had to face up to numerous groups in Parliament, all with different interests. There may have been some MPs who were genuinely scared of a resurgent German militarism. But there were also a considerable number of Communist deputies who voted against the treaty because it did not fit with Moscow's plans. Finally, it is often forgotten that just three months earlier the French army had lost its jungle fortress at Dien Bien Phu, its last stronghold in Indochina, which led to the end of French colonial rule there; and to the independence of Vietnam, Laos and Cambodia. At the same time, there were the first signs of unrest in French North Africa. Signing up to the EDC would have meant the end, or at the very least a considerable weakening, of independent French military power, since the EDC was to create a European army. Without a national army France would have been unable to hold those territories and would have simultaneously lost the claim to great-power status.

Whatever the reasons for the French National Assembly's rejection, the bad news hit the German government like a bombshell. Herbert Blankenhorn, Adenauer's foreign-policy advisor and confidant was on the way to the Chancellor's holiday retreat when he received the news and recorded the reaction in his diary.

Doc 81 Blankenhorn on EDC failure

Monday, 30 August 1954
In the evening in Ettlingen on the way to Bühlerhöhe, Hallstein and I received the news about the French National Assembly's voting results in which 319 deputies against 264 had voted to cancel the treaty's further readings. In the debates prior to the vote mainly opponents to the defence community had spoken. The Minister President had only supported the acceptance of the ratification bill half-heartedly. This means the end of the EDC.

Tuesday, 31 August 1954
With the Federal Chancellor at Bühlerhöhe. The news has hit him hard. Until the very last minute he had hoped that the French Parliament would accept the treaties, even if only by a small majority. Now a good deal of work in the European unification project has been destroyed. Had the enemy been underestimated? Had one tried to achieve too much too fast? Despite all disappointment the Chancellor under no circumstances wanted to aggravate the situation through harsh criticism of the French Government. His line was: continuation of the work on European integration, postponement of plans for an integrated European defence, achievement of full sovereignty for the Federal Republic and entry into NATO. The Cabinet, which the Chancellor had gathered at Bühlerhöhe on 1 September, made a decision accordingly.

Trans. from: H. Blankenhorn, *Verständnis und Verständigung: Blätter eine politischen Tagebuchs 1949–1975*.

Despite the disappointment about the failure of this particular policy of European integration, Adenauer stuck to his long-term aim of reconciliation with France and did not criticise the French for the failure of this important European project. Instead he quickly took up the only other possible solution: West German integration into NATO. On 23 October 1954, in the so-called 'Paris Treaty' (see

Doc 70), the Federal Republic joint NATO and received qualified sovereignty once the treaty came into force on 5 May 1955.

On 12 November 1955 the first soldiers of the new West German forces were sworn in. The day had been deliberately chosen, since it was the 200th birthday of the Prussian military reformer Scharnhorst. Making this link was meant as a symbol of the new army's loyalty to the democratic state. Since the overwhelming majority of the new army's first volunteers had already served in the Nazi Wehrmacht, certain safeguards were put in place in an attempt to prevent diehard Nazis from entering the new force, and to try to guarantee the loyalty of the new soldiers to the democratic state. One of the most important of these safeguards was the Personnel Appraisal Committee.

Doc 82 Personnel Appraisal Committee (*Personalgutachter-Ausschuß*)

Task and Work of the Personnel Appraisal Committee

...

It is due to the same endeavour that the Personnel Appraisal Committee (PC) for the Bundeswehr is in existence. It is a 37-member-strong body elected by the Bundestag, made up from the most different groupings, political camps and professions [*Berufen*]. There the Social-Democrat minister sits next to former generals and other high-ranking officers; next to the Catholic priest sits a member of the Protestant synod; next to the female German UNESCO delegate the widow of the resistance fighter who was executed after the 20th July. The circle of resistance against National Socialism and of the politically persecuted is effectively represented by a number of individuals. Apparently these individuals have been selected from the viewpoint of a watchful experience of the latest period of German history and an increased sense of responsibility for the future of our national order. Political parties, authorities of the Federal Government and the Bundesrat with three members participated in the selection process. This committee, elected by Parliament, which is in terms of party politics and all other aspects completely independent of Government and Parliament, has been given the task to draw up guidelines for the preconditions to be fulfilled by a volunteer for the Bundeswehr – regardless of rank. Furthermore, the Committee is called upon to judge on the personal qualification of candidates for the highest officer ranks – colonels and generals – on an individual basis. If it is at all possible to compare the Personnel Appraisal Committee with similar institutions in other democratic countries, the Committee is most closely comparable to the Royal Commission which has proven itself in British constitutional life ...

It is very important to the Committee to find out about a candidate's efforts after 1945 to integrate into civilian life through his own work. Here, his efforts and steadiness of the job do count. 'Birds of passage' or even those men who limit themselves to spending their maintenance and have the sulks will find little approval. Candidates that have proven that they did find the right tone with their colleagues and their subordinates will guarantee that as officers they will satisfy the demands of considerate behaviour and that they will respect the soldiers' human rights. In regard to citizenship the Committee obviously runs checks to determine whether the applicant had been an ardent follower of the NSDAP during the 'Third Reich' to a degree that an honest embrace of the concepts of law and order [*rechtsstaatliche Gesinnung*] cannot be expected. It will be established whether he has tried to open himself to democratic thinking or if he has even been actively participating in the rebuilding of political life at all, be it in his local community, ... the European Union or similar institutions. The number of refused applicants or those who had withdrawn their application themselves or had been declined by the Federal Ministry of Defence is nearly 15 per cent ...

However, the Committee has always held the view that nobody has a claim to become an officer in the Bundeswehr; and that for the judgement of all applicants the basis of absolute equality is to be applied, regardless of whether he worked before in the *Amt Blank* or not. In our view only one group has priority: it is those who were persecuted by the National Socialists and those who resisted against the rule of the illegal state [*Unrechtsstaat*] ...

One question with which the public, public authorities, Parliament, the political parties and the Committee dealt with quite keenly over recent months is the question of allowing former members of the SS into the Bundeswehr. The Personnel Assessment Committee's guidelines distinguish between 'Allgemeine SS' [General SS] and 'Waffen SS' ... Members of the 'Allgemeine SS' had been without exception convinced and fanatical National Socialists who regarded themselves, with some justification, as the innermost core of the National Socialist regime ... During the war an increasing number of ordered transfers [*Kommandierungen*], forced transfers and drafting into the Waffen SS occurred, such that by the end of the war it comprised some 600,000 men. The guidelines passed by the Personnel Appraisal Committee deal ... with those Bundeswehr applicants who were members of the Waffen SS at any time. The guidelines state first of all that persons who had evidently been forced into or taken on by the Waffen SS not of their own wish – the burden of proof lies with the applicant – will be subjected to the same

173

scrutiny as the other applicants ... No former member of the Waffen SS who, for example after a temporary transfer to the *Verfügungstruppe*, had ever participated in guarding a concentration camp, no former Waffen SS soldier who had ever participated in a mass liquidation or a similar hideous act will find entry into the Bundeswehr ...

The Personnel Appraisal Committee in its consultations had been fully aware of the burden of the SS question. But it has refused to pass collective judgement over the entire SS in the knowledge that collective judgements will always contain flaws and are unable to do justice to such a complex case as a totalitarian state. Even the Nuremberg Trials have refrained from a collective judgement on the SS. However, on one point the Personnel Appraisal Committee has passed a collective decision: it has decreed that former Waffen SS applicants with the rank of colonel or general are absolutely excluded from being accepted ...

The Personnel Appraisal Committee realises the responsibility with which it has been burdened. This body is made up of the most heterogeneous elements, but its members all agree in their determination to contribute with their work to a healthy spirit within the Bundeswehr. The Committee has developed into an amazingly united unit. Most decisions, often after a hard struggle, are taken unanimously or near unanimously ...

Trans. from: *Bulletin der Bundesregierung*, 8 February 1957.

While the Committee may have been a good idea in principle, it also helped to create an image of a break with the past that was simply not possible in reality. The Committee's actual impact can be challenged – as a fairly derogatory comment from a high-ranking officer who was to be vetted shows. In regard to the 'widow of the resistance fighter' his statement was simply 'So, now I'll be scrutinised by a housewife!'

During the debate on West German rearmament prior to the Paris Treaty, the 'Without me' movement posed a political challenge for the government's plans. However, once facts had been established, the movement lost its significance. In 1957, after the intentions of the ambitious new Defence Minister Franz Josef Strauß to arm the Bundeswehr with nuclear weapons had become public, a new movement emerged. Its aim was similar to that of the British CND, the Campaign for Nuclear Disarmament, namely nuclear disarmament, or in the German case, the prevention of such weapons. The Easter marches organised by the movement once more attracted a significant number of participants. What was more important was the fact that this time the movement gained the active support of publicly well-known men and women – including MPs, bishops, and Nobel laureates who on 10 March 1958 publically spoke out against nuclear weapons in national newspaper advertisements.

Doc 83 Appeal by the Working Party

'Fight Against Nuclear Death'

The German people on this side and on the other side of the zone border will, in the case of war, face certain nuclear death. There is no protection against it. Participation in the atomic arms race and the provision of German territory for launch sites for atomic weapons can only increase this threat. The aim of German policy, therefore, has to be to ease tensions between East and West. Only such a policy can serve the safety of the German people and the national existence of a liberal, democratic Germany. We ask the Bundestag and the Federal Government not to participate in the atomic arms race but instead to support all attempts for a nuclear-free zone in Europe as a contribution to détente. We call upon the whole German people – regardless of rank and status, denomination or party – to oppose a life-threatening armaments policy and instead support a policy of peaceful development. We will not rest as long as nuclear death threatens our people.

[40 Signatures by writers, politicians, Trade Unions leaders, academics, clergy]

Trans. from: *Keesings Archiv der Gegenwart* (1958).

Although it gained the capability to deploy them, the Bundeswehr never had nuclear weapons in their arsenal, although ultimately this was more due to political concerns by the Allies than because of the movement's activities. The 'Fight Against Nuclear Death' campaign was the last significant public attempt to prevent any kind of armament in West Germany until the debate about the stationing of new NATO missiles in Europe that developed after 1979.

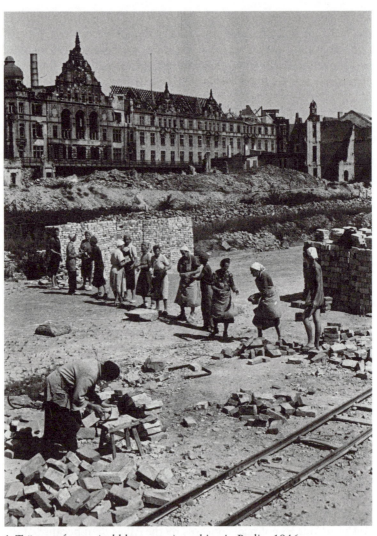

1 Trümmerfrauen (rubble women) working in Berlin, 1946

2 Currency reform 1948: Passers-by staring at newly available goods in a shop window

3 A family enjoy their new prosperity in their living room, admiring the new television

4 Ludwig Erhard, the 'father of the economic miracle' with his trade-mark cigar and his book Wohlstand für Alle (Prosperity Through Competition), 1957

5 Relatives awaiting returning POWs from the Soviet Union to find out about the fate of their sons or husbands, 1955

6 'Loitering' teenagers on a moped and a pushbike, 1959

7 West Berliners watch the construction of the Berlin Wall at Sebastian-strasse, 13 August 1961

179

8 Adenauer and De Gaulle embrace each other after the signing of the Franco-German treaty (the Elysée Treaty), 1963

9 The Auschwitz trial. In front of a map of the Auschwitz concentration camp two of the accused are escorted away by police during a break in the proceedings

Part III
'We are somebody again ...', life and politics in the 1950s

If one wanted to put a date on the beginning of West Germany's 'miracle', then 1954 would be the best year. In June that year, against all odds, the country's national team won the football world cup in what became known as *Das Wunder von Bern*, or the 'Berne Miracle'. This event caught the public imagination on a massive scale and the catch phrase *Wir sind wieder wer* or in English 'We are somebody again' became a widespread motto in West Germany from the mid-1950s onward. At first, the phrase had been used in the business community, which had greatly profited from the Korea boom that had massively invigorated West German exports; and from there the phrase spread to the rest of the economy. Together with Adenauer's foreign policy successes that helped to turn the country from an international pariah in 1945 into a valued member of the Western community, the now emerging 'economic miracle' began to spread to wider sections of the population.

By the mid-1950s many West Germans had begun to refer to 8 May 1945 as *Die Stunde Null*, the Zero Hour, to emphasise that a new era in German history had begun. This *Schlussstrich Mentalität*, the attitude of drawing a line under the Nazi period, was challenged in the late 1960s when the Adenauer era was seen by rebellious students and by some political scientists as a period of restoration. This restoration claim referred not only to attitudes but even more so to the continuing occupation of positions of power and influence by people who had held or gained such positions during the Third Reich. Those accusations were made in particular against industrialists and members of the judiciary, but also against some politicians and civil servants (see chapter 15). Old attitudes did not disappear overnight, especially in regard to gender roles, not least because the government advocated a traditional family policy. In contrast, considerable liberalisation and challenges to the establishment appeared in arts and culture, though not without strong resistance from the traditionalists. The biggest impact on West German society derived from the trickling down of the economic success to the wider population in the form of higher wages and falling living cost, in real terms. This led to the development of a modern consumer society against the background of what Abelshauser has termed the 'corporate state', in which the state, trade unions and employers worked closely together.

Political developments during the second half of the 1950s, in particular in the field of foreign policy, were a continuation of Adenauer's previous strategy of ongoing European integration on the one hand and attempts to keep the GDR internationally isolated outside the Eastern Block on the other. The climax and at the same time the dead end of this dogmatic position was reached in the years after the announcement of the Hallstein Doctrine, which during the 1960s became more and more a political cul-de-sac.

7

Visit to Moscow and the Hallstein Doctrine

Adenauer's official foreign policy towards the East was based on a 'policy of strength'. The claim was that if the West – of which the Federal Republic had to be a part – showed strength against the Soviet Union and its satellites, then Germany, including all its Eastern territories (i.e. even those under Polish administration), would be reunited in the near future and remain part of the Western camp. However, since Adenauer was one of the twentieth century's greatest *Realpolitiker*, there is some doubt as to whether he believed his own public statements on this matter, or simply made them for political convenience. Yet there can be no doubt about the validity of one aspect of this policy: Adenauer claimed that by right the Federal Republic was the only representative for all Germans and the whole of Germany, since the FRG had the only democratically elected government in Germany. It is not surprising that one of his first statements on governmental policy (*Regierungserklärung*) in parliament, on 21 October 1949, emphasised this point.

Doc 84 Adenauer's claim for sole representation

Contrary to the Potsdam Agreement of 2 August 1945 in which it was decided that Germany should be regarded as a political and economic unit during the period of occupation, differences soon began to emerge among the Allies concerning their attitude towards Germany. As early as 1945 Central Administrations were set up in the Soviet Zone in contrast with the other three zones. These Central Administrations had the unmistakable purpose of organizing the whole of the Soviet Zone into an administrative *(staatliche)* whole. These tendencies were strongly reinforced by the creation, on 12 June 1947, of an Economic Commission. The economic and political separation of the Soviet Zone from the rest of Germany was further promoted by the appointment of the

so-called First People's Congress on 6 December 1947, the summoning
of the Second People's Congress on 18 March 1948, the creation of a
Peoples Council on the same day, its instruction to work out a Constitution, and finally the passing of this Constitution by the People's Council
on 19 March 1949. These People's Congresses were not the result of
elections – that is to say, of free elections – in which everyone could freely
have taken part ... The People's Council established itself on 7 October
1949 as the Provisional People's Chamber, contrary to the Constitution it had itself passed. Simultaneously it was stated that the elections
which had already been planned several times would be postponed until
15 October 1950. After the unconditional surrender and the complete
collapse of all the state institutions in Germany, it is not possible for
any organization in Germany to claim that it is a legitimate state unless
it rests on the freely expressed will of the people. Nobody can claim
that the organisation now created in the Soviet Zone rests on the freely
expressed will of the people of that zone. It has come about on the orders
of Soviet Russia with the participation of a small minority of Germans
devoted to it.

In contrast with the Soviet Zone, there was no sign among the
Western Allies in the Western Zones of an endeavour to create a unified
state *(staatliche)* organisation for these three zones until the London
Conference of the six Powers – England, France, the USA, and the
Benelux countries – which was held from February until June 1948 ... As
a result of the recommendations of the London Conference, the Parliamentary Council was called together on 1 September 1948. The Basic
Law passed by it came into force, after ratification by the *Landtage* on
23 May 1949. Elections for the first Bundestag were held on 4 August
1949. About 25 of the 31 million Germans entitled to vote took part in
them. After deducting the 1.5 million Communist votes which alone can
be regarded as having been cast against the new organization of the state,
roughly 23 million voters are left who in this election confirmed their
approval of new political organization of the three Western Zones, the
creation of the Federal Republic of Germany.

I must emphasize the following: there is no free will of the German
people in the Soviet Zone. What is happening there now has not the
support of, and is therefore not recognized as legitimate by, the population. The Federal Republic, on the other hand, is supported by the recognition and the freely expressed will of about 23 million Germans who
are entitled to vote. Thus the Federal Republic is – pending the achievement of German unity – the sole legitimate political organisation of the
German people. This has certain consequences for internal and foreign
policy on which I cannot dwell in detail today.

The Federal Republic of Germany also feels a responsibility for the
fate of the 18 million Germans who live in the Soviet Zone. It assures

them of its loyalty and care. The Federal Republic of Germany is alone entitled to speak for the German people. It does not recognize declarations of the Soviet Zone as binding on the German people.

Trans. from: *Verhandlungen des Deutschen Bundestages, 1. Wahlperiode.*

During the first years of the 1950s, Adenauer's claims were vehemently supported by the three Western Allies. In one instance in 1950, for example, the British leaned heavily on the Swiss, who had considered recognising the GDR. After the death of Stalin in 1953 and the end of the occupation status for the FRG, along with the country's accession into NATO, the new Soviet leadership under Khrushchev and Bulganin in June 1955 took the initiative to shake things up. They invited Adenauer to come to Moscow and to establish diplomatic relations between both countries. Once more, it is not clear what the true Soviet intentions behind the move were: whether a recognition of the new status quo or an attempt to make the GDR politically presentable. The offer certainly caused a stir, not only in the West but also in the Eastern Block, as a telegram by the US Embassy in Poland to the State Department shows.

Doc 85 Polish fears

20 June 1955

... Germany: Although USSR bid [for] relations [with] West Germany was [an] admission of weak Soviet faith in [the] possibilities [of] reunification East-West Germany, interesting confirmation [was] provided recently to [a] reliable Western colleague by East German Ambassador Heymann, who stated that since reunification [was] impossible for [a] long time, [the] two Germanys 'should' have relations and that he consequently 'welcomed' [the] invitation Adenauer['s] to Moscow. [The] statement [is] particularly interesting from [the] standpoint that satellites, including East Germany, will presumably follow Moscow's lead promptly in attempting to establish relations [with] West Germany when and if Soviet-West German relations become fact. Embassy has heard [in] this connection that some Poles fear Adenauer trip to Moscow may result in [a] Soviet offer [to] return some 'recovered' territories to Germany. Department has probably already foreseen [the] problem which would arise if [the] USSR, having established relations [to]

West Germany, would insist[on] inviting both West Germany and East Germany (which Western countries have refused to recognise) to [a] conference on reunification ...

From: *FRUS 1955–57*, vol. XXV.

For Adenauer the visit came with certain political risks, not necessarily in the form one of his advisers foresaw, who feared that the whole German delegation would be arrested instantly on their arrival in Moscow and sent to a Siberian Gulag. The risk was not to lose the trust of his Western allies. As Adenauer stated later in his Memoirs, he had to make it absolutely clear to the Western Powers that he would remain loyal to the West and not begin a seesaw policy between the two power blocks. For him, even the idea of West German neutrality in return for the country's unification was out of the question.

Doc 86 Adenauer's political preparation for the Moscow visit

The highest requirement of my negotiations in Moscow would be my absolute faith in the treaties with the West. Our firm integration into the West was not to be shaken. Marguerite Higgins, a renowned American journalist wrote on the 28 August in a report on my Moscow visit very accurately: 'Dr Adenauer's consultations with the Russians will without a doubt be the most delicate ones of his long political career. He has to do everything possible to convince the German public that every chance for Germany's reunification is used, and on the other hand he can't do anything that would threaten his connection with the Western Allies.' For understandable reasons Washington, Paris and London were very interested to learn more about the aims of my negotiations in Moscow. Dulles in particular tried to explore how I imagined the negotiations in Moscow would proceed ...

I let Dulles be assured that the Federal Government would stand unswervingly by the signed contracts ...

In Paris I let Herbert Blankenhorn inform Minister President Antoine Pinay about my intentions for the Moscow talks. Pinay was very grateful for the statement and requested to meet me after my Moscow visit ...

I informed the British Government as well about the intentions I had for the Moscow talks. From London's perspective it was of particular importance that the Germans in Moscow should avoid anything that could negatively influence the Geneva Conference of Foreign Ministers. London's opinion was similar to my own, in that we considered my Moscow talks and the Geneva Conference as one connected round of talks. It appeared expedient to the British Government that in Moscow I would emphasise the reunification question.

Trans. from: K. Adenauer, *Erinnerungen 1953–55*, Stuttgart 1994 (5th edn).

The excerpt from his memoirs also shows the ranking in importance Adenauer gave to the Western powers. For obvious reasons, the protecting power, the USA was the most important; second came France, which he regarded as the crucial partner for further European integration, while the United Kingdom to him played a less significant role. The actual visit to Moscow took place 8–14 September 1955, and tough negotiations were held. Other than the establishment of diplomatic relations, the visit brought two results. The most celebrated outcome was the release of the last 10,000 German POWs that had remained in Soviet camps. Many people saw this as the greatest of all of Adenauer's achievements. The second outcome, politically more important and longer-lasting, was the Hallstein Doctrine; it was more a necessary construct for Bonn than an intended outcome. By taking up diplomatic relations with the Soviet Union, a precedent was created. For the first time, the FRG had agreed to full diplomatic relations with a country that had recognised the GDR. This deviation from the previous policy carried the risk that countries outside the Eastern Block would now recognise the GDR, which would have meant an end to the FRG's claim of sole representation. To prevent this from happening, Wilhelm Grewe, a high-ranking official in the German Foreign Office came up with what seemed to be a good formula on the flight back from Moscow. The FRG would regard the establishment of diplomatic relationship with the GDR by any state as an unfriendly act by that country. In diplomatic language, an unfriendly act meant almost automatically the termination of political relations. As a former occupying power, the Soviet Union was labelled a special case and as such exempted from the doctrine.

Immediately after his return, on 20 September, Adenauer wrote to the Soviet Premier Bulganin. In the letter he confirmed his Government's view on the basic conditions under which they had established diplomatic relations.

Doc 87 Adenauer letter to Bulganin

On the occasion of establishing diplomatic relations between the Government of the Federal Republic of Germany and the Government of the USSR, I declare:

1. The establishment of diplomatic relations between the Government of the Federal Republic and the Government of the USSR does not represent any recognition of present territorial possessions on both sides. Final determination of the German boundaries remains reserved for a peace treaty.

2. The establishment of diplomatic relations with the government of the Soviet Union does not signify any change in the legal standing of the Federal Republic regarding its authority to represent the German people in international affairs and the political relationship in those German areas which presently lie outside of its effective jurisdiction.

These reservations eliminate the possibility that third nations misinterpret our decision to establish diplomatic relations with the Soviet Union. All states having diplomatic relations with us can clearly see that the standpoint of the Federal Republic toward the so-called 'GDR' and to boundary issues has not changed in the least ...

A settlement of Germany's territorial situation that is binding under international law does not yet exist. Such a settlement can be made only within the scope of a peace treaty to be concluded with a freely elected all-German government. The position of the Government of the Federal Republic toward the government of the Soviet zone – as follows from the first reservation – will not be affected by the establishment of diplomatic relations between the Soviet Union and the Federal Republic. The government of the so-called 'GDR' was not formed on the basis of truly free elections and therefore has not received any real authorization by the people. In fact, it is rejected by the overwhelming majority of the population; there is neither legal protection nor freedom in the Soviet occupied zone, and the constitution exists only on paper.

The Federal Republic therefore remains the only free and legal German government, with sole authorization to speak for all of Germany ... We have notified the Soviet government of our viewpoint in order to remove any doubts whatsoever as to the firmness of our position. If the Soviet government nevertheless establishes diplomatic relations with us, it is doing so, though without granting approval, with full knowledge of our stand toward the so-called 'GDR' and our claim to speak for all of Germany. Where third nations are concerned, we also maintain our standpoint regarding the so-called 'GDR'. I must clearly and in no uncertain terms declare that the government of the FRG will interpret as an unfriendly act the establishment of diplomatic relations with the 'GDR' by third nations with which it has official relations, as this act would serve to deepen the division of Germany.

Trans. from: Bundesministerium für gesamtdeutsche Fragen (ed.), *Die Bemühungen der Bundesrepublik um Wiederherstellung der Einheit Deutschlands durch gesamtdeutsche Wahlen*, vol. 2, Bonn, 1958.

When Adenauer referred to 'the so-called "GDR"' in his letter, he followed his government's common practice of not even lingualistically recognising the GDR. In West Germany, the East German state was usually called either Central Germany (*Mitteldeutschland*) or Soviet Occupation Zone (*Sowjetische Besatzungszone*), or Eastern zone, or simply just 'the Zone'.

On 22 September, in a speech to the Bundestag, the Chancellor confirmed that the establishment of diplomatic relations with the USSR did not mean the acceptance of the territorial status quo; nor did it necessarily imply amicable relations with the Moscow government. Obviously he had to reiterate once again the strong ties to the West, but when he stated that with a West German Ambassador at the Kremlin the West's voice there would be stronger, he clearly over-exaggerated the impact of his move. Pointing to the support he had received on this issue from the other NATO members when the Paris Treaty had been signed, he repeated that the Federal Government was the only legitimate representative of the German people and repeated the warning that diplomatic relationships with the GDR would be regarded as an unfriendly act by his government. However, what consequences such an 'unfriendly act' would have was actually never spelled out.

Doc 88 Adenauer statement to the Bundestag

In the talks with representatives of the Soviet Government, the Federal Republic's delegation has clearly pointed out that the normalisation of relations can under no circumstances mean a legalisation of the abnormal state of Germany's division. Furthermore, it has been pointed out that the existence of diplomatic relations between two states does not equate to amicable relations [*freundschaftliches Vertragsverhältnis*]; our Soviet negotiation partners have themselves declared that they have diplomatic relations to states with which they have serious political and ideological differences.

On the other hand the following has to be considered: the Soviet Union is one of the four victorious powers and without its co-operation our most noble political aim, the creation of our country's unity, cannot be achieved. The absence of a relationship between these two countries, which made it impossible for us to present our national concerns ourselves in Moscow, is an anomaly ... With the establishment of diplomatic relations, the Federal Republic, with an effective power of sovereignty encompassing three-quarters of our people and 80 per cent of its productive powers, the politics of which – of this we are convinced – is backed up by at least 90 per cent of the population of Central Germany [*Mitteldeutschland*], will now also be recognised by the Soviet Union ...

Not only do the treaties of integration into the West [*Westverträge*] not impede normal relations with the Soviet Union, they are instead a forward-looking opportunity for international détente which will bring peace to the world and national unity in freedom to Germany. We won't accept the slightest doubt in our loyalty to the treaties. Germany's belonging to the West lies much deeper than in the political constellation, it is founded in its inseparable belonging to the cultural sphere of the Christian West [*christlich-abendländisher Kulturkreis*]. I formally declare on behalf of myself, the Federal Government, the whole German people in West and East that Germany is part of the West, as determined by its intellectual and social structures, by its historical traditions and due to the will of its population. (*Applause from the CDU/CSU, from the FDP and the DP*) ...

The establishment of diplomatic relations between the Federal Republic and the Soviet Union does not contradict Western interests. I believe I may go as far as to say that they serve Western interests. With the Federal Republic as a clearly Western, Europe-oriented power, now also having a representative in Moscow, the West's voice there will be strengthened further. The establishment of relations has further significance. It contributes to the difficult task of easing international tensions and thus contributes to world peace ...

All other states of the free world that have diplomatic relations with us accept our claim explicitly or implicitly ... If the Soviet government established diplomatic relations with us despite this fact they do so not in approval of, but in knowledge of our point of view regarding the so-called German Democratic Republic and our claim to speak for the whole of Germany ... We also confirm our point of view on the so-called GDR with regard to third-party countries. I have to declare unequivocally that the Federal government will continue to regard the establishment of diplomatic relations with the GDR by third countries with which it has diplomatic relations as an unfriendly act

(*Applause from the government parties*)
since it could deepen the division of Germany ...

I conclude: as a result of the travel to Moscow we have decided to establish diplomatic relations with the Soviet Union. We have the word of the Soviet leaders that the detained persons will be returned in the very near future. We have the acknowledgement of the Soviet government that, based on the Four-Power status, they are committed to German national unity. We have made the reservations necessary under international law to protect our legal point of view and the Soviet Union has recognised them ... The scope of the decisions to be taken has induced me to make the effectiveness of the Moscow agreements dependent on the approval of the Bundestag ...

Trans. from: *Verhandlungen des Deutschen Bundestages, 2. Wahlperiode.*

Making the establishment of diplomatic relations with the USSR conditional on a Bundestag majority was an extremely clever move, since it bound the opposition to his policy. The vote that took place the day after his speech unanimously confirmed the establishment of diplomatic relations.

It can be assumed that for the next two years the Hallstein Doctrine played a small part in preventing other states in recognising the GDR, but in October 1957 things changed dramatically. After Stalin's death in 1953, the new Soviet leadership had successfully tried to mend their bad relationship with Yugoslavia. On 15 October 1957, in a gesture of good-will towards Moscow, the Yugoslav government recognised the GDR and announced the establishment of diplomatic relations. Adenauer called the Cabinet for an emergency session and on 17 October Foreign Minister von Brentano summoned the Yugoslav Ambassador. In a memorandum for the Chancellor, he described what happened.

Doc 89 Brentano on meeting with the Yugoslav ambassador

This morning at 11 a.m. the Yugoslav Ambassador called on me at my request. I handed to him the note from the Federal Government which I briefly explained. I emphasised that the Federal Government's decision was not the expression of a hostile feeling against the Yugoslav people, but the expression of a deep disappointment with the decision by the

Yugoslav Government that stood in total contrast to the vital interests of the German people ...

The Yugoslav Ambassador read out a brief statement that he had drafted himself. He stated the following: The Yugoslav Government and the Yugoslav people could not understand the German decision. As a sovereign state, Yugoslavia had reacted to a political reality ... The Yugoslav Government is still convinced that their decision was the right one. Very frankly the Ambassador stated that Belgrade had not expected this reaction from the Federal Government!

I told the Ambassador that he and his Embassy staff would receive any necessary support and that I would leave it up to him to prepare the wind-up of his Embassy's operation and the departure of his staff. For this, the Federal Government will not impose a deadline. A reciprocal action is expected from the Yugoslav Government.

Then the Ambassador asked about the fate of the economic agreements and economic relationships. I replied evasively that, according to international law, the termination of diplomatic relations would not necessarily lead to the termination of existing treaties. I pointed out that France had been willing to act as a protecting power in Belgrade and represent Germany's interests there and that the necessary talks could be conducted through the protective power ...

It was very obvious that the Ambassador was deeply shocked by the German decision although he had known about it by the time he came to see me. His whole attitude was totally impeccable and correct and I had the impression that he tried very hard to hold back his personal feelings. Finally he spontaneously expressed his wish that the general political developments would make it possible to renew the diplomatic relationships at a later time.

Trans. from: Bundesarchiv Koblenz, BA B 136/6169.

For the Yugoslavs, who had not expected such a drastic move, the termination of diplomatic relations came obviously as a shock although it did not turn into a catastrophe for them. The West German government acted somewhat inconsistently by not terminating the economic relationship between both countries, as well. Nevertheless, this incident sent a clear message to all those countries which had been playing with the idea of recognising the GDR. Very few now seriously considered antagonising the new economic great power for the sake of diplomatic relations with a state that had been recognised only by countries from within the Eastern Block.

There were few dissenting voices in the Federal Republic that criticised Adenauer's foreign policy. Erich Kuby, a journalist and keen observer of West German politics and society who was always ready with his pen, indicated some of the flaws in the claim of West Germany's leadership and mainstream public opinion.

Doc 90 Erich Kuby: sovereign states?

In our part of the fatherland legend has it that the other part is no state at all. When, after hundreds of conversations and thousands of impressions, I emerged out of the depth of the GDR at the West Berlin barrier at Wannsee, a policeman checked a list for my car registration in order to cross it off. He looked in vain, I did not come from Marienborn. 'I see', he said, 'you're from the Es-Be-Zett' [SBZ, Soviet Occupation Zone]. 'From where'? I said and then I had to laugh when the penny dropped. It has something touching about it, this superstition that what is not named does not exist ... On what grounds do we conclude that the GDR is no state? Because it carries out the policy of its protecting power? God knows, then the Federal Republic is no state either. Because its military is equipped by the protecting power? Then the ... Because its leading politicians sometimes discuss the next political steps with the protecting power's leading politicians? Then the ... Because they accept money from the protecting power? Good heavens, the Russians won't put so much money into the GDR than we have accepted from our protecting power. Because, as far as the ruling minority is concerned, it agrees ideologically with its protecting power? Then ... No, this is all nonsense. There is no criterion according to which the Federal Republic is a sovereign state and the GDR is not. Neither is a sovereign state, luckily. But states they are. Therefore there is a capital of the GDR. It is not possible to say where exactly in East Berlin this capital is located. Certainly not in Pankow. Nobody knows why in the West [*bei uns*] 'Pankow' is called 'Pankow'.

Trans. from: Erich Kuby, *Das ist des Deutschen Vaterland: 70 Millionen in zwei Wartesälen*, Stuttgart 1957.

Obviously, there were plenty of other voices who believed strongly in Adenauer's policy, as the following report by Klaus Mehnert shows. Mehnert was a highly influential conservative writer and political broadcaster who visited East Asia in January 1960. India was of particular interest to him on his travels since the country had just launched its second five-year plan to modernise itself. In this process India had accepted aid from both the East and the West, and in particular from the FRG. Together with Yugoslavia, India was the self-proclaimed leader of the movement of the non-aligned countries and it was a role model for former European colonies that had gained independence, or would gain it soon. In New Delhi, Mehnert was received by the Permanent Undersecretary to the Indian Foreign Office and afterwards he wrote a report on the meeting for the CDU Parliamentary Group.

Doc 91 'Advice to India'

... Then Mr. Dutt of his own accord (I had not intended to address the issue) changed the topic to talk about *the German Question*. Beginning with the assumption that the summit meeting scheduled for May would hardly bring a solution to the question he said: 'He is not talking to me as a member of government but as an Indian who thinks about this question. He hoped I would understand when he said that the Federal Government had not convinced him that they tried all possibilities to achieve reunification. Despite this it was Bonn's wish that India had no relations to the East German Government. He felt it increasingly difficult to accommodate this wish because it went against the principle of Indian foreign policy to have a diplomatic relationship with all de facto existing states. He did not want to say that the diplomatic recognition was to happen very soon but that I had to understand that the solidification of the German division ... was strengthening India's intention to recognise East Germany.' I replied: 'I certainly do not speak as Government, I speak as an independent writer, but I want to answer you not less candidly. I could understand your views. However, I'd also ask for understanding of my position: if your Government recognises Pankow I will – and with me many of my friends – use all journalistic means possible to make my Government terminate diplomatic relations with India. I did this two years ago in the case of Yugoslavia, although with some regret, and I would do it again, in India's case with bigger regret, even pain.' Perhaps nobody had told him in such a sharp tone; he certainly yielded and said that in the Yugoslavia case Bonn had not been very consistent, leaving a consul in Yugoslavia.

I replied: 'I do not regret this inconsistency; I believe it was the right step to keep consular representation. However, I do regret another inconsistency, namely that we did not terminate our economic services and financial payments to Belgrade.'

Mr Dutt did not respond to this remark although he clearly understood what I meant in regard to India; however, he indicated that the termination of the economic relationship would have severe consequences for the German economy. I replied that in this situation we cannot make our decision depending on whether we would deliver some more machines to a country or not; in this case a decisive principle was at stake for us; that the Federal Republic that had emerged after free elections was the only state that was legitimised to speak for the German people and that we were prepared to suffer economic disadvantages to sustain this principle.

Trans. from: Bundesarchiv Koblenz BA B 136/3637.

It is difficult to say what impact Mehnert's threat had on the Indian decision not to recognise the GDR. The loss of West German development aid and industrial know-how would have been a serious blow to India's modernisation plans. However, here the flip-side of the Hallstein Doctrine comes to the fore, which would haunt West Germany for the next nine years: the Federal Republic became prone to political blackmail, in particular from developing countries and especially from such influential ones such as India. Just by 'considering' recognition of the GDR, India had a powerful lever to demand more development aid from West Germany. If India had recognised the GDR, other developing countries would have followed, which would have meant a fatal blow to Bonn's claim for sole representation. By providing more and more aid to an increasing number of countries, the Federal Republic was able to sustain the sole representation claim until it was eventually abandoned under the Chancellorship of Willy Brandt in 1969. The only exception to the rule occurred in 1963, when Cuba fell out of line.

Doc 92 Memo by the German ambassador in Cuba

12 January 1963
Record on the discussion with Foreign Minister Roa on 11 January: shortly after 10 a.m. the Cuban Foreign Ministry protocol called me with the request that I should call on them at the wish of the Foreign Minister ... Accompanied by *LR I* Gracher I went to the Foreign Ministry at the requested time where Minister Roa received me after a short delay.

He told me in a very clear but friendly manner that he had received the task from the President of the Republic and Prime Minister, Fidel Castro, of informing me prior to making it public at the weekend, that the Revolutionary Government had decided to diplomatically recognise the Soviet zone. He stated that two German states existed and because of the co-existence term, they felt obliged to recognise the Soviet zone as a state equal to the Federal Republic. He regarded such recognition as politically justified because East Germany belonged to the communist states. I replied that I very much regretted this decision since I had done everything humanly possible during my three years in office to not only maintain the existing relationship but also to deepen it in as cordial a manner as possible ...

The Minister wanted to express a certain human understanding, but regarded the decision he was instructed to convey to me as logical and hoped that the Federal Republic would retain diplomatic contacts to Cuba regardless. To this I replied that the Cuban Government was mistaken in this belief since the Federal Republic ... had to respond to any recognition of Pankow with the termination of diplomatic relations, since they regarded themselves as successor to the German Reich and, as such, represented the whole of Germany.

Minister Roa pointed out that economic ties with the Federal Republic had become insignificant. My objection, based on publication from the Ibero-American Bank showing an increase of German exports to Cuba during the last year, was ignored by the Minister as he referred back to his instructions ...

... he hoped for the continuation of the – as he expressed it – good relationship between the Federal Republic and Cuba. To emphasise this good will the Minister cited the fact that the Cuban Government had not reacted to the sharp declaration by the Federal Chancellor and the Federal Government during the crisis in order not to damage the good relationship. He also indicated that the same was true for the other states that were a member of NATO ...

Trans. from: Auswärtiges Amt (ed.), *Aussenpolitik der Bundesrepublik Deutschland. Dokumente 1949–94.*

In the wake of Fidel Castro's revolution, Cuba's move was more ideological than political, so it is fair to say that the Hallstein Doctrine did achieve its aim – particularly once it had been applied for the first time against Yugoslavia. However, this achievement came at a financial cost and no one could hide the fact that from the early 1960s onward the doctrine became more and more anachronistic, and the symbol of an intra-German policy that would not recognise the reality on the ground; something even the Western Allies began to see, although they never opposed it publicly.

8

European integration: from Messina to the Elysée Treaty

When the Federal Republic gained its sovereignty and joined NATO in 1955, a significant aim in Adenauer's foreign-policy concept had been accomplished. During the remaining eight years of his chancellorship he tried to build on what had been achieved to reach his final aim: a full reconciliation between France and Germany that would make the wars of the past impossible in the future. The Coal and Steel Community was seen as a major success both in political and economic terms. Many commentators at the time, as well as historians during much of the 1960s and 1970s, saw it as the expression of an idealistic attempt to prevent future slaughter on the battlefields. Politicians began to see the success as an example for further integration, most notably the 1957 Treaty of Rome which established the European Economic Community (EEC), for the sake of economic growth in Europe and increased influence between the two superpowers. It was Alan Milward who in the 1980s and early 1990s challenged this mainly idealistic view by pointing out the more narrow nationalistic intentions behind the move for further European integration. Regardless of the motives, it was the continuing process of European integration – which found its next climax in the signing of the Franco-German Treaty in 1963 – which also marked the fulfilment of Adenauer's foreign-policy objective.

Although the German coal and steel industry had to make considerable concessions and had to give up some of its traditional structures, it had been one of the main beneficiaries of the ECSC. Despite those gains, there were some of the politically more conservative industrialists who remained fundamentally opposed to the idea, since they regarded it as a politically motivated abandonment of German industrial competitive advantages. One of the strongest critics remained Hermann Reusch of the *Gutehoffnungshütte* steel trust. While on the one hand Reusch had been an outspoken opponent of the Nazis, he was nevertheless an arch-conservative, and held social views and some business attitudes that belonged more in the nineteenth than the twentieth century. In January 1955 he explained some of his criticisms of the ECSC to Franz Etzel, the German ECSC Vice President.

Doc 93 Industrialists' criticism of the ECSC

At our company's annual general meeting on 11.1.1955 alongside other things, I made the following statement:
'The Coal and Steel Community, of which the Federal Republic has been a member for more than two years, serves the increase in economic power. We believe that the expansion of the market and an increase in competition in the long run will not fail to deliver their positive impact, even if at present the treaty's faults nearly out-weight the benefits ... German industry has always acknowledged the aim of an economically united Europe. Unfortunately, our expectations have been disappointed in several respects, and the aims that the European Coal and Steel Community is supposed to realise have recently become more problematic.' ...

I am happy to explain my viewpoint in more detail. Like the majority of German industrialists, in particular President Berg, I am of the opinion that European economic integration is necessary, if only to give sufficient room to the strong impulses that originate from the German economy. I therefore welcome the Coal and Steel Community where it serves this aim. But it appears to me as if achieving this aim has recently become more problematic again for the Coal and Steel Community ...

In my opinion here yet another essential point in the judgement of the Coal and Steel Community treaty has become obvious, namely its dependence on the limited interpretation of it by lawyers. You will agree with me that the viewpoint 'The treaty, the whole treaty, and nothing but the treaty' as it is especially widespread in France will not create very favourable prospects for the achievement of European economic integration through the Coal and Steel Community. Therefore, when I said in my speech that the aims the Coal and Steel Community was supposed to achieve had recently become problematic again; this was to be understood as a statement on the situation that arose after the French rejection of the EDC and the resulting re-emerged problems of partial integration. Indeed, it appears to me that the possibilities which only a short time ago seemed evident in this form of integration were overestimated ...

Trans. from: Rheinsch-Westfälisches Wirtschafts Archiv, RWWA GHH 130/40010146/47.

Reusch's concerns were based on old fashioned group egotisms. The overall experiences of The Six countries participating in the ECSC were far more positive and the politicians began to think beyond coal and steel. In June 1955 a delegation of The Six met in the Sicilian city of Messina to discuss what had been achieved so far and how those accomplishments could be expanded. Again, Great Britain did not fully participate in the negotiations but only sent an observer delegation. The final resolution that was passed at the end of the conference on 3 June laid out a framework in which further European co-operation would be achieved through the creation of a co-ordinated energy, infrastructure, and eventually a common economic policy.

Doc 94 Final resolution of the Messina Conference

The Governments of the Federal Republic of Germany, Belgium, France, Italy, Luxembourg and the Netherlands believe that the moment has come to initiate a new phase on the way to creating a unified Europe. They regard it as necessary to continue the creation of a united Europe through the development of common institutions, the gradual fusion of the national economies, the creation of a common market and the gradual harmonisation of their social policies.

Such a policy appears to be imperative to retain the place Europe has in the world, to re-establish its influence and its aura [*Ausstrahlungskraft*], and to steadily increase the living standards of its population.

To achieve these aims the six ministers have agreed the following objectives:

1. The increase in the exchange of goods and the freedom of movements of people calls for the common expansion of the major transport routes ... with the wider common aim of creating a European traffic network of canals, motorways and electrified railways and a standardisation of equipment ...

2. More substantial and cheaper energy is a fundamental element of economic progress. Therefore, everything possible has to be done to enhance the exchange of gas and electrical power that is suited to increasing the profitability of investments and to lowering prices for consumers ...

3. The development of atomic power for peaceful purposes will soon

open up the possibilities for a new industrial revolution on an even bigger scale than the one of the last hundred years ...

The Six Governments declare that the aim of their action in the field of economic policy is the gradual creation of a free common European market that is free of any tariff barriers and quotas. Its realisation demands the investigation of the following questions:
a) The question of how and in what period of time, procedures are to be applied in the relations between countries involved, during the gradual elimination of trade barriers. How to achieve a gradual unification of the tariff system against third states also has to be addressed.
b) Measures for the harmonisation of the member states' general policy in financial, economic and social fields.
d) A system of protective clauses.
f) The gradual introduction of movement of labour.
...
The creation of a European investment fund is to be examined. This fund would serve the common economic development in Europe and, in particular, that of the less favoured regions of the participating countries
...

The Six Governments agreed on the following procedure:
...
6) The Government of the United Kingdom as a member state of the Western European Union and as an associated member of the European Coal and Steel Community will be invited to participate in this work.

Trans. from: *Europa Archiv 10* (1955).

Opinions on exactly how this new European policy should look differed even within the Federal Government. The biggest fault line was the question whether European integration should be motivated and driven by, and be in the service of, politics, or whether pragmatic economic concerns should determine the process. Economics Minister Ludwig Erhard, the government's most popular minister thanks to his reputation as the supposed 'Father' of the economic miracle, and some of the FDP ministers supported a free market approach, with a free flow of goods, services and labour and with little or no state interference. Erhard expressed this whenever he had the opportunity, for example on 21 July 1955 in a press article for the *Deutsche Korrespondenz*.

Doc 95 Erhard on European integration

I myself have made it clear in talks and public announcements that it is necessary to distinguish between two possible forms of an ongoing integration: in one form the emphasis lies more on the institutional side, in the other more on the functional side. Others refer to the same problem when they talk about horizontal or vertical integration. With my criticism and my doubt as to whether Europe can really emerge with the creation of new (sectored) partial integration [*Teilintegration*] with simultaneous supranational administration ... I have, as some comments show, brought suspicion on myself not to be, or at least only a bad, European ...

Anyone who wants Europe has to remember consequently the commendable work of other institutions such as the OEEC, the EPU, GATT or the International Monetary Fund; they have developed – although not limited to the sphere of the ECSC countries – in a geographical comprehensive way, an extraordinarily fruitful activity, and have achieved great successes in the functional area I have already mentioned. If each of those six countries offering itself for European integration today would be prepared to be even more liberal in its trade with each other, to accept more stringent trade rules, liberalise its payment transactions even further and – in order to implement these efforts – create an institutional co-ordinating body to oversee this endeavour, I would be their most ardent supporter of such ideas. But at the same time I doubt very much that one would find such good Europeans anywhere ...

The question of who is a good or a bad European has been phrased wrongly. I, for my part, am not willing to let myself be deprived of my fundamental European attitude and belief just because I phrase the question differently; and because I have suggested to all those involved to see if there is only *one* way and *one* method towards Europe; or if not, other means would perhaps lead more quickly and more efficiently towards that aim. I want to say it clearly and want to declare that I do not wish less, but more Europe than is expressed in the proposals for further partial integration ...

Furthermore, I do not resist European commitments but like to create the necessary preconditions for them whenever I warn that first the internal order of a national economy has to be achieved in national responsibility, otherwise the integration is to lead towards a supranational statism ...

The institutions and persons responsible for economic matters have the obligation to create, in their fields, the preconditions for political decisions and to allow the necessary material conditions for these to mature quickly ...

There is hardly another way left to us but to achieve, in ever quicker succession, in *all* questions of trade and services, money and capital transfers, in matters concerning tariff policy and regarding freedom of movement and ever advancing and increasing liberty; and to renounce any state manipulation which would be contrary to those principles ...

The idea that the Common Market demands equal conditions for competition in the sense of equal burden, equal wages, equal working hours or equal component costs, and thus requiring a system of balancing accounts [*Ausgleichskassen*] towards a general levelling, cannot be brought into line with the practical experiences and theoretical knowledge of the nature of an international division of labour. One will get caught in the techniques and operates on the periphery if one believes it possible to reach the core by means of individual solutions on a case-by-case basis. This path of least resistance will not lead towards Europe, but, I am afraid to say, away from it ...

Trans. from: Ludwig-Erhard-Stiftung, NE 43.

Unfortunately for Erhard, his liberal free-market approach was motivated by his particular economic theory which did not much correspond with the *Realpolitik* motives of the Chancellor. By early 1956 Adenauer had had enough of talks about Europe based on economics, and made it clear to his Cabinet that he regarded further European integration first and foremost as a political process. Everything else was to be subordinated to this political process, in particular Erhard's economic theories and ideas. Adenauer did this by pointing out that the Basic Law gave him the right as Chancellor to determine the guidelines and direction of politics, *Richtlinienkompetenz*, to which every Cabinet member had to adhere.

Doc 96 Adenauer directives on European policy

19 January 1956
To the Federal Ministers
The current foreign-policy situation contains extraordinary dangers. In order to prevent them and initiate a positive development, decisive measures have to be taken. This includes above all a clear, positive German position towards European integration.

The decisive Western statesmen regard the European integration as the pivotal point of the development; in particular my talks with Pinay and Spaak and very specific American political statements have shown this. This opinion is without a doubt correct. If integration is a success, we will be able to throw in the weight of a united Europe during negotiations about security as well as reunification. Conversely, no serious concessions from the Soviet Union can be expected as long as European discord gives it the hope to pull the one or the other state on its side, thus to break up the West's unity and gradually begin to annex Europe to the satellite system. Add to this the fact that the long-term consolidation of our relationship with France is only possible through European integration. If the integration were to fail because of our reluctance or our hesitation, the consequences would be unforeseeable.

It follows from this, as the guideline for our policies, that we have to carry out the Messina decision resolutely to the letter. The political character of the decision has to be heeded much more strongly. This calls not only for technical co-operation based on specialist subject-matter considerations [*fachlichen Erwägungen*], but needs to establish a community which – also in the interest of reunification – guarantees the same direction of political will and action. For this the OEEC framework is insufficient. All specialist subject-matter considerations have to serve this political aim.

For the implementation of the Messina programme, the following aims have to be adhered to in particular:

1. The integration, initially among the Six, is to be supported by *all* means possible, both in the areas of general (horizontal) integration and in regard to suitable (vertical) partial integration.

2. In this, the possibility for the creation of suitable common institutions has to be an aim from the start in order to achieve, in the spirit of the greater political aim, the firm linking of the Six.

3. The consultations on the creation of a common European market – i.e. a market similar to an internal market – which have gone well, have to be brought vigorously to a conclusion. In the process European institutions with decision-making powers have to be established in order to guarantee the functioning of the market and at the same time support ongoing political development.

4. Based on the idea of the common market, one should strive to achieve a real integration of the Six's transport policy. This is the case particularly in aviation; a rejection on principle or a delay of plans for integrating production, procurement and management in this field is politically irresponsible.

5. The same is true for power, especially nuclear power. It is a compelling political necessity to erase any doubt that we are still standing by our Messina declaration according to which an European atomic institution with decision-making powers, common organs and common finance and other means of implementation is to be established. As they have officially declared, the Americans see in a European atomic community with – in contrast to the OEEC – its own rights and responsibilities a decisive moment of political development. They are prepared to support such an atomic community with all necessary vigour.

On the other hand, according to world opinion, the peaceful use of atomic energy is practically inseparable from the possibility to produce atomic bombs. A German attempt of a purely national atomic settlement would be taken with a great deal of mistrust abroad. We cannot, in particular, refuse the common European management of individual substances if it is necessary for security reasons, although it goes without saying that Germany is not to be discriminated against and German research and industry have to receive as much room to flourish as possible.

I request that you regard the above-said as a political guideline by the Federal Government (Art 65 Basic Law) and to act accordingly.

Signed Adenauer

Trans. from Auswärtiges Amt (ed.), *Die Auswärtige Politik der Bundes-republik Deutschland*.

Without a doubt, Adenauer's letter to his ministers was a direct rebuke for those who played with the idea of a less political European free trade area – Erhard in particular. Four months later, in May 1956, Adenauer would disavow his Economics Minister in a public speech at a BDI meeting in Cologne which caused the so-called *Gürzenicher Affäre*. Erhard threatened to resign and Adenauer had to publically apologise. The relationship between the two men would deteriorate over the next years (see chapter 14) not only because of the different opinion they held on Europe. On 25 September that year, at the Grandes Conférences Catholiques in Brussels, Adenauer outlined some of the reasons why he wanted a united Europe, namely to regain some of Europe's lost influence in the bipolar world of East–West conflict.

Doc 97 Adenauer on European integration

... I would like to talk to you in the first instance not about the common economic interests but about the responsibility which we carry in politics because of the Christian culture that is common to all European peoples. I would like to speak about the urgent necessity of a common European policy of the European states ...

The development and the course of the Suez Canal question is not concluded and therefore I will not draw them into my considerations. However, the development in this question shows for everyone with eyes in his head how things currently stand for Europe and its political and economic influence in the world ...

After the Council of Europe and the Coal and Steel Community, the idea of a European defence community arose. Its realisation has failed partly because of the excessive perfectionism in the creation of the treaty. It has also failed because the conviction for the necessity of a military-political union of the European people for defence purposes has not yet been generally accepted ...

I see the beginning of a new political development in the world as the following elements start to take effect:

1. Soviet Russia consolidates itself more and more due to the West's political division ...

2. Over the course of the last decades the political and economic power of the free peoples has concentrated more and more on the United States. I recognise with gratitude and admiration that the United States is aware of the responsibility .... This is not to develop into a permanent state because Europe's powers will, in time, grow weary; and because the United States is in the long run not of the mind to take care of Europe to a degree that simply cannot be expected of them ...

3 ... I don't know if it is still justified to speak of any European state as great power in the sense that was completely justified at the beginning of the century. But if a big one and a small one, or a big one and several small ones try together to conduct politics, then automatically the big one develops a claim for leadership and the small one a feeling of dependency ...

4. A fourth element ... is the appearance on the global political stage of non-white peoples ....

We have to learn one more thing from the experiences of the last ten years: the realisation of the European integration should not be made

impossible by the disease of our time, perfectionism. European integration is not rigid – it has to be as flexible and as elastic as possible. It is
not to be a suffocating armour for the European peoples but it has to be
a common hold for them and their development and a common support
for the healthy development of their justified peculiarities ...

Trans. from: *Bulletin der Bundesregierung*, 26.9.1956.

In the face of the decline which all European great powers had
suffered on the world stage since the Second World War, Adenauer
proposed European co-operation so that traditional nineteenth-
century great-power nationalism could continue in a different
form. In his mind, the European countries could play only a significant role on the world stage if they co-operated on the basis of
Europe's common heritage and culture. There were some critics in
Germany who had sectarian objections to the way the European
integration seemed to work. The driving men behind closer integration, Adenauer, DeGaspari, Spaak and Schuman, were all Catholics
and of The Six countries only the Netherlands had a Protestant
majority, though with a large Catholic minority. Delivering the
speech at the 'Grandes Conférences Catholiques' was grist to
the mill for those critics who accused him of wanting to create a
'Catholic' Europe made up only of the Catholic countries of Italy,
France, Belgium and Germany (where since the loss of the Eastern
territories and the GDR, there was a small Catholic majority).
The accusation had a major flaw because Europe's big Protestant
countries, most notably Britain, deliberately decided not to join the
emerging community.

Less than two years after the Messina Conference The Six countries had completed their negotiations. On 25 March 1957 the
Treaty of Rome was signed with great fanfare, laying the foundation for the establishment of the European Economic Community.

Doc 98 Treaty of Rome

Article 1
With this treaty the High Contracting Parties establish among themselves an European Economic Community.

Article 2
It is the task of the Community – through the establishment of a Common Market and the gradual convergence of the member states' economic policies – to support the harmonious development of economic life within the Community. The Community is also tasked with promoting continuing and balanced economic growth, greater stability, an increased rise in the standard of living and closer relations between the states that make up the Community.

Article 3
The activities of the Community as indicated in article 2 include, according to the Treaty's stipulation and the timeframe proposed therein:
a) the abolition of tariffs and quotas for imports and exports of goods and all measures of similar effect between the member states;
b) the introduction of a common tariff policy and a common trade policy towards their countries;
c) the removal of all hindrances for the free movement of persons, services and capital between member states;
d) the introduction of a common agricultural policy;
e) the introduction of a common transport policy;
f) the creation of a system that prevents competition within the Community from being distorted;
g) the application of procedures that allow for the coordination of the member states' economic policy and the restoration of balance of payment imbalances;
h) the convergence of member states' legal rules if it is necessary for the proper functioning of the Common Market;
...

Article 4
The tasks assigned to the Community will be carried out by the following organs:
An Assembly
A Council
A Commission
A Court of Law
...

Article 5
The member states take all necessary steps of a general or specific nature that are necessary for the fulfilment of contractual obligations .... They abstain from all measures that could endanger the realisation of the Treaty's aims ...

208

Article 8
1) The Common Market will be realised gradually over a 12-year transitional period. The transitional period consists of three periods of four years each; the length of each period can be altered according to the stipulations in the following rules.

…

3) The transfer from the first period to the second depends on the verification that the aims for the first period explicitly laid down in this Treaty were essentially and factually fulfilled …

Trans. from: Auswärtiges Amt (ed.), *Aussenpolitik der Bundesrepublik Deutschland: Dokumente 1949–94*.

There can be no doubt that Adenauer believed in the idea of European unification, but at the same time his most important aim was to achieve a full Franco-German reconciliation. He had shown this when he demonstratively continued with a state visit to France at the height of the 1956 Suez Crisis, thus giving moral support for the French government. While Adenauer had worked hard to bring about reconciliation, it was clear that, due to the history between the two countries, the decisive step had to come from the French. France had to embrace Adenauer's gesture if reconciliation was to work. It was no one less than General Charles De Gaulle who would bring about this acceptance, although during 1960–61 he had ended further European integration by launching his idea of a 'Europe of the nation states'. Despite this setback for Europe, De Gaulle received a rapturous welcome when he visited Germany on a state visit in 1962. Adenauer himself commented on that event in the government's *Bulletin*.

Doc 99 Adenauer on the De Gaulle visit

A week of deep historic significance lies behind us. A duel of two great peoples that lasted over 200 years – as President De Gaulle said so impressively in Hamburg – has come to an end. Statesmen have to act but there are also the rare moments in which the peoples themselves speak. I believe that President De Gaulle has felt this moment in all German cities in which he has spoken to thousands who had crammed the squares up to the roofs to listen to him. From the first day onwards one could feel that these crowds had not come out of curiosity but that they wanted to confirm with their applause that a new chapter in the book of the long German-French history has been opened. What my government has striven for in nearly one and a half decades of the post-war period, and often with considerable effort I might add, has thus become reality. In the communiqué on my talks with M. De Gaulle it was emphasised once again that both Governments will take practical measures to effectively strengthen the bonds between our two countries that already exist in many areas. The French President's journey through the Federal Republic has received more and more attention abroad the more it began to appear as an impromptu triumphal procession. Reserved judgements, too, even sceptical ones, spoke in the end of a 'historic milestone'. At the same time the question of how a reconciled France and Germany would react towards the rest of Europe and the wider Atlantic Alliance came up ... Immediately voices were heard which said that these days have ultimately witnessed the creation of the 'Paris-Bonn-Axis', around which the rest of Europe – whether bigger or smaller – should or even must gather. I regard this as false, outdated and even dangerous terminology .... Today we can't use terms that derive from a totally different, and for Europe disastrous, time ... A 'Paris-Bonn-Axis': that could only mean that the rest of Europe has to link itself to the French-German core until it has eventually melted into it. If one compares this image with the living European reality, one sees how unrealistic it is ...

We in Europe should stop breeding out ever newer and misleading alternatives. If for example someone says 'either close German-French co-operation or Great Britain's entry into the EEC', he has obviously little insight in the real and certainly difficult problems that concern us currently. Together with President De Gaulle, my government and I are aspiring to achieve the close and possibly most reliable connection between Germany and France. But by doing so we – French and Germans – aspire at the same time to Europe's unity within the wider protective community and alliance of the Atlantic world ...

Trans. from: *Bulletin der Bundesregierung*, 14.9.1962.

Only four months later, Adenauer achieved his ultimate aim. On 22 January 1963 the Franco-German treaty, also often called the Elysée Treaty, was signed. On the eve of the signing, the Chancellor indicated in a speech how big a historic event the treaty was, and paid tribute to General De Gaulle. Above all, Adenauer praised the new Franco-German friendship.

Doc 100 Adenauer on Franco-German friendship

... I come, so I was told by one of my gentlemen, to Paris for the eighteenth time. But the reason for this journey to Paris is a special one. In the next few days we want to sign a treaty between France and Germany which has slowly developed in its elements and which is now to be completed. This is a historic event of global significance. I want to emphatically stress its importance: it is an important event in the history of the world, a historic event. If we read our newspapers we see the big bold headlines of all that was and which now is ... But today, in this treaty a period of quarrelling, of contrasts and of wars that lasted more than 400 years will be ended and ended for good. The special thing about this treaty will not be that it ends acute difficulties or differences or similar things or clears them out of the way. Rather, the special thing is that it takes care that such tensions can never arise again, thanks to the common work of both peoples, by the French people together with the German people, for an unlimited future. Principally, it is not the task of two governments in the future but the task between both peoples in the future. The visit by the German Federal President, Lübke, in 1961, the visit by the State President, De Gaulle, in Germany and my visit in France in the summer of 1962 have demonstrated that both peoples agree to what was planned and to what is now to be completed. Tonight I would like to send a particularly friendly word to your State President, De Gaulle. He has something exceptional. He has a sense of history. He sees [*überschaut*] distant pasts and he sees future spaces. He has recognised what France and Germany mean for Europe, for the world, what they mean for the French and German people. The consequences of this closeness between the two peoples that lie as neighbours in the middle of Europe are not so easy for the two peoples. This is because they will demand a huge responsibility of both of them, a responsibility not only for the good of the French and German people but also a responsibility for Europe and for world peace.

Trans. from: H.P. Schwarz, *Konrad Adenauer, Reden.*

The Elysée Treaty did indeed mark a milestone in Franco-German relations. The treaty was passed into legislation by both parliaments so that the new friendship had a lasting legal foundation, too. It not only furthered cultural and youth exchanges but stipulated regular ministerial meetings and regular meetings of the heads of government and state respectively, as well as military exchanges at all levels. Considering the countless wars both countries had with each other over centuries, the treaty truly was the expression of a new era and stands unique in modern history.

Doc 101 Elysée Treaty

I. Organisation

1. The heads of state and government will issue, when necessary, the relevant directions and continuously observe the implementation of the programme that has been laid out below. For this purpose they will meet as often as is necessary and always at least twice a year.

2. The Foreign Ministers are responsible for ensuring that the programme is implemented in its entirety. They meet at least once every three months. Regardless of the normal contacts via the embassies, the leading officials of both foreign ministries who are in charge of the political, economic and cultural matters will meet monthly – alternating between Bonn and Paris – to determine the state of the current issues and to prepare the meeting of the ministers ...

3. There will be regular meetings between the relevant authorities of both states from the areas of defence, education and youth issues. They will not interfere in any way with the already existing body – the German-French Cultural Commission, the permanent groups of the General Staff – whose activities will actually be extended ...

a) The Defence Minister and the Army Minister will meet at least once every three months. Furthermore, the French Minister for Education will meet at the same interval with his named counterpart on the German side ...

b) The Chiefs of the General Staff of both countries will meet at least once every two months ...

c) The Federal Minister for Family and Youth Affairs or his deputy will meet the French High Commissioner for Youth and Sport at least once every two months ...

II. Programme

A. Foreign Affairs

1. Both governments will consult with each other prior to each decision on all important issues of foreign policy, and first and foremost in questions of common interest, to reach a uniform position as far as possible. This consultation concerns, among others, the following areas:

- Questions regarding the European Community and European political collaboration;
- East-West relations, in both the economic and political areas;

- Matters that are dealt with in the North Atlantic Treaty Organisation and the various international organisations in which both governments have an interest, especially in the Council of Europe, the Western European Union, the Organisation for Economic Co-operation and Development and in the United Nations and its affiliated organisations ...

B. Defence

I. In this field, the following topics will be pursued:

...

2. The exchange of personnel between the armed forces will be increased; this concerns in particular the teaching staff and students of the general staff college; the exchange can extend to the temporary secondment of whole units ...

3. In the area of armaments, both governments undertake to organise joint efforts from the stage of suitable armaments projects to the preparation of financial plans ...

C. Education and Youth Affairs

...

2. All opportunities should be offered to the French and German youth so that the bonds that exist between them can be strengthened and their understanding of each other deepened. In particular, group exchanges will be extended further ...

Trans. from: Auswärtiges Amt (ed.), *Aussenpolitik der Bundesrepublik Deutschland: Dokumente 1949–94.*

Although the Bundestag welcomed the treaty, there were members of parliament who were worried that Adenauer and the Federal Republic could follow De Gaulle in his anti-American policy. The Chancellor was critical, even suspicious, of the policy of rapprochement the new US President Kennedy was pursuing towards the Soviet Union, especially after the Cuban missile crisis. He feared that this could lead to a sell-out of German interests; thus the Franco-German treaty can also be seen in part as an attempt to find another ally. Ultimately it is rather unlikely that Adenauer really would have sacrificed the good-will and friendship of his American protective power but some deputies were not so sure about this. Subsequently the German Parliament added a preamble to the treaty which explicitly confirmed the transatlantic alliance. The preamble therefore signified the division within the government party between the so-called 'Atlanticists' and 'Gaullists' and took away some of the

213

effect the Chancellor and the French President had hoped to achieve with the treaty.

Doc 102

Preamble to the Elysée Treaty, 15 June 1963

In the conviction,

that the treaty of 22 January 1963 between the Federal Republic of Germany and the French Republic will deepen and build up the reconciliation and friendship between the German and French people;

With the conclusion,

that through this treaty the rights and obligations of the multi-lateral treaties concluded by the Federal Republic of Germany remain unaffected;

With the will,

to promote, through the application of this treaty, the great aims which the Federal Republic of Germany in co-operation with its allies has been aspiring to for years and which determine its policy,

Namely

the maintaining and deepening of the coming together of free peoples, in particular in a close partnership between Europe and the United States of America ...;

the common defence within the framework of the North Atlantic Alliance and the integration of the armed forces of those states linked in this alliance;

the unification of Europe, along the path which was embarked upon with the creation of the European Community, with the inclusion of Great Britain and other states willing to join, and the further strengthening of this Community;

through the dismantling of trade barriers through negotiations between the European Economic Community, Great Britain and the United States of America and other states within the framework of the 'General Agreement on Tariffs and Trade';

Conscious,

that a French-German co-operation that is guided by these aims will benefit all nations, will serve peace in the world and thus will be beneficial to both the French and German peoples, the Bundestag has passed the following bill; ...

Trans. from: Auswärtiges Amt (ed.), *Aussenpolitik der Bundesrepublik Deutschland, Dokumente 1949–1994.*

9

Art and culture in the miracle years

Arts, culture and cultural policy provides a good reflection of a society. Only fairly recently has more thorough research into the arts and culture of the Federal Republic's post-war years begun. There remain considerable gaps in the research of aspects of arts and culture in the miracle years, perhaps with the exception of the more fashionable topic of film studies. On the whole the area remains, perhaps due to its very nature, full of contradictions and clichés.

In the immediate aftermath of the war the cultural and arts scene in Germany experienced a wide boom not seen before or after. It was driven by people who felt free of the Nazi cultural strait-jacket; others who sought a cultural way to deal with the moral bankruptcy the war and its devastation had brought; and those who simply tried to come to terms with their war experience. Despite acute and severe paper shortage literally hundreds of new cultural or philosophical journals and magazines sprang up all over the country in 1945 and 1946. A new genre of *Trümmerfilm* (rubble or ruin film) emerged, often supported by the Allies in their attempt of cultural re-education. In literature, *Trümmerliteratur* (literally: rubble literature) created a lasting impression on German writing. Short stories like *Draussen vor der Tür* (The Man Outside) by Wolfgang Borchert, the most famous writer of *Trümmerliteratur*, became and remained part of the modern German literature canon, as did the works of Heinrich Böll, who would eventually win the 1972 Nobel Prize for Literature.

The currency reform of 1948 meant the end to the plethora of cultural magazines and newspapers. The new money was scarce compared to the inflated Reichsmark. People had to economise again and the cultural scene dried up because people could no longer afford to pay for magazines. The biggest losers in this process were publications that had advocated a return to God and Western culture (*Gott und Abendland*) as the basis of German renewal.

One magazine that escaped the cull was *Frankfurter Hefte*. Founded in 1946 in the spirit of Christian socialism by Walter Dirks and the Buchenwald survivor Eugen Kogon, it became a leading intellectual magazine of the post-war era. In its first issue the editors attempted an explanation of what they were trying to achieve.

Doc 103 Frankfurter Hefte, no. 1

To Our Readers!
We write it down thoughtfully, this phrase '*To our readers*'. Who will they be? We are standing in a circle among whom we are known; but we pass through it into the people, into the world, into the unknown. It is an adventure like everything else today that starts afresh.

Will the teacher who has a transformed youth in front of him pick up our magazine to feel the stream of thought that is supposed to renew Germany? The returned soldier who in streets and in railway stations had looked with tired but alert eyes for traces of sympathy and under-standing? The student with many unspoken demands, claims and expec-tations? The priest who knows himself to be on a rock but feels the flood around his feet? The woman who drifted into the '*Volksgemeinschaft*' and who is now trying to get on new ground? Or her fellow sister who out of the unwavering of the female feeling put up resistance and now is looking to the certainty of her heart for the security of understanding? The politician with high aspirations and nagging doubts in his heart, the worker with the thinking shaped by the party and the ability to distin-guish between utopia and real possibilities, the businessman with the drive for normal activities and the pessimistic mood in face of the rubble that surrounds him and the diminishing instead of replenishing stocks? The intellectual believing in the power of the mind and the 'practical' man who only wants to take a look at 'what the theorists are stitching together yet again' [*wieder zusammenschreiben*]? Or will those only-keen-to-read as well take our magazine because today books are still in short supply, to browse through them, curious and sceptical?

We don't know anything about our readers, who are supposed to become our partners, participants and friends.

But perhaps this is a good thing. Determined anyway not only to say what they want to hear, we want to take no false considerations but say what we regard as right and necessary. This will quite often sound harsh and uncomfortable ...

Thus we expect 'thoughtful' readers. We believe that in this way we can provide a service to Germany's renewal – we, that means the editors, colleagues and employees and those readers already included.

The darkness around us shall be lifted. We all want to help to clear the obscure and the mysterious which threatens us, as far as this is possible, for us who have just emerged out of an abyss and have been granted a human mind.

But we want more: that is, to take the reader whom we made thoughtful out of his thoughtfulness towards the necessary separation and decision, to give him courage for the No and even more the courage for the Yes. We repeat, because it is important: courage for the No and even more courage for the Yes, and we want to nourish with insight the power of the heart and the mind which are necessary for this. This cleansing and nourishing word, which will be read here, shall be determined by the Christian conscience; the world, however, to which it is to relate is not 'the religious' but the whole, multi-layered, rich, poor reality.

Trans. from the 'Introduction', *Frankfurter Hefte, Zeitschrift für Kultur und Politik*, April 1946.

The second cultural institution of lasting fame that survived for decades was *Gruppe 47* (Group 47), named after the year it first met. Despite its name, it was not a group at all but rather a gathering of young writers who were invited by the main initiator, Hans Werner Richter, to read and discuss their works and to award annual prizes. The list of participants to their twice-annual meetings reads like a who's-who of post-war German literature. Heinrich Böll lauded their achievements.

Doc 104 Heinrich Böll on Group 47

The Group was (and in part still is) what Germany was missing after 1945: a meeting point, mobile academy, literary substitute capital; and long before it became fashionable, it was what the Federal Republic's society now takes for granted: pluralistic. The Group remained pluralistic, society became so. By now, pluralism is only a buzzword, a club in everyone's hand with which individuals can be beaten to death as what they least are: individualists or anarchists ...

The Group belongs to this state, it fits it, it is politically as helpless as the state, it has not all but a few attributes in common with the Federal Republic's society and thus it is in the real and only danger of becoming an institution and taking on a function; that is: to function per se ...

Exactly because it never became that which threatened it (that is:

becoming 'representative') it managed what no party and no Federal Government could achieve: establishing relations, though non-diplomatic, to GDR authors. And there is an amazing, almost mythical correctness in that, that they gave their latest prize to Johannes Bobrowski, again not to a realist .... In the meantime, Bobrowski has received the Heinrich Mann prize 'on the other side of the Wall' [*drüben*] – anyone who has eyes to read has read it. In a state like the GDR this is neither pure chance nor an act of pure justice. Writers should manage to fully abstain from the rich Western brother's terrible condescension; for even the Federal Republic's 'literary wealth' is probably connected to the 'Look-how-wealthy-we-are' saying political non-commitment of this state which is by far not as sovereign as it presents itself to be ... That part of Germany, too, that is called Federal Republic, has not liberated itself .... The local freedom, of which literary freedom is only a tiny part, has not been achieved by *Germans*.

Apart from some Church authorities (there is a good deal of unavoidable irony in this parallel), the only team that has a chance to determine – without the big-mouthed attitudes of West- or East-German politicians – whether there already exists a border between GDR-German and FRG-German and where it possibly lies, is Group 47. The fact that the Group is apolitical and not corrupt will help in this respect. What is to happen politically is determined neither in Bonn nor in Pankow, in any case. It is also not for political reasons either, that the credit which the German post-war literature has earned the Federal Republic has to be rated more highly than anything the foreign ministers have achieved. And that is not the foreign ministers' fault. They are, as are we all, only liberated, not free [*Befreite, nicht Freie*].

It would be wrong to believe that Group 47 is 'in crisis'; it was permanently in crisis and from year to year its imminent doom had been prophesied. The danger is that its state becomes less critical, that it institutionalises and functions ... It was not Group 47's fault that there was no creation of literary movements and directions after 1945; ... No, Group 47 has remained what it was: an instrument for publication, a forum, a medium and naturally a market, too. And it still consists of Hans Werner Richter plus unknown – its mythical character is unmistakable.

Trans. from: Heinrich Böll, *Werke: Essayistische Schriften und Reden 1964–72*, Bd. 2., Hg by Bernd Balzer.

Group 47 and the *Frankfurter Hefte* were shining beacons of avant-garde and critical intellectual post-war German culture. They stood increasingly in contrast, and sometimes even in opposition, to the more conventional middle-class culture which often became influenced by Cold War developments and more traditional bourgeois cultural conservatism. A good example for this trend can be seen in a speech by the Federation of German Industry Vice President Otto Vogel, about Culture and Civilisation, given in 1950. This is not only a thinly disguised re-run of the old debate about German 'culture' versus Western 'civilisation' but also bears undertones of the East-West conflict and something that would become more prevalent during the 1950s: self-praise for businessmen.

Doc 105 BDI Vice President Vogel on Culture and Civilisation, 1950

Will the culture of the West [*des Abendlandes*] overcome the storm of the masses from the inside and outside one more time? Is the West, positioned between the old and the new world, still an idea that carries itself? Is culture still possible at all? Culture, this result of psychological-physical efforts by the self-maintaining individual, that constantly renews itself in life? Wherever culture sprouts, maintains and develops itself, this miracle only occurs by combining the efforts of the individuals that consciously suffer – often in contrast to the spread of civilisation that intends nothing but to get rid of life's inconveniences – all those little pains in the world. Will culture and civilisation have to fight each other when the latter, through an excess of the comforts it has produced, has turned into a peaceful monster? And will civilisation, detached from cultural sense – that is, free of any transcendental bonds – level everything in the automatism of its impersonal functionality [*Zweckleistung*] and leave to the human being only that 'pitiful contentment' as a pipe-dream that does not long for great achievements from the individual? ...

Despite this we need not despair! Because the history of all peoples shows us that these times we are currently living through only lead to mankind's long infirmity if the magical and faithful [*glaubensstarke*] power of the individual is prevented from having its effect, if the individual fails in his mission and task or if the populace lacks the necessary interspersion of wilful and powerful, self-assured personalities who take responsibility ...

Trans. from source reprinted in Bührer, *Die Adenauer Ära.*

In his speech, Vogel displayed the typical pseudo-elitism of the conservative upper middle class in which the word *abendländisch* (Western) had replaced the now discredited *germanisch* that had been used a decade earlier. Ordinary people would have followed neither the intellectuals of the *Frankfurter Hefte* nor the elitist middle-class ideas of people like Vogel. A good example of their cultural preference is a carnival song from the 1948/49 season. Carnival had a centuries-old tradition in Germany; and nowhere more so than in the Rhineland, where it had always been used to lampoon the rulers and the ruling classes. While the song snipes a little at the Allies, on a deeper level it expressed first and foremost a wish to return to normality. The past is not challenged but suppressed; instead Germany's past cultural highlights are put at the centre.

Doc 106 Eingeborenen von Trizonesien

My dear friend, oh dear friend,
With the old days gone that we may be
Whether we laugh, whether we cry
The world goes on one, two, three.
A small group of diplomats makes high politics today
Creating zones and altering states
And what about us in this very moment?
(Refrain): We are the natives of Trizonesia
Hey! Heidi-tschimmella-tschimmella-
Tschimmelle-tschimmella-bumm!
We got lassies with character and a fiery way
Heidi-tschimmella-tschimmella-
Tschimmelle-tschimmella-bumm!

Yet actually cannibals we are not
But we kiss right on the spot.
We are the natives of Trizonesia
Hey! Heidi-tschimmella-tschimmella-
Tschimmelle-tschimmella-bumm!
In America Columbus had been
A new part of the world he found
What Marco Polo first had seen
Our culture would some day hold sound.
Sven Hedin was o'er the Himalayas
His traces from desert sand blown

Amundsen's shout Heeyiya!
But so far as people we'd be unknown;
(Refrain)

So stranger, hark that you hear it
A Trizonesian has humour
He has culture he has spirit
And of these nobody has more.
Even Goethe hails from Trizonesia
From Beethoven's cradle we all know
Nothing like this exists in Chinesia,
It's pride in this land we show
(Refrain)

From: Fred Ritzel's '"Was ist aus uns geworden? – Ein Häufchen Sand am Meer": emotions of post-war Germany as extracted from examples of popular music', in: *Popular Music*, vol. 17, no. 3.

A similar trend appeared in the cinematic field, where the *Trümmer-film* – which had often dealt with aspects of the Nazi past – became replaced by the often ridiculed *Heimatfilme*, which presented a *heile Welt*, a rosy and cosy picture of reality. With a setting usually in one of Germany's more picturesque regions, such as the Luneburg Heath or the Black Forrest, the story line dealt with the protagonists' personal problems, had a love interest and, of course, a happy ending. However, hidden under a layer of escapism and schmaltz the *Heimatfilme* often also carried a message about the integration of refugees and expellees or the fate of those men who returned late from the POW camps. The trend of rosy escapism that hit the cinemas since at least 1950 was bucked one last time in 1951 with the making and the screening of *Die Sünderin* (The Sinner). The film depicted the life of a young woman from a middle class family who became a prostitute before falling in love with a terminally-ill painter. Moral outrage was caused not only by a very brief scene that showed a naked female breast but also because the story ended in euthanasia and suicide. Public order disturbances as the one described in a newspaper article happened all over the Republic wherever the film was shown in cinemas.

Doc 107 Newspaper report on *Die Sünderin*

For and against 'The Sinner'
Riots and demonstrations in Regensburg
Mass demonstrations for and against the Willi Forst film *The Sinner*,
which developed into a major disturbance, caused the film to be banned
by the Lord Mayor in the city of Regensburg. The two last screenings
at the Bavaria picture house were prevented by police intervention. This
caused violent protests by cinema goers who had already bought their
tickets. They demanded the Lord Mayor's attendance. After attempts by
the police which lasted for hours and in which rubber truncheons and
fire hoses were used, the cinema was cleared. Shouting in unison 'We
want to see the film' and 'Freedom for the Press and film' a large crowd
moved outside the archbishop's palace – since the diocesan authorities
had previously protested against the screening of the film. Before police
protection arrived, a wooden door in the walls surrounding the palace
was kicked in by the crowd. The demonstration in the street lasted until
about 11 p.m. The cinema manager sent a telegram of complaint to the
Bavarian interior ministry and requested ministerial protection.

Trans. from: *Kölner Stadtanzeiger*, 23 Feb 1951.

After 1950 some excellent literary adaptations came to the cinemas
but by and large the thorny issues of the past were not touched
barring a few notable exceptions. For example, *Rosen für den Staat-
sanwalt* (Roses for the State Attorney, 1959) satirised the continuity
of personnel in the judiciary from the Nazi to the post-war years,
while *Die Brücke* (The Bridge, 1960) told the story of the senseless
slaughter of teenagers in the last days of the Second World War.

A significant change in the cultural and social attitudes of the
mid-1950s which went hand in hand with a generational conflict
was brought about by American music. While many in the so-called
'establishment' and many parents denounced Rock n' Roll as
'uncivilised negro music', the young had found a cultural expression of their own. Bill Hayley's music and more importantly his film
Rock Around the Clock led to local rioting after cinema screening.
Elvis Presley's arrival in Germany for his military service marked the
high point of a teenage frenzy (see also chapter 11).

When looking at the West German cultural scene in the 1950s,
there is one big surprise. Some of the most conservative (if not
even reactionary) individuals at the time acted as strong supporters

for cultural development and cultural patronage. In August 1951, under the leadership of Herman Reusch, the Federation of German Industry set up their *Kulturkreis* or Cultural Circle, a body dedicated to supporting young artists. The list of recipients of their scholarship and prizes reads like a who's who of the German postwar cultural scene, including writers, painters, musicians and sculptors, many of whom criticised 'the establishment' in their works. Representatives of modernist and abstract arts were also supported. The Federation accorded the Circle a spot in its monthly bulletin, demonstrating how important they regarded the promotion of the arts to be. Furthermore, in order to instil the importance of arts and culture into the next generations of business leaders, they incorporated regular talks on arts and culture into their seminars for future top managers. One of these talks was given by the Bavarian State Secretary for Cultural Affairs, who enlightened his audience with eight theses on cultural policy.

Doc 108 Eight theses on cultural policy

Hypothesis 1: Culture serves the development of the inner forces of a people. Cultural policy is not to be conducted as an aspect of foreign policy.

Hypothesis 2: Culture is an intellectual dimension [*geistige Größenordnung*]. Cultural policy is not to be measured with ordinary external measures [*äußeren Masstäben*].

Hypothesis 3: Culture is maintained by the few. Cultural policy is not supposed to leave decisions to the masses.

Hypothesis 4: Culture is seeds of hope. Cultural policy must be able to wait.

Hypothesis 5: Culture is not opposed to the economy; but economics is not to be a starting and finishing point of cultural policy.

Hypothesis 6: Culture is varied. Cultural policy needs the participation of experts.

Hypothesis 7: Culture wants to develop in freedom. Cultural policy is not to appear as guidance or preferential treatment.

Hypothesis 8: The best cultural policy is the one that feels more responsible for culture than for politics and therefore puts the emphasis on the former and not on the latter.

Trans. from: RWWA 130/40010146/576.

Considering the industrialists' usual conservative stance, they remained extremely liberal when dealing with culture. Little was heard from them in public when in 1963 Rolf Hochhuth's book *Der Stellvertreter* (The Deputy) about Pope Pius XII's knowledge of the Holocaust caused a massive outcry in the country. The limits of their cultural liberalism were only reached in 1965 when things came closer to home with Peter Weiss's play *Die Ermittlung* (The Investigation). Based on the transcripts of the recent Auschwitz Trial, the play attacked industrialists' knowledge of what happened at Auschwitz, and for keeping quiet about it for the sake of profits. The industrialists' propaganda mouthpiece, the *Deutsche Industrie Institut*, stated that such an accusation was not only an attack on them but also an attack on the whole order of society and private property.

Doc 109 DII on P. Weiss, 'The Investigation'

German Industry Institute
To all members of the Board, the Curatorium and the Advisory Council
14 October 1965
Dear Sirs!
On 19 October 1965 various theatres in the Federal Republic will perform a new play by Peter Weiss, 'The Investigation'. The author abuses the Auschwitz trial to attack industry and to defame the social order which supports free entrepreneurial activity and private property as the breeding ground of National Socialist crimes.

Radio and TV broadcasters in the Federal Republic also want to participate in the dissemination of the play. In face of the anticipated reaction these performances and broadcasts will cause, we are sending for your information documentation about 'The Peter Weiss Case.'
With best wishes

Trans. from: RWWA 130/40010146/326.

Some industrialists had a genuine interest in cultural affairs. Nevertheless, this incident confirms the suspicion that propaganda was a significant motivation for the BDI to support arts and culture during the 1950s. First, it helped them to present themselves as good citizens who supported the nation's cultural heritage and future. Secondly, supporting arts and culture created some distraction from the Nazi past, since many people still believed that arts and Nazis did not fit together. Sponsoring an artist who was controversial in some way would only increase this image. Only when artists or writers directly associated them with the Nazis did cracks appear in their impression of cultural liberalism.

There were other signs that towards the end of the Adenauer era a change in mentality began slowly to appear, reaching a first climax in the public outcry in connection with the Spiegel affair (Docs 148, 149). One year before the affair, in 1961, the historian Fritz Fischer published his seminal work *Griff nach der Weltmacht* (English translation *Germany's Aims in the First World War*) in which he outlined that the German leadership in 1914 did not fight a 'defensive war' but was set on imperial hegemony. The book caused an outcry among conservatives and led to the longest and fiercest historical debate in post-war German history. The historian Gerhard Ritter would become Fischer's strongest critic and he tried to savage the book in a 23-page review.

Doc 110 Ritter's Review of Fischer's *Griff nach der Weltmacht*

A New War Guilt Hypothesis?
The Documents of German diplomacy 1867–1945 have finally ... been returned from England and made available to German researchers in their original form. The first comprehensive book which German academic historians (*Fachhistorie*) ... have made out of these documents has the screaming title *Griff nach der Weltmacht* ... The book is intended to reinforce the theory that official German war politics 1914–1918 had right from the beginning ... abandoned the character of a defensive war which had been noisily and openly proclaimed in August 1914 ...

The author leaves it to the reader to conclude that our war policy was therefore pure madness as early as September 1914 ...

The question is whether he has been successful, whether his book will contribute to a better understanding of German history or whether it misunderstands the past and distorts it ...

Fischer also explains that he does not want to deal with the war-guilt question as such again, but still does this in practice. Only he knows beforehand what he has to prove and is not very picky in his choice of evidence ...

At the same time [the book] reaches a first climax in the current political-historical fashion trend: the self-darkening [*Selbstverdunkelung*] of

225

German historical consciousness which after the catastrophe of 1945 has replaced the earlier self-deification and which is now increasingly more and more prevalent and biased. According to my conviction this will be no less fatal than the former hyper-patriotism. Thus I am not able to put the book aside without great sadness: sadness and concern for the coming generations.

Trans. from Gerhard Ritter in: *Historische Zeitschrift*, vol. 194 (1962), pp. 646–68.

10

Leisure and consumers

Within less than ten years, the Federal Republic had turned from a country of desperation during the immediate post-war years into a modern prosperous consumer society. This process has been described by contemporaries as appearing in three waves, the *Fresswelle* (wave of gluttony); the *Konsumwelle* (wave of consumption); and the *Reisewelle* (wave of travel). The wave of gluttony was initially only for the more affluent, who right after the currency reform could afford the newly available yet still relatively expensive foodstuffs. Only after the Korea boom had brought an upturn in economic activity that led to a significant rise in real incomes from about 1953 onward could the broader population participate in this first wave. One must also recognise the considerable impact the massive structural change that took place during the 1950s had on the growing national income. In 1950, the agricultural sector employed some 25 per cent of the workforce, often on small and unprofitable farms that generated hardly any income beyond subsistence level. When those farmers moved to work in industry or their children into the tertiary economic sector, they were able to earn considerably higher wages, which allowed them to increase their standard of living. Two items became symbols of the new consumer society. The first was the television set, which had its first boom year in 1954, when West Germany unexpectedly won the football World Cup; the second item was the motor car, symbolised by the Mercedes for the rich, or the VW Beetle for ordinary people. Rapid motorisation (see Doc 44) then allowed the third wave to take place, the *Reisewelle*. Italy became *the* fashionable holiday location, with some people making the trip, including the crossing of the Alpine passes, on motor scooters! Hire-purchase and catalogue mail order revolutionised consumer habits and aspirations. The largest mail-order firm, Neckermann, became synonymous with the fulfilment of average consumers' dreams before the name eventually became a derogative term for package holidays.

In 1957, one of the great scourges of industrial society, poverty among the elderly, was all but eradicated by the introduction of the so-called 'dynamic' pension. This, too, was a further step towards a more egalitarian society that developed during the 1950s. This general trend was described by a sociologist in a provocative study as the 'levelled-out middle-class society', the *nivillierte Mittelstandsgesellschaft.*

Although the currency reform established itself as the seminal event in the public memory of the immediate post-war years, the large majority of people had initially very little hope of a significant improvement of their situation; they certainly did not dream about a consumer society. Even in 1949, the basic supply of clothes could not be guaranteed, despite the fact that the bizonal Director for Economics, Ludwig Erhard, had initiated the *Jedermann Programm* (everyman programme) that was supposed to provide old American military clothing at low, fixed prices in an attempt to combat the existing profit inflation. The Staatliche Erfassungsgesellschaft für öffentliches Gut (StEG), a state-owned company that had been given the task of utilising any old military equipment and running the programme, was badly criticised for its inefficiency and wastefulness in the face of still massive demand even for basic clothing.

Doc 111 Need for clothing

StEGreif – Ökonomie [ad-lib economics]
'In Sandhofen, near Mannheim, ten million pieces of American textiles, jumpers, socks, underpants and vests, coats, blankets and tarpaulins are stored. Ten million pieces, one each for ten million people. Hurry those of you who are naked and get clothed with what is bestowed upon you ...'. Thus called the Economic Council, thus called the StEG, the trustee for the American army-surplus material that got stuck on German soil. Ten million came, everyone took a piece, wore it over or underneath their clothes and the StEG depot at Sandhofen near Mannheim was distributed to the needy. Ad lib so to speak [*Stegreif*], just the way it was supposed to have been taken over by the improvised 'Staatliche Erfassungsgesellschaft für öffentliches Gut m.b.H.'. Alas, however, it was not done like that. Because the StEG could not be convinced of such an

ad-lib economy. They did not believe in the justice of such a conventional method of distribution. Thus they took care of the matter(s) in their own way and dealt with them according to the acknowledged principles of economics and accounting. These principles are: the economic-technical provision of goods, rationalisation of labour and tools, establishment of a technical-economic unit within the company; evaluation of goods, price formation, getting the retail trade involved for interpersonal and inter-local goods transfer, etc. And the StEG organised, made an inventory, sorted, demilitarised, calculated, balanced so that every good paymaster was really happy and satisfied, and, yes, they even improvised when things didn't quite go according to plan. Now it *had* to work. Alas, it didn't. Although the organisation worked, the rest did not. The distribution, that is, as it appeared to the final customer who was longing for new socks because he did not understand economics. On rotten wooden frames, just about ten centimetres above ground in the mud of the Sandhofen depot, by January five million jumpers, socks, underpants and undershirts, coats, blankets and tarpaulins were still stored. Anything that is not yet rotten, filthy, decayed, decomposed after three years of American administration followed by four months under StEG control soon will be. By now, here and there, some StEG commodities have appeared, but apparently so few that one only hears about them and believes in them so as not to appear malicious. The simple consumer, however, far at the back, hardly reachable, silently wrings his hands for socks and begs for an explanation. He hasn't a clue about economics, though.

Trans. from source reprinted in: A. Kuhn (ed.), *Frauen in der deutschen Nachkriegszeit.*

At least for some, change was on its way. By 1950, more affluent people who had been able to afford the high prices for foodstuffs, especially non-staple items, had made up for the wartime restrictions and the starvation rations of the post-war years. During the ensuing *Fresswelle* those who could afford it seemed to have tried to 'catch up' for the years of want, and the results had become quite visible, as a small article in a household magazine shows.

Doc 112 Getting slim

Getting Slim

Together with whipped cream and ham sandwiches, chocolate and smoked eel, concerns about one's figure have re-emerged. Concerns – that is something different from those deep sighs arising from a good life and which we had better called 'pangs of conscience', resulting out of joy over the return of the good things in life in which we have over-indulged slightly.

Be that as it may, the coat is too tight, the suit jacket doesn't fit any more, the dress seams are splitting and the dinner jacket – yes, you too are affected this time, gentlemen – can't be expanded by either moving the button or extending the seams. Our face approaches full-moon format, the chin has turned into at least two. We'd better cover our posterior and hips with the coat of compassion, and Herr Müller has always to ask his little son to tell him if his shoes are dusty, since the father's belly blocks his own view of them.

One thing is certain: recently we have eaten too much, or rather, the wrong things. Always that which we craved for and could not resist after the long years of managing without – and which puts on fat so nicely. It is not the quantity of food, so that the classic 'F.d.H.' diet (in plain German: scoff half!) has only a limited effect. In order to become slim and to remain so we only need a natural way of living and a sensible mixed diet. We put vegetarian food before meat dishes, prefer vegetables (cooked without flour and eaten raw if possible), salads (without oil and bacon, but with lots of herbs), fruit and fruit juices. We avoid fatty and fried meat, deep-fried fish or fatty fish such as eels and courageously say good-bye for some time to sweet savouries, cakes, chocolates and other sweets. Quark and milk, boiled fish, boiled eggs enrich our shopping list. Instead of beer we enjoy a glass of Moselle wine and make it a rule to drink only before or after meals but never during them and to never drink too much.

Trans. from: *Ratgeber* 1950, no. 9.

While the advice given may sound very familiar in today's society, at the time it was a novelty. The food industry had been quick to react to the improving situation and the changing eating habits and benefited from the wave of gluttony with extra marketing publications. Even before the economic miracle was in full swing, advertisements tried to entice customers to buy products which not too long ago would have been the purest luxury items for ordinary people.

Doc 113 Dr Oetker advertisement

Today's modern woman has to ask herself two essential questions: 'What am I going to wear today?' and 'What shall I cook today?' Men who have a sweet tooth have a good character. A man has to be won anew every day – cook him Dr Oetker's custard [*Pudding*].

Trans. from Dr Oetker advertisement, early 1950s.

The advertisement not only shows a changing pattern of food consumption away from the traditional daily basic staples (as seen in Doc 34) to more extravagant products, it also highlights a return to the traditional gender roles of women cooking and charming their husbands. This also meant that 'modern women' had to be appropriately dressed in the latest fashion. The mail-order shops of Josef Neckermann and Werner Otto contributed to this trend with their catalogues, enabling customers who lived outside the big cities (the largest part of the West German population lived in rural areas or small towns) to have the latest fashion as well. Neckermann prices were calculated very tightly so that more traditional retailers and even some of the department-store chains had to cut their prices to stay competitive. It was this kind of market economy, where competition led to falling prices, Erhard had talked about. Alongside mail order was another new American form of shopping – hire purchase – which allowed Germans to benefit from ever-increasing consumer satisfaction, although this kind of business was heavily criticised by some.

Doc 114 Defence of hire purchase

In his report on the hire-purchase problem Prof. Röpke gave his inclination towards unconventional [*eigenwillig*] phrasing unlimited space: 'Hire purchase as a mass habit is therefore nothing but a sign of a false, that is unreasonable, planning of life. It is the expression of an un-bourgeoisie [*unbürgerlichen*] conduct of life.'

This view is in remarkable contrast to the opinion of all those who accuse the modern worker, with his trend towards owning a radio and a motorbike, of displaying a tendency towards 'bourgeoisisation' – since the attributes of becoming bourgeois are made available only because of hire purchase! And especially in North America, where the 'bourgeoisi-sation' penetrates the broadest levels of the working classes to whom the thinking in classes is much more alien than in the Old World, the hire purchase orgy has reached new heights ...

The neo-liberal view culminates in the nanny-ish exhortation that the individual should kindly behave in a respectable, bourgeois manner until he has saved the money needed to buy a refrigerator, for example ...

The fluctuations of hire purchase loans are basically a secondary symptom of those changeable public moods that play a part in the economy's [der Konjunktur] ups and downs. If the public mood is on the up, then it is contagious – even when the upswing is not really secure. These are mainly credits that only rest on one base: on the presumption that the debtor keeps his current income until he has repaid the loan. But once there is a downturn, not only debtors get nervous – because they have to ask themselves if the next day they will be able to pay their instalments – but the creditors even more so. If the previously reliable customer becomes unemployed, they will be stuck with a fridge that is only half paid-for, assuming, of course, that they can get it back at all ...

It has to be emphasised: the condemnation of hire purchase cannot logically be derived from liberal thoughts ... However, it seems that here – as in many other areas – the neo-liberal view shrinks back from conse-quent economic policy [konjunkturoplitischen] measures. Not least for this reason it will be necessary to emphasise the significance of the hire purchase problem for the economic development.

Trans. from: *Gewerkschaftliche Monatshefte 5* (1954).

The article's author takes a firm stand against the middle-class critics of hire purchase, throwing out the bourgeois notion of only buying what one can pay for in cash, usually only after a long time saving up. He also slammed the most outspoken critic of hire purchase, the neo-liberal economist Röpke, for abandoning his liberal doctrines for the sake of traditional bourgeois sentiments on purchasing.

Mail-order businesses that guaranteed their prices for at least six months and hire purchase contributed to the development of a consumer society in the Federal Republic; the economic boom began to trickle down the social ladder and brought higher wages, falling prices did the rest. The German equivalent of 'keeping up with the Joneses' played a role in the consumer boom as did the overall feeling of 'we are somebody again'. That feeling was expressed through the purchase of radios, record players, television sets, new furniture and kitchen appliances, and, of course, motor cars. By 1955, the millionth VW Beetle had left the assembly line at Wolfsburg. Collective bargaining achieved higher wages, falling weekly working hours and increased holiday periods, which all allowed for more leisure time. Traditional German holiday areas such as the Black Forrest, the Rhine valley or the Luneburg Heath benefited from free publicity in form of the *Heimatfilme*, but the 1950s dream holiday remained a trip to Italy. As a matter of fact, the outflow of currency spent on holiday trips abroad was an important factor that kept West Germany's overall balance of payments from rising even higher. The amazing rise in the spending on tourism is another sign of how much the German economy had changed for the better.

Doc 115 Increased spending on tourism

Balance of payments in tourism, 1950–1970 (in million DM)

Year	Income	Expenditure	Balance
1950	135	85	50
1960	1672	2651	–976
1970	4953	10330	–5377

Trans. from: Harald Winkel, *Die Wirtschaft im geteilten Deutschland 1945–1970*, Wiesbaden 1974.

In 1957 the situation of one group that had usually been pushed to the sidelines of society, where many suffered relative and even real poverty, was dramatically changed. The reform of the pension system in January of that year had a dramatic impact: raising average pensions by 65 per cent, it changed the principle of pension payments from being a subsidy to one's own savings into a payment that would guarantee a pensioner's standard of living. The timing of the pension law was not an accident but part of one of the biggest 'electoral gifts' (or bribes) ever made in the FRG. It contributed significantly towards the CDU's absolute majority in 1957. The reform had been strongly opposed from several sides: by Finance Minister Fritz Schäffer, who feared about growing national debt; by the Bundesbank, which feared it would cause inflationary pressure;

and by Economics Minister Erhard who saw it as a first step away from a system based on prudence and self-reliance to one where people began to rely only on the state for their livelihood in old age. All of them were overruled by Adenauer and sections of the CDU for political reasons linked to the election. On 13 September, just two days before the federal elections, the Minister for Labour, Anton Storch, from the CDU's left wing reminded people of the reform in a press article.

Doc 116 Pension reform

With the promulgation of the two pension insurance bills ... a year has passed that took us a decisive step towards social security for our population's working people ... the new pension insurance is exactly tailored to workers' life situation [*Lebensschicksal*] as we see them daily and on the needs of our working people whose lifelong existence depends on the availability of work for them to do. In particular the means-testing of pensions has to be rejected and a legal right for pensions has been acknowledged. The pension, too, belongs to the equivalent of the work done during one's lifetime. In the same way as a worker's wage is his only means of income during his working life, so this law assumes that in old age or invalidity the pension becomes available to him to secure his basic needs [*Lebensgrundlage*]. The legal claim for a pension rests deeply in the belief that the worker during his time at work receives his wage as consideration and after his retirement from work he receives a pension which is commensurate with his working wage. The size of the pension is calculated in such a way that after a normal working life it is not only sufficient to sustain a living in old age [*zum Lebensunterhalt ... ausreicht*] but that it also guarantees a standard of living that can withstand the comparison to the lifestyle of someone still working ...

Now many will point out that they became unemployed, perhaps as a result of the Big Depression in the 1930s or due to military service and fighting; because of illness or a longer school and technical college education. These instances will be cited as reasons for individuals not being able to work as long as others. For all these cases and further ones, care has been taken in the law. These periods [*Ersatz- und Ausfallzeiten*] which count towards pensions but for which no contribution had been made will be considered by calculating the pension in such a way as if the insured person had indeed been in work ...

A productivity pension that after 40 years of insurance amounts to

60 per cent and after 50 years of insurance to 75 per cent of the average when applied to the current wage levels [*Gegenwartshöhe*] means a sweeping success ...

Trans. from: *Bulletin der Bundesregierung*, Sept. 1957.

The reform did not follow the Scandinavian and British models of a state-guaranteed minimum pension but was calculated according to the average pension contribution one had paid during one's working life. The higher the payments, the higher the pension would be. Nevertheless, the reform was heavily criticised by neo-liberals as the first sin against the market economy.

As long as there was full employment, economic growth and an expanding population the system would work and contribute to a more egalitarian society. There was indeed a trend towards a more equal society, a development which had been pointed out by the sociologist Helmut Schelzky as early as 1953. In his famous and often cited article he described and explained the Federal Republic's move towards a 'levelled middle-class society.'

Doc 117 Helmut Schelzky: *Nivellierte Mittelstandsgesellschaft*

1. In the last two generations of German society extensive social upward and downward movements took place. First the broad upward mobility of industrial workers and secondly the more individual, but altogether the still class-forming [*schichtbildend*] rise of technical and clerical white-collar workers into the new middle class constituted the broad upward mobility of industrial-technocratic society. These processes of upward mobility were counteracted in somewhat more recent times by broad social downward movement and declassing processes, beginning in the First World War, which – in the years after 1945 – found its culmination in the existence of expellees, the politically declassed etc. and particular affected sections of the former property-owning and educated bourgeoisie [*Besitz- und Bildungsbürgertum*]. The combination of these opposing movements of social mobility initially caused an extraordinary increase in social mobility in itself. But beyond that, in particular, they precipitated a relative reduction in class antagonism, with no differentiation of the old professional groups still characterised by status. Thus these movements created social levelling in a relative uniform layer of society that is neither proletarian nor bourgeois, but is characterised

instead by the loss of class tensions and social hierarchy. A comprehensive and continuously expanding social policy on the one hand, and a strict and increasingly tough tax policy, in terms of its income levels, on the other, become constant factors of this social levelling process which only a few small groups can escape today.

2. The levelling of the true economic and political status mainly follows a standardisation of the social and cultural patterns of behaviour in a way of life which could be – when measured against the old classification – located in the 'lower middle', and thus be called petit-bourgeois-middle-class [*kleinbürgerlich-mittleständich*]. This relatively standardised lifestyle of the levelled-middle-class society [*nivellierten Mittelstandsgesellschaft*] is no longer characterised by the substance of a socially somehow hierarchically ordered or layered social structure [*Gesellschaftsverfassung*] in any way. Rather this 'middle-class' form of life fulfils itself by uniformly participating in the material and spiritual commodities of civilisation's comforts. The universal consumption of industrial and journalistic mass production takes care to ensure that materially and spiritually, nearly everybody, according to his ability, can develop the feeling that he is no longer 'at the bottom', but is instead already able to participate in the wealth and in the luxury of life.

In this way, within the industrial mass production of consumer, comfort and entertainment products – which nowadays even the former upper and bourgeois classes use – lies the most effective means surmounting industrial society's class structure, but also to make lifestyle and social needs uniform ...

4 ... The petit-bourgeois and middle-class [*mittelständische*] people's social consciousness fights most against the lack of social position [*soziale Standortlosigkeit*], with no social status or significance; thus typically in this levelled society the old class society's ranking order is being preserved and kept. In many cases belonging to a certain old prestige group is more stressed today than in the past, although there are hardly any social realities behind these 'imagined' forms. This desperate maintenance of outdated social models corresponds to the adherence of the – already largely changed – society in its old political ideas and positions in the way that the levelled-middle-class society tends ideologically towards any form of restoration ...

Trans. from: H. Schelzky, *Die Bedeutung des Schichtungsbegriffs für die Analyse der gegenwärtigen deutschen Gesellschaft* (1953), in: H. Schelzky, *Auf der Suche nach Wirklichkeit*, 1965.

11

Gender and youth

West Germany's development in regard to gender relations and the so-called youth rebellion of the late 1950s is not different from the experience of other Western countries, perhaps with the exception that due to the impact of the war, some encounters were stronger and others were slightly more hypocritical. In the absence of the men during the war years, women had worked in most sectors of the economy; in the post-war period they had cleared the rubble of the destroyed towns and cities while having to cope with the meagre rations for themselves and their children. The *Trümmerfrauen*, or 'rubble women', became one of the iconic images of the immediate post-war years. However, once the men began to return from war and captivity, most women also returned to, or were forced to return to, their traditional roles. The war's impact on demographics had also affected the Federal Republic like no other country west of the Iron Curtain. By 1950 there was a considerable imbalance in the ratio of women to men, with the former outnumbering the latter by nearly 2.5 million in the age group of the 20- to 55-year-old. Wives whose husbands had been killed in action received war widow pensions. In the case of officers' widows those pensions could be considerable. However, if a widow wanted to remarry, she would lose the pension entitlement. This led in many cases to the so-called *Onkelehen*, literally uncle marriages, where the woman lived under one roof with her new partner, who was to be addressed by his de facto stepchildren as 'uncle' to preserve the image of moral decency, since in the 1950s cohabitation was hardly socially acceptable for the middle classes.

Interestingly, this kind of social deviation for economic reasons was by and large tolerated in a society that had returned to pre-1933 moral values in its search for normality. The obvious moral double standards may have had an impact on how teenagers experienced, and reacted towards, post-war society. The legacy of the war on 1950s German youth in creating insecurity and/or juvenile challenges of authority again was stronger than, say, in Britain. Somebody born in 1940, for example, would most likely have been raised, either permanently or at least for some time, without a father and, more dramatically, would have experienced first the collapse of the traditional system of authority and then of the German state itself. In the face of widespread adult moral double standards during the 1950s many youths began to challenge traditional authorities. This happened not least under the influence of American films, such as James Dean's *Rebel without a Cause* or Marlon Brando's *The Wild One* with their theme of juvenile rebellion against the adult world. The economic miracle and the consumer society had an impact, too; for the first time, teenagers had their own financial means which gave them (though still limited) unprecedented economic freedom. Many of them could afford to purchase the juvenile status symbols of the time, such as transistor radios, record players and records, jeans and in some cases even motor scooters.

In the immediate post-war years women usually bore the brunt of the desolation, even more so when they had to care for a family. In cases where the husbands had not (yet) returned from the war, they had to find work, queue for food and heating material, and take care of the children while often living in insufficient and desolate housing. In many cases, as described in a report by a social worker in the town of Wuppertal from summer 1947, they gave up part of their own meagre rations for the sake of their children or the husband if he had work to go to, with predictable results.

Doc 118 Mothers' sacrifices

As a consequence of insufficient nutrition, the population as a whole [*Geamtbevölkerung*] no longer has any resistance at all. Diseases are spreading. The number of tuberculosis sufferers is increasing at a frightening rate as does the number of patients with boils. Infants cannot be fed properly because of a complete lack of vegetables and fruit. Mothers sacrifice most, giving up everything to satisfy their husbands and children so that in time the mothers themselves lose all their strength. Silence [*Stummheit*] and hopelessness are spreading more and more. In many families there are arguments resulting from insufficient food supplies.

Individual family members are stealing each other's ration cards. Husbands who are barely able to work any more are demanding their pregnant wives' supplementary ration cards. Because of this marriages and family lives are being ruined.

Linked to the increasing weakness is a great unwillingness to work [*Arbeitsunlust*]. Many people drift into working on the black market, where the essentials can be obtained and where indeed everything is available. Most at risk are juveniles some of whom have no regular work at all but conduct black-market deals, organise small thefts and thus become criminals. The little children, too, suffer neglect because their mothers have to leave them unattended while they queue for hours on end for the most essential foodstuff such as bread, meat etc. In spite of everything, some women and mothers bear this desperate situation with a bravery that deserves admiration. They put all their strength into keeping their households and their family lives in order.

Trans. from source reprinted in: Kuhn (ed.), *Frauen in der deutschen Nachkriegszeit*.

When husbands returned from war and captivity, they too, were confronted with new situations that had derived from the experiences of their wives. Many women found it difficult to return to the old subordinate role after they had learned to cope on their own. For the men it was often difficult to re-establish their traditional role, not least because of the psychological impact the lost war had had on their masculinity. Certainly not many men would have been prepared by their own upbringing to respond in a compassionate way when their wife told them about her experience of being raped by Allied soldiers – assuming the women were courageous enough to tell their husbands about it.

Doc 119 Family reunion

... and when I returned in 1949 she had already restored our flat and everything was reasonable ... When I returned, I didn't know if she would need me again.
Peter Kl., returned from Soviet captivity in 1949.

And then I told him that at the end of the war in Pomerania I had been raped several times. It was terrible for me to talk about it once more but

I thought he had to know. I then asked him if he would still be able to live with me. He was shocked about what I had lived through, he said he needed time to think about it. He couldn't tell how he would decide. Those events were grave enough to not continue a marriage.
Gisela K.

Trans. from source in: Kuhn, Pitzen and Hochgeschurz (eds), *Politeia: Szenen aus der deutschen Geschichte nach 1945 aus Frauensicht.*

Undoubtedly, circumstances and events like those described in documents 118 and 119 put huge strains on marriages. The brutalisation of the war and the long separation had led in many cases to such estrangements between partners that divorce rates more than doubled compared to levels before the war.

Doc 120 Divorce rates

Divorce rates in the FRG (without Berlin and Saarland) 1939, 1946–58

Year	Total	per 100,000 inhabitants
1939	29303	7.5
1946	48422	9.9
1947	76091	17
1948	87013	18.9
1949	79409	17
1950	74638	15.9
1951	55862	11.8
1952	50833	10.6
1953	47383	9.8
1954	44438	9.1
1955	42538	8.6
1957	41187	8.2
1958	42726	8.4

Trans. from source in: Kuhn, Pitzen and Hochgeschurz (eds), *Politeia: Szenen aus der deutschen Geschichte nach 1945 aus Frauensicht.*

When looking at these figures, one has to remember that divorce had been made easier by the Nazis, so that the 1939 figure would have been above the longer-term trend. In contrast, in the post-war years the legislation had been reversed and it had once again become more difficult to get divorced. Furthermore, divorce had regained some, but clearly not all, of its old social stigma.

With more and more men returning home and then looking for jobs, and life returning to its more traditional ways, there was an increasing trend of pushing women out of their employment and, where possible, back into their customary role. In many cases, some pathetic excuses were produced to justify the process, as demonstrated in the next document.

Doc 121 Female conductors causing unrest

From now on, both the Essen and Mühlheim tramways want to fill job vacancies only with men. The main reason given is that the loss of working hours is much higher with women than with men. Essen tramways, for example, claim that because of high absenteeism among women, 140 women are needed to do the work of 100 men. Furthermore, both companies stated – but only in passing – that female conductors were an element of unrest within the workforce. Male tram drivers and female conductors strongly depend on each other which creates a certain familiarity [*Vertraulichkeit*] that, because of the large amount of freedom and independence the job entails (late shifts and shared way home), can too easily lead employees to stray into unprofessional territory.

Trans. from source reprinted in: Kuhn (ed.), *Frauen in der deutschen Nachkriegszeit.*

The reasons given for the reduction of female employment or the reason for women's dismissal were typical of the gender roles at the time. No-one seemed to have taken into consideration (or just ignored the fact) that most of those absentee women would have families to look after, something male drivers obviously could have left to their wives. The claim about the 'unrest within the workforce', by the same token, disregards the fact that it takes a man and a woman to 'behave unprofessionally'.

The demographic reality of a surplus of women was acknowledged but in many cases this acknowledgement only led to them being pitied, patronised and moralised in the tone of traditional bourgeois self righteousness as this example from the *Ratgeber* magazine (translated as *advice manual*) shows.

Doc 122 'Surplus women'

A lot has already been said and written about the problem of surplus women (what an unkind word), about 'threesome marriages' [*Ehe zu dritt*] and other consequences of this problem; and yet so often it is passed by thoughtlessly, it is passed over, hushed up ...

Time and again you can hear that 'a woman's natural destiny' (by which womanhood and motherhood are usually meant to be only physical-sexual experiences) has not been given rights because of lack of men. In contrast to this I say: the prime quality and task of a woman is motherliness [*Mütterlichkeit*]. I know women who probably radiate more of that caring, selfless goodness without ever having conceived a child than those who could experience motherhood. In addition, there are a fair number of girls and women who don't show any 'natural destiny': fun, superficiality, pleasure of all kinds form the basis of their lives! – To awaken motherliness in themselves and turn it into a serving power would thus be the 'woman's natural destiny'. Whether she lets this destiny prevail by being a nurse, welfare worker, warden of a hostel, nursery school teacher, in another job or being a wife and mother is not immaterial. Maybe the last task is the most beautiful – but it also is the most difficult. And how many unhappy or at least indifferent marriages are there! Such a life is worse than one without a companion ...

The term 'threesome marriage' could only be created because, once again, the matter had been judged only from its physical side. Is not marriage so much more – a mental and spiritual union, a life-long relationship [*Lebensgemeinschaft*] between two people? How can there be harmony between two women and a man? The women will always be rivals and gradually destroy themselves and him emotionally in the process. A woman who breaks into an already existing marriage may well be called egotistical – she only wants to be made happy [*beglückt*] by the man. Does she know for sure her existence makes him happy in the long run as well? Does she know what she is probably going to destroy and what will remain of her conscience? It is only such a relationship that evokes the tragedy of the lack of men ...

From what has been said so far, the following should have become clear: you are pitied, you so-called surplus girls – but you will be helped only with perilous escape routes, with slogans which are meant to take you away by force from the right path that has been laid out for you by destiny. Such straying from the straight and narrow will only plunge you into deep spiritual distress and hopelessness and will avenge itself because it is unnatural. Think of yourselves – seek pleasure and strength in good books and in all beautiful things that were left to us on this earth, fight to overcome. Do not fear loneliness – essentially everyone is lonely, even in the most happy marriage. I know it myself ...

Trans. from *Ratgeber* 1950, no. 10, p. 289 f.

At the end of the Adenauer era the traditional gender roles were more entrenched than ever. Although there remained a considerable number of women and even mothers that still had to work, the ideal was that the man was the breadwinner and the woman stayed at home and looked after the children and the household. The economic boom which had brought rising wages and living standards contributed to this development. Even most husbands whose wives had to contribute to the household income wished – in the typical cliché of the traditional patriarchal society and male psyche – that they, the men, could be the sole provider to their households, as a 1964 survey published in the magazine of the employers' organisation shows.

Doc 123 Cooking-pot marriages

German fathers don't like to see their wives working. This is the astounding result of a representative survey ... on 'The Situation of West German Mothers'. Astounding, since of the 6.7 million mothers with children under 14 years of age 2.3 million – that is more than one-third – are working. According to this, one in four women in the Federal Republic who is working is a mother with a child of school age or younger. Mothers tend more towards working than fathers would like, and they get their way. German fathers' ideas are trailing well behind reality. The wishful thinking of the ideal wife and mother that they harbour in their inner selves needs urgent reform. According to the survey of 1,000 husbands ... 30 per cent of them expect from their wives first and foremost good housekeeping and cooking skills. The trend towards the cooking-pot marriage is unmistakable. The remainder emphasise the women's economical, housekeeping and practical sense, praise her willingness to work [*Arbeitsfreudigkeit*] and her diligence. A large proportion of the men questioned indicated a woman who had homely-familiar sides and – would you believe it! – even turn against mothers who like to go to the cinema or the hairdresser's or even like to smoke cigarettes. Only 1 per cent would like to have a wife who is working. However, the husbands whose wives are working recognise the wife's threefold burden of job, household and childcare. But in most cases they are not prepared to take on some of the burden of household or childcare. Their solution to the problem is that: a husband should earn enough so that his wife shouldn't have to work. A woman's realm is the household. Everything else is men's business. This all in a time when the economy needs all workers, even female, in which all kinds of ideas are considered as to how to enable mothers to have a job alongside their family commitments. It seems appropriate to include in these deliberations the husbands' conservative views.

Trans. from *Der Arbeitgeber* 1964, no. 18, p. 452.

The conclusion drawn from the survey was that women would not be available in large numbers to fill the companies' job vacancies. Consequently, employers would have to look elsewhere for labour, a trend that would increase the recruitment of workers from abroad, the so-called *Gastarbeiter* or guest workers. In 1964, the millionth of these workers received a motorbike as a welcome gift.

Without a doubt there were women who welcomed the end of their treble burden of work, childcare and household chores, even if those had become easier with the increasing availability of appliances. The fact remained that in such a male-dominated society 'emancipation' and 'gender equality' or 'female self-fulfilment' had little chance of becoming a reality.

In contrast to gender roles, relationships between the generations experienced greater upheaval and challenges to the traditional and largely unquestioned authority of parents and institutions. It was during the 1950s that West Germany, like most of the Western world, witnessed the emergence of an independent youth culture. The impact of the lost war and its aftermath helped to erode state and institutional authority to an extent never seen before. Teenagers began to adore and copy all things American, not least rock and roll music, which was seen as an invigorating contrast to the schmaltz of the contemporary German music world, the *Schlager*. In the economic boom of the 1950s, a 17- or 18-year-old boy or girl could expect to instantly find a well-paid job as soon as they had completed their apprenticeships; thus they had money available to spend on the new lifestyle. However, this new spending power was not matched by the availability of sufficient and adequate leisure-time activities or venues. The resulting frustration often found an outlet and was discharged after concerts or after rock and roll films were shown in cinemas. *Rock around the Clock* in particular became notorious for sparking off disturbances. Describing one such incident, the newspaper report in the next document gives a good illustration of the bewilderment many adults felt when faced with such unfamiliar and rowdy behaviour.

Doc 124 Youth unrest

On 4 December 1956 there was a rock and roll brawl in Mannheim. After watching the film 'Rock Around the Clock' numerous juveniles [*Halbwüchsige*] left the cinema in an atmosphere of adventure [*Unternehmungslust*]. One part – especially the 'Hobby' group – was determined for action, they wanted to 'shout, sing and howl'. Initially, the majority remained in a state of wait-and-see and followed only out of curiosity. At first they went to the old fairground where soon some 400 to 500 adolescents [*Halbwüchsige*] had gathered. Then the crowd moved over the Kurpfalz bridge towards the city centre where four particular adolescents stood out as ringleaders and set the examples for others to follow. After failing to open the 'Hobby' bar by force or to enter the 'Café Rheinland', a group of some 40 adolescents forced their way into the 'Rondo' bar where the glass panel of the entrance door, tables, chairs, glasses and ashtrays were damaged or smashed. This happened partly because of the consumption vouchers usually demanded by the proprietor, whom they wanted to show 'how tough we are' and that 'we are who we are', and partly because some people wanted to dance. When it became known that the police were approaching, the adolescents left the bar and ran towards the 'Prinz Max' dance hall. A group of 200 or so adolescents forced their way into the dance hall, ripped down a curtain that was fitted at the door and, according to witnesses, shouted 'like idiots'. On the way to the 'Hobby', 'Rondo', the 'Prinz Max' dance hall and eventually towards Jungbusch bridge, the noisily rampaging crowd threw stones through the windows of several houses; residents who were looking out of the windows were shouted at and insulted ...

A small car parked at Luisenring was pushed onto the middle of the road and left there causing another vehicle to nearly crashing into it ... The 18-year-old Y. attempted, as in the movie 'Rebels Without a Cause', to slash the tyres of a car with a knife .... Near the 'Drei Kronen' inn, 16-year-old Z., together with some other adolescents, displayed a threatening attitude towards two policemen and hurled abuse at them ... Further actions had been planned but were prevented by the early arrest of the ringleaders. Following the main trial on 23 January 1957, the district juvenile magistrate's court [*Bezirksjugendschöffengericht*] sentenced eight of the main offenders, that is four ringleaders and four other participants ...

Trans. from source in: G. Kaiser, *Randalierende Jugend*, Heidelberg 1959.

In the German language the now old-fashioned term '*Halbwüchsiger*' – roughly translated as 'half-pint' – is intended to be derogatory in the sense that a person so described is not to be taken seriously, since they have not reached full maturity as an adult. The other term used to describe and deride those teenagers involved in disturbances was *Halbstarker*. It implied more willingness to use violence than *Halbwüchsiger*; and for some time *Halbstarke* became the scourge of the upstanding citizen. In contrast to the British 'Teddy Boys' phenomenon of about the same time, the social make up of *Halbstarke* was more varied and much less limited to the working class. *Bravo*, the leading youth magazine at the time, commented on the causes of, and reaction to, the new attitudes among youths.

Doc 125 *Bravo* on Halbstarke, 1956

Halbstarke (Rowdies), Halbstarke, Halbstarke, nothing but Halbstarke, the newspapers are full of it, books are published about them and movies made. The term has become a catchphrase, a plague ... Every young man wearing drainpipe trousers, roaring around with some other young people on their mopeds or motorbikes or who just acts a bit more provocatively than had been normal in the past has suddenly become a Halbstarker. *Bravo* demands that this be stopped! There is no Halbstarken generation and these young people pose no danger or threat. There are indeed a few hooligans as there have always been some. And if there are really more around than in the past then it's the fault of all of us. Simply because several no-hopers ['*Flasche*'] who had never dared to become one of the few hooligans now dares to be one of the Halbstarke ...

Nobody talks about the fact that the biggest German sports clubs had never before experienced such a surge in youth membership as at present. There are not enough sports grounds. A city such as Munich does not even have a decent stadium. The sports clubs complain bitterly and mostly justifiably that the state and the communities do not do enough to support them. Authorities' incompetence, fussing and doing nothing is ignored with refined silence. But over some crazy young people who left their brains in the last pub and now want to overturn a car such fuss is made as though a national state of emergency ought to be declared. Instead of acknowledging that in this generation, whom nobody really cares about, there are a great many respectable, diligent and great guys [*ordentliche, fleißige, patente Kerle*], whole year groups are held responsible [*Sippenhaft*] for the actions of a few criminals. And what is the result of this psychosis which we have worked ourselves into? If policemen see a group of young men their eyes narrow and suddenly the rubber truncheons sit very loosely. If the youths see the police they take a deep breath clench their fists and wait for the brawl. One side will start it, either the youths or the police … It can't go on like this! In every better crime film any policeman who had been attacked only with bare hands blows loud and clear on his whistle and his colleagues come running from everywhere. Are our policemen unable to blow their whistles – or run? And if there are indeed so few policemen that they can't hear each other, then the night patrols should be equipped with walkie-talkies (wireless radio sets). The money needed for this can easily be saved during the construction of the next ministerial building or the next villa for political officials … The Federal Interior Minister and his regional colleagues should not only discuss what can be done against the youth but what can be done for them. So far both money and ideas have been insufficient …

Trans. from: *Bravo*, 16.9.1956.

In the field of sexuality and sexual education, the Adenauer years meant a step back, even beyond the attitudes of the Nazi years. Although Nazi ideology had reduced sexual activity and mother-hood to a mere function of the state, their display of a naked (mostly female) body as the symbol of the healthy race was a far cry from the prudishness of the 1950s. Four short excerpts from advice manuals on manners and sexuality make the point.

Doc 126 Advice on manners and sexuality

The man is characterised by his typically male behaviour (in contrast to that of a woman) and his typically male (also in contrast to that of woman) interests. Fearlessness and courage respectively, are further criteria. But to be a gentleman the following qualities have to be present as well: good manners, good education [*Bildung*], good composure (not just physical posture). Further: being able to command because one has learned to obey.

Trans. from M. Heinz, *Der gute Ton für meinen Sohn*, 1959 (Good Form for my Son).

She (the woman) should not herself attempt to influence the course of arousal. It is most favourable if she surrenders herself completely to her feelings without being active in the slightest.

Trans. from Dr Rolf Verthen, *Enthüllte Geheimnisse der Liebe und Erotik*, 1955 (Unveiled Secrets of Love and the Erotic).

For a real kiss the most important thing is that the performers are a man and a girl. Kisses among men are un-aesthetic and – what is worse – taste bad. It lies in the idea of a kiss that the man kisses the girl, not the girl kissing the man.

Trans. from Fritz Tanner, *Von Liebe, Verlobung und Ehe*, 1959 (About Love, Engagement and Marriage).

Does one think differently today about pre-marital virginity? People think the same as they always did, namely that a virgin girl has something to give a marriage that another girl no longer has. Translated into current language: if a driver has the choice between a used car and a brand new one, he will prefer the new.

Trans. from Ottilie Moßhammer, *Leben und Liebe mit 17*, 1965 (Life and Love at the age of 17).

While to the amazement of adults, a youth culture did emerge in the 1950s, a full-blown restoration took place with regard to gender roles and in matters of sexuality which took the Federal Republic back to the inter-war years. The mould of this restoration would be broken only in the late 1960s, by the feminist movement and the student rebellion.

12

The 'Corporate' State

During the 1970s, after the West German economy had truly become a global economic player, the term *Deutschland AG*, (Germany plc) emerged to describe the specific German way of running the economy. More specifically for the 1950s, Werner Abelshauser coined the term 'corporate state' to describe the open or clandestine co-operation between state, businesses and trade unions in the running of the economy. In this line of argument, the 'corporate' economy would be nothing else but the twentieth-century version of 'Rhineland Capitalism' a century earlier. Those definitions stand in contrast to the view of other economic historians who think that in the 1950s and 1960s West Germany underwent a process of 'Americanisation'. Recent detailed studies of companies and business leaders suggest that during this period 'Americanisation' took place mainly in the production process. The root cause for the economic success lay, apart from the peculiarity of the time, in the close co-operation of state, industry and trade unions, despite sometimes bitter verbal disputes and fundamental differences between trade unions and businesses on how the economy should be organised.

It was the dire economic situation and the shortage of investment funds that led to the establishment of the Kreditanstalt für Wiederaufbau by the bizonal Economic Council in 1948. Both its task and the composition of its supervisory board exemplify how the system of the 'corporate' state worked.

Doc 127 Law on the Kreditanstalt für Wiederaufbau

The Economic Council has adopted the following Ordinance:

Article I
A corporation under public law to be known as the Reconstruction Loan

249

Corporation (Kreditanstalt für Wiederaufbau) with its seat at Frankfurt/ Main shall be established for the purpose of promoting economic reconstruction.

Article III
1. It shall be the function of the Corporation to enable the carrying-out of reconstruction projects by supplying all branches of the economy with medium and long-term credits to such extent as other credit institutions are unable to raise the necessary capital. The credit requirements of the individual economic areas shall be given consideration when adjusting the regional differences in the accumulating of capital (Kapitalbildung). Credits shall be granted through credit institutions. In exceptional cases and only with consent of the Board of Directors (Art VII) the Corporation may also make direct loans. Short-term loans shall not be made without the approval of the Bank deutscher Länder ...

Article IV
1. To achieve its objectives the Corporation shall:
    1. issue bearer bonds;
    2. borrow money from the Administration of the Combined Economic Area and raise loans abroad;
    3. take over Deutsche Mark funds arising from the proceeds of foreign goods supplied to the Combined Economic Area, and which have been placed at the disposal of the Corporation to be used for its purposes;
    4. in particular cases, borrow short-term funds from the Bank deutscher Länder ...

Article VII
The Board of Directors of the Corporation's supervisory shall consist of:
1. The Chairman and his deputy; they shall be appointed by the Bizonal Executive Committee; they shall be persons with special experience in the field of credit matters;
2. One representative each of the Bizonal Departments for Finance, for Economics, and for Food, Agriculture and Forestry;
3. Three representatives of the Länder, who should be experienced in the field of credit matters, to be appointed by the Bizonal Länderrat;
4. A representative of the Bank deutscher Länder;
5. One representative each of the real estate credit institutes, the saving banks, the co-operative credit institutes and a leading credit institute in the field of industrial credits to be appointed by the Board of Directors (Zentralbankrat) of the Bank deutscher Länder upon recommendation of the parties concerned;

6. One representative each of industry, agriculture, handicrafts and housing, who shall be appointed by the Bizonal Executive Committee upon the recommendation of the parties concerned;
7. Three representatives of the Trade Unions to be appointed by the Bizonal Executive Committee of the Combined Economic Area upon recommendation of the parties concerned ...

Article XII
The Corporation is under the supervision of the Bizonal Executive Committee. The supervisory authority is entitled to issue orders to safeguard that the Corporation's business is carried out in line with all laws, bylaws and other regulations.

From: *Military Government Gazette, Germany, British Zone of Control, Gesetzblatt des Vereinigten Wirtschaftsgebietes*, 18 November 1948.

The bad economic situation in 1948 made it necessary to establish a financial institution that was able to provide long-term investment finance for the most crucial reconstruction projects, and only a public body could fulfil this task. The people to decide on the priority of projects irrespective of short-term profitability were top representatives from all walks of the economy, including trade-union representatives.

Before the summer of 1949, Allied restrictions had prevented the establishment of any organisation on a national level. The first groups that were allowed to convene on a national stage were the German trade unions when they established their umbrella organisation Deutscher Gewerkschaftsbund (DGB, German Trade Unions Federation) in October 1949. In their Basic Principles for Economic Policy they outlined how they wanted to organise the German economy for the future.

Doc 128 DGB Economic principles

1. The trade unions as organisations of workers, white-collar workers [*Angestellten*] and civil servants look after the economic, social and cultural interests of all working people [*Werktätigen*]. They fight for an economic order in which social injustice and economic need are eliminated and in which for everyone willing to work, a job and their exis-

tence are secured. Economic policy is one of the most important means for the improvement of the total economic performance. At the same time it is the arena in which decisions are made concerning how much the various interest groups have to raise in terms of labour and effort for the totality [*Gesamtheit*] and to what degree they participate in the gross domestic product. Starting from these facts the trade unions claim the following
Basic Demands:

I. An economic policy that guarantees: the full employment of all those willing to work; the purposeful utilisation of all the national economy's productive forces; and the securing of the national economy's most important demands, while safeguarding the dignity of free men.

II. Co-determination of the organised workforce in all issues of management and economic structuring [*Wirtschaftsgestaltung*] that concern personal, economic and social matters.

III. Transferral of key industries into public ownership [*Gemeineigentum*], especially mining, iron and steel industries, major chemical companies, energy companies, the most important transport services and the credit institutions.

IV. Social justice through appropriate participation of all working people in the gross domestic product and granting of a sufficient livelihood for those unable to work due to old age, invalidity or illness.

The formation of such an economic policy idea and economic conduct calls for a centrally planned national economy so that private egotism cannot triumph over the needs of the national economy.

Economic planning has nothing to do with the forced economy of recent years. The aims of the war economy, under the motto 'guns instead of butter', prevented the production of essential consumer goods and led, because of the preference of unproductive armaments and despite the mobilisation of all capacities, inevitably to the rationing of all scarce economic goods. The forced economy that remained after the war was unable to change this emergency since all productive capacity was exhausted, state had disintegrated and the German currency had been destroyed.

The forced economy of the past years was nothing but an emergency measure for the distribution of essential goods which were insufficient for a full supply; without economic controls [*Zwangsbewirtschaftung*] that part of the population unable to pay would have been doomed.

Where the lack of goods has been rectified, coupons and ration cards lose their purpose. The sufficient supply of goods will be achieved and retained more quickly the better the economic planning is able to achieve the utilisation of all productive forces.

Economic planning is also in contrast to the chaotic market economy that has been in place in Germany since the currency reform and which has led to an incredible waste of capital through misinvestment and the production of luxury goods. It has led to the exploitation of consumers through unjustified high prices, short-term work and unemployment as well as social injustice and the large-scale collapse of economic cohesion. These kinds of economic circumstance are not an inevitable fate but are instead consequences of an imperfect economic order and a poor economic management ...

Economic planning is completely compatible with the basic rights of human freedom. The most important freedom for the majority of people – freedom from poverty and the fear of poverty – will only be achieved through economic planning. Planning of the national economy and free consumer choice, the right to change one's workplace and free choice of jobs are aims which do not oppose each other. Private initiative and competition within management structures retain a considerable amount of scope and freedom within the framework of the plan ...

1. Overall economic planning at national level

...

2. Transferral of key industries into public ownership

...

3. The necessary democratisation of the economy

...

Trans. from source reprinted in: Abelshauser, *Die langen 50er Jahre.*

Due to their persecution by and resistance to the Nazis, the trade unions had a high moral standing in the post-war years, quite in contrast to many industrialists who as a group had come under suspicion for bringing the Nazis to power and profiting from the war. Nevertheless, in December 1949 businesses followed the trade unions and formed their own top association, the Bundesverband der Deutschen Industrie (BDI, Federation of German Industry). Its task was to act as a political lobbying body for economic and business interests; industrial relations and collective bargaining, however, were handled by another organisation, the Bundesverband deutscher Arbeitgeberverbände (BDA, Federation of German

Employer Associations). The reason for the functional division was simply the expectation that two bodies would be able to assert more influence than just one body alone. Of the two associations – there was a third one representing trades – the BDI would be the more influential and more outspoken one. The inaugural speech for the BDI was delivered by Hermann Reusch, the director general of Gutehoffnungshütte, one of the country's largest steel combines. Despite some sugar-coating Reusch implicitly made the old claims for the industrialists' privileged status in German society.

Doc 129 BDI Foundation statement

Dr Hermann Reusch, Oberhausen, opened the meeting at 16:20. In the name of the Preparations Committee he welcomed all in attendance and expressed his pleasure that the relevant top associations had accepted the invitation almost without exception … Herr Reusch set out the following:

Gentlemen, …

At the beginning of my explanation allow me please once again to explain the aims that are pursued by the establishment of this leading organisation [*Spitzenverband*]. The purpose is to create a coherent, powerful representation of industrial entrepreneurs' [*Unternehmer*] economic and economic policy interests that encompasses, if possible, all economic sectors …

We want to represent the interests of *industrial* entrepreneurs. That means that on the one hand we have to guard against conducting an interest policy that attempts one-sidedly to look after the points of view of industry without taking into consideration the common good. On the other hand it demands that the whole economy flourishes to represent the interests of industry with complete clarity so that they get sufficient input concerning the big economic and economic-policy decisions. In this respect, we regard ourselves as the industrial entrepreneurs' trustees. We are convinced that a healthy economy is only possible if the creative industrialist's free initiative is able to develop. In this regard, we want to represent entrepreneurs who are upholders of manufacturing industry, which is the actual basis of the economy …

The necessity for a top association arises for several reasons: It is of the utmost importance for industry to have the opportunity for an exchange of views and to arrive at common statements in regard to questions that concern all economic sectors in the same way. Without a uniform development of opinion, the representation of industry's interests is unthinkable. In the age of coalitions, industry's views will only have a chance to be heard and to be carried through if they are brought forward with the combined weight of all industrial sectors ...

A central concentration of industrial associations corresponds further to the needs of the State and especially of the Ministries concerned with economic issues. Independent action by individual associations at each of the relevant authorities will lead to an avoidable multiplication of work. The combined presentation of general economic-policy questions will provide the guarantee that the views of the various industrial groups will be brought to a common denominator and will be taken to the economic administration in a focused form. That is a particular necessity for the State and the administration because this is the only way the State can remain in contact with the economic reality and the demands and wishes of industry. The State can consider the opinion of the whole economy when making economic-policy decisions only if these views are presented not by individual companies or groups but rather as the truly established opinion of the whole economy following comprehensive agreement ...

The establishment of a representative general association [*Gesamtverband*] is an undisputed necessity when considering the relationship with the trade unions. You know that the trade unions have expressed a wish to talk to management [*Unternehmertum*] not only about social-policy matters but about all economic-policy issues. We basically agreed to this wish but pointed out that as a precondition the economic associations as representatives of the industrial management would first need the opportunity to unite under a general umbrella association [*Gesamtorganisation*], which, combined with the existing general association of the management, can then act as a partner for comprehensive economic-policy talks with the trade unions. I believe I have the support of all of you when I stress that one of the aims of the industrial top association is the intention to cultivate the exchange of ideas with the trade unions.

Last but not least, the less important issue of our relationship with our foreign colleagues deserves due consideration. Top associations as we have intended them exist in all countries of the Western world. Like us, they have a strong interest in establishing talks with the relevant groups in other countries. Only in this way will it be possible to examine the international correlations from the perspective of industrial production, enabling us to find solutions that serve a European community. We declare our support for this European co-operation which is the only way to save Western culture [*abendländische Kultur*]. Nowadays the general consensus confirms that this European community is unthinkable without Germany and without a strong German economy. In my opinion, it is not in the interests of European co-operation if the questions related to it are dealt with only by governments. The problem of the European economy and the precondition for the existence of a united Europe is productivity increase to the highest level …

Trans. from: BDI Archive, HGF Pro 1 K 786.

When many of the industrialists spoke about working towards the 'common good', they had first and foremost their own good in mind. They also spoke of the common good in order to deflect from the accusations that linked them to the rise of the Nazis and to war profiteering. In the same way, the more conservative industrialists had little interest in co-operating with the trade unions unless it was on their terms or to their benefit. This became most obvious in the question of co-determination. In an attempt to democratise the heavy industry in the Ruhr and to curb the influence of the industrialists, in 1946–47 the British occupation authorities had introduced a law that stipulated that the supervisory boards of the big coal and steel companies had to be filled equally with representatives from capital and labour. The measure had also been initiated to counteract the American-driven suspension of the socialisation of the Ruhr industries. Obviously, co-determination on the supervisory boards strengthened the power of the trade unions immensely and they tried their utmost during 1949–50 to get it extended into other sectors of industry. The management, for their part, tried their hardest to get the statute repealed. Eventually, in 1951, and partly because Adenauer needed the political support of the trade unions to get the ECSC project approved, co-determination in the iron and coal industry was passed into Federal Law.

Doc 130 Co-determination law

Article 1: Companies subject to the law
(1) According to this law, employees have a legal right to co-determination in the supervisory boards and in company organs that have power of legal representation in the following cases:
a) companies whose main purpose [Betriebszweck] is in the production of hard coal, soft coal or iron ore or in the transformation of these raw materials into coke, [Verkoksung], briquettes [Brikettierung] or into a carbonised form; and whose operation is supervised by the mining authorities [Bergbehörde];

(2) This law applies only to those companies mentioned in paragraph (1) that are joint stock companies, limited companies or mining unions with their own legal status and which, as a rule, have more than 1,000 employees or are unit companies.

Article 3
(1) If a limited company or a mining company with its own legal status operates a business as defined in article 1, this law decrees that the company must establish a supervisory board according to this law.

Article 4
(1) The supervisory body consists of eleven members, comprising:
a) four representatives of the owners and one additional member
b) four representatives of the employees and one additional member
c) one additional member.
(2) The additional members mentioned in para. (1) must not:
a) be representatives of a trade union or an employers' association or any of these associations' leading organisations, nor are they allowed to be in permanent service of, or have business links with them;
b) have had any employment as defined under subsection a) within one year prior to the election;
c) work in the company either as employee or as employer;
d) have a considerable economic interest in the company.
(3) All supervisory board members have the same rights and obligations. They are not bound by directions or orders.

Article 12
The appointment of the members for the body of legal representation and the revocation of their appointment occurs in accordance with Article 75 of the Stock Company Law through the supervisory board.

Article 13
(1) A personnel director [*Arbeitsdirektor*] is appointed as an equal member of the body of legal representation. The personnel director cannot be appointed against the majority votes of the supervisory board members elected under Article 6. [Article 6 deals with employees' representatives.] The same applies for the revocation of the appointment.
(2) The personnel director, like all other members of the body of legal representation, has to fulfil his duties in closest co-operation with that entire body [*dem Gesamtorgan*]. Details are laid down in the company regulations.

Article 15
The Federal Government is authorised to pass, through statutory orders, regulations on:

a) the adaptation of by-laws and company contracts to the regulations of this law;
b) the procedure for the nomination proposals mentioned in Article 6.

Trans. from: *Bundesgesetzblatt (I) 1951.*

This outcome of the fierce dispute between capital and labour confirmed the status quo, but it was only achieved because of Adenauer's need for trade-union support. For the trade unions it meant a failure of their overall political strategy and demonstrated some of industry's regained political influence, although the managers in the iron and steel industry were outraged about the law.

In the wake of the Korea Crisis, heavy industry's influence grew considerably. With the outbreak of the war in East Asia came a sudden risen in demand for German investment goods and semi-finished products from abroad. Now it showed that Erhard's economic policy so far had a crucial flaw, namely that basic industries (coal, iron and steel and electricity) were not able to supply the increased demand from customers. As a result, serious bottle-necks appeared, in particular because of coal shortages. During the winter of 1950/51 the situation grew so severe that electricity had to be rationed and power-cuts introduced for industry and households. Ludwig Erhard was faced with what he regarded as anathema: the reintroduction of economic controls. The industrialists, too, tried to avoid those at all costs. Their reaction was to offer a 'voluntary' contribution by industry to the tune of DM 1 billion, which was to be invested in the bottleneck sectors. For this they submitted a proposal to the government which would lead to the *Investitionshilfegesetz* (IHG, Auxiliary Investment Law). Once the principle was agreed with the government, the three top associations of the German economy wrote to their members on 27 April 1951.

Doc 131(I) IHG principles

Principles for the arrangement of the German economy's investment aid according the declaration for a legal settlement made by the chairmen of the top association of German entrepreneurs.

1.

To facilitate the necessary funds for replacement, supplementation or expansion of fixed assets to increase production and output in the basic industries according to the Federal Government's memorandum regarding new economic measures ... the necessary funds will be raised by industry [*gewerbliche Wirtschaft*] on its own responsibility and by itself ...

2.

From 1 July 1951 to 30 June 1952 industrial commercial enterprises and the Government will raise the sum of DM 1 billion by issuing bonds or shares.

3.

The funds raised will be utilised for investment needs in the basic industries – coal, iron, steel and the energy sector.

...

8.

The utilisation of the funds raised under this law will be determined by a committee appointed by the top associations that are involved in the process.

9.

For industry damaged during or after the war, as well as refugee businesses and the export industry, special rules will apply.

10.

The process will be conducted in agreement with the Federal Government

Trans. from: Rundschreiben des DIHT, 27.4.1951, reprinted in Adamsen, *Investitionshilfe für die Ruhr.*

Despite some delays it took an astonishingly short period for the bill, which had been drafted by the BDI's legal department, to pass through the legislative process. It became law as early as January 1952, which highlights the economic pressures at the time.

Doc 131 (II) IHG law

Article 23

Special Asset [*Sondervermögen*]

(1) The revenue form the auxiliary investment constitutes a special asset exclusively dedicated to the purposes outlined in this bill. The special asset is a legal entity in its own right [*eigene Rechtspersönlichkeit*] and bears the name '*Industriekreditbank*-Special Asset Auxiliary Investment'

...

Article 26

Curatorship

(1) For the special assets a curatorship will be established that consists of a President and 19 members, eleven of which will have only an advisory capacity.

(2) The President is appointed by the Federal Government on the proposal by the Joint Committee of German Industry [*Gemeinschafts-ausschußder deutschen gewerblichen Wirtschaft*]

(3) Thirteen members will be appointed by the Federal Minister for Economics, eight of which will be proposed by the Joint Committee of German Industry and five will be proposed by the German Trade Union Federation. The proposals have to take account of the Federal Republic's federal structure.

(4) One curatorship member is appointed each by the Federal Ministers for Finance, Economics and Transport as their representatives, three more members are appointed by the *Bundesrat*.

…

(6) Those entitled to vote are the President, five members appointed by proposal from the Joint Committee of German Industry, and three members appointed by proposal from the Trade Union Federation. These members must have no links with, or be close to the industrial sectors named in Article 1. [Coal, iron and electrical power industry]

…

Reestablishment of structured pricing conditions

Article 37

Article 1 of the Pricing Law of 10 April 1948 … is amended by the following third sentence:

'This consent [*] is not necessary, if the price amendment's sole purpose is to remedy an obvious bad state of affairs in the market without adversely affecting general levels of prices or the cost of living in particular.'

Trans. from: *Bundesgesetzblatt 1952* I, pp. 7–14.

[* Previously, the consent of the *Bundestag* had been necessary to raise any of the (fixed) prices the basic industries could charge.]

The IHG increased the industrialists' reputation quite considerably, not least because the law created the image that they actually had to pay the DM 1 billion. As a matter of fact, everyone who was required to contribute to the fund received bonds in the nominal amount of the contribution and those bonds were guaranteed a generous rate of interest. The IHG was not an imposed levy, more an involuntary loan on generous terms for the lender. Although there were trade-union representatives on the committee which administered the funds, they were more a token gesture. The law made it fairly clear that the IHG was an affair for industry run by industry with the committee's voting power divided six to three in industry's favour. The Economics Minister for his part was happy with the law. For one, it saved him from introducing direct state control into the economy; secondly, he had been able to insert Article 37 into the law. This allowed him to raise prices in the basic goods sectors without the consent of Parliament, as had been necessary before.

Quite in contrast to the unity displayed between Economics Minister and the Federation of German Industry in this case, they had totally different, if not hostile, approaches to another legacy of German economic history, namely cartels. For Erhard cartels were a perversion of the markets; in contrast, for the majority of industrialists they were a guarantee of an 'ordered' market, which meant price arrangements and a renunciation of competition. However, Erhard could fall back on one of the Allies' 'four D's', decartelisation, for his policy, and justify the draft of an anti-cartel bill with Allied demands. When the draft Anti-Cartel Bill was made public, BDI chairman Fritz Berg responded with the following open letter.

Doc 132 Berg defending cartels

... In contrast to this it is claimed time and again by the advocates of a cartel ban that cartels equal 'a planned economy' [*Planwirtschaft*] and that price cartels especially constitute a 'forced economic measure' [*Zwangswirtschaftsmaßnahme*]. But cartelisation functions essentially in a different way, as can be seen from the following arguments:

a) There is no forced satisfaction of somebody's needs [*Bedarfsdeckung*] but rather the consumer's full freedom to decide on a purchase. However, what the 'dictatorship' of purchasing power and consumers' and clients' purchasing desire mean for the supplier has been proven time and again by the market.

b) The silent or open struggle before and during negotiations for the conclusion of a cartel ensures that to a large extend agreements are reached that conform with the market. Until now, any cartel that forced market conditions or tried to escape the natural turns of the market has broken down.

c) For the duration of a cartel treaty, persistent and constant latent competition exists between the cartel members regarding the imminent danger of the cartel's disintegration. Every cartel member – especially the 'strong ones' – closely monitors proceedings, ensuring that the competition is not earning too much and that no firm that seems to be doomed is dragged through in the long term.

d) Usually there are outsiders, and the emergence of new competitors has to be expected. They constitute an important counterbalance towards ensuring that a cartel's pricing policy conforms to market conditions.

e) Even in fixed-price cartels, the competition plays a very significant role in the areas of quality, service and advertising.

f) It is of particular significance that the 'classic' competition of new goods (substitution competition), new techniques, new uses of raw materials etc. is being replaced. New textile fibres compete with old ones, plastics compete with metals, glass, china etc.

Our remaining large firms are dwarfed by [sind Zwerggebilde] the sheer enormity of foreign competitors. (For example, the turnover of the General Electrics trust equals that of the whole German electrical industry!) Under those circumstances, ... how can we ... speak about 'market-dominating businesses' at all? ...

Based on my explanations I would like to summarise my ideas on the organisation of a future German cartel law by offering the following constructive solution:

a) Any 'limitation of competition' has to be licensed and registered. This allows the cartel authority to verify proceedings easily. The compulsory publication of proceedings would effectively prevent any misconduct in the first place.

b) The cartel authority constantly checks the existing marketing agreements and carries out market investigation, and has to propose to business and the State any measure that serves as far as possible to support and preserve free competition.

c) Cartels that limit competition unjustifiably or are not in the interest of the national economy can be declared inoperative, i.e. they are to be dissolved or to be restructured ...

A legal ruling on the principles stated above would suffice with a fraction of the authority apparatus necessary to sustain a law banning cartels [Verbotsgesetz], which would also have to be manned by qualified personnel [qualifizierte Sachkenner]. This solution would guarantee the effect that is intended by the law: the elimination of misconduct while upholding the creative entrepreneurial initiative ...

Trans. from: *Handelsblatt* no. 124, 24 October 1952.

Some of Berg's arguments were quite obviously a severe distortion of the reality, and industry's resistance against anti-cartel legislation continued. It would take until 1957 for Erhard to get the legislation passed, but he could hardly consider it as a success. The eventual law was a considerably watered-down version of what he had had in mind originally; it was full of exceptions and exemptions. Only in the 1960s did German businesses eventually lose their interest in cartels.

Meanwhile it had taken the trade unions some time to realise that their fight for co-determination in sectors other than coal and steel had been lost. It was only after 1953 that they began to look for new strategies. During their 1954 Federal Congress such a new direction was agreed. In a flyer which was published on 1 May 1955, Labour Day, Otto Brenner, the head of the metal-worker union *IG Metall* outlined their visions.

Doc 133 DGB 1955 action programme

What came afterwards [after the co-determination]? It became more and more obvious that the forces of restoration in the Federal Republic asserted themselves. This development of restoration found its expression in our failure to get a progressive Company- and Personnel Representation Law, in the 1953 federal elections, in the attempt to undermine trade-union unity, in the defamation of the unions and their officials who were accused of being power-hungry and, last but not least, in the re-establishment of the old large companies and in an increasingly excessive and impudent appearance of former Nazis and war criminals. This was the situation at the end of 1953 until August 1954 when many of us – partly from a certain feeling, partly out of a realisation – asked the question: What can we do now? How can we overcome this situation? Out of the discussions, clear realisations gradually became apparent: one realisation was that the balance of power between capital and labour had changed in such a way that it would be utopian to believe that we would be able to carry through our Munich basic demands for the reform of the economy in the near future. The other realisation was that the balance of power in Parliament was such that one could not expect any support for trade-union issues from the current majority in the *Bundestag*. These realisations made it clear to us that it was necessary to find new means and ways which could be achieved through the unions' own united strength. That was the intention of the Action Programme. At the heart of the programme should be those demands which express the burning interest of all employees and their families and thus of the large majority of our people as well.

These demands were:
I.   Shorter working hours
     A five-day working week with no decrease in wages and/or salaries, with an eight-hour working day

II. Higher wages and salaries
     Raising of the standard of living by increasing wages and salaries for blue-collar workers, white-collar workers and civil servants
     1. Equal pay for men and women
     2. Holiday pay
     3. Safeguarding the Christmas bonus
     4. Sick pay for blue-collar workers as well

III. Improved social security
     Security of the workplace
     Sufficient support in cases of unemployment, accident and illness
     Old age without poverty

IV. Guaranteed co-determination
     Legal regulation for parity co-determination in the holding companies
     Equal co-determination in all firms and administrations

V.   Improved industrial health and safety standards
     Sufficient opportunities for youth apprenticeships

Trans. from source reprinted in: Abelshauser, *Die langen 50er Jahre*.

The same year, the eminent political scientist Theodor Eschenburg published his influential book *Herrschaft der Verbände?* (Rule of the Associations?), in which he questioned whether or not interest groups, lobbying bodies and in particular the big industrial associations had too much influence on the running of the state. By this time many industrialists, or 'entrepreneurs' as they liked to call themselves, claimed to be the state's new 'aristocracy of merit', but Eschenburg's book and other, more hostile claims had hit a nerve. Industry found it necessary to respond and explain its role in state and society.

Doc 134 BDI on state–industry relations

Especially because the BDI regards a proper order in our state as imperative, it has watched with concern the debate about the Associations which, at times, created the impression that it is not about the co-operation of state and associations but about the deepening of conflict that, in reality does not actually exist ...

Since there are hardly any common interests, not even in the same economic sectors, consequently there can be generally no increased one-sidedness as compared to when the interests are represented by the individual themselves. It is much more likely that the opposite is the case, as demonstrated by an industrial sector's top association. Under the compulsion within an association to balance out the different and often even contrasting interests and unite them under a common approach, the Associations actually fulfil a task in the interests of the common good. The necessity of finding a common solution leads furthermore to an understanding by the members of the variety of mutual interests within an economic sector ...

Naturally, the Associations' main task is to establish with the public the determined interests, and, at the same time, based on the exact knowledge of the facts, advise the authorities which make political decisions and give suggestions for the legal framing of certain economic processes. The fact that in this process political problems are addressed derives inevitably from the close interconnection of the economic and the political spheres ...

It should be noted here that the Associations' statements reduce Parliament's dependency on the opinion of administrative specialists and thus provide an opportunity for the MPs – especially Select Committee members – to form their own opinion. However, the criticism of the Associations' public activity overlooks in particular the fact that in a democratic state the development of an informed opinion [*Willensbildung*] occurs in an open way such that not only the individual but also groups formed by individuals have the right to contribute to a general development of public opinion which is committed to the greater good. Incidentally, the Associations' real area of operation lies not here but in the public debate with the most diverse opinions ...

Trans. from: BDI Jahresbericht 1956/57.

In 1958 the Deutschmark and most other European currencies had become freely convertible into dollars under the Bretton Woods Agreement. As a result of the Federal Republic's continuing export boom since 1951, the country had begun to accumulate a considerable surplus in foreign currencies and gold. By 1960 the surplus had become so large that economists began to fear that it could lead to imported inflation. Rumours of a revaluation of the DM began, which in turn increased the pressure. More and more economists and politicians supported the call for a revaluation of the Deutschmark against the dollar and other leading currencies in order to reduce exports so as to limit the rise of currency reserves. Obviously the export industries were totally opposed to such a move, since their goods would become more expensive on foreign markets, with the effect that they would have sold fewer products. Once more, industry proposed a private initiative to raise DM 1 billion for capital exports. The aim was to reduce the balance-of-payment surplus slightly in the hope that this would prevent the revaluation. Although the DM 1 billion was raised and Adenauer had assured Berg that revaluation would not happen, the pressure became too strong and in March 1961 the Deutschmark was revaluated by 5 per cent: from DM 4.20 to the dollar to DM 4.00.

As the minutes from the following BDI Board Meeting reveal, the industrialists were furious about the government's decision, in particular Fritz Berg, who had relied so heavily on Adenauer's word in this matter.

Doc 135 Berg on DM revaluation

... Herr Berg then went straight over to the agenda, the only point of which concerned the decision by the Federal Government to revaluate the DM by 5%, and declared: 'Gentlemen! You know that I declared myself in public against this decision ... Since autumn our economy has certainly not heated up any further, on the contrary, clear signs for a gradual slowdown [*Abkühlung*] had become apparent. But before the measures we had intended for the safeguarding of the economy and which had at first been accepted by the government could take effect, the government decided on the revaluation of the DM ...

When I now have to read about these aspects of our export economy [*Außenwirtschaft*] in the press, that finally the word has to be said that 'the export industry is not to be seen as a sacred cow, the privilege of which it is to hold back the domestic standard of living', then I have to say I am very bemused about these kinds of unrealistic claim. I am very sorry about the dangerous demagogy with which the export industry is discriminated against. The export industry has not held back the nation's standard of living. On the contrary, without exports we would have neither achieved nor obtained our present standard of living.

Gentlemen! It is too early to address the effects of the revaluation in detail. But I can say as much that industry, which has already signed large amounts for development aid, will have to carry the main burden of the revaluation. In the face of this industry is being accused of conducting self-interest policy [*Interessenpolitik*], a claim repeated in regard to the revaluation ...

I am aware that, after what has happened, a lot has been asked of you. Our willingness to act in the interest of the general good has certainly not been increased by the misgiving and even discriminating judgements the manufacturing industry has been faced with in recent days.

...

Trans. from: BDI Archive, HGF Pro 787–8.

As a matter of fact, the BDI leadership was so annoyed that they stopped their monthly donations of DM 100,000 to the CDU. The revaluation itself brought only a temporary reduction in the size of German exports and the balance-of-payments surplus continued to grow. Industry's anger was also short-lived. During the general election campaign in the autumn of 1961, industry was once again the biggest donor for the CDU.

Part IV
Kanzlerdämmerung and the Nazi past

The term *Kanzlerdämmerung* is often used in regard to Adenauer's last years in office. It is an analogy to Richard Wagner's *Götterdämmerung* (Twilight of the Gods), the last opera from his Ring cycle, and is meant to describe Adenauer's fall from power. Konrad Adenauer had reached the zenith of his public esteem in 1955 after his visit to Moscow, which had led to the much publicised release of 10,000 German POWs. Not least because of this success, he reached the high point of political success in 1957 when he led the CDU to the first and so far only absolute majority in the Bundestag. By this time, Adenauer was less than four months away from his 82nd birthday. What followed over the next six years was a slow political dismantling and more often self-dismantling due to mistakes, miscalculations, scandals and outright stubbornness on his part. Today, few politicians would survive the aftermath and fallout from the various affairs for long. That Adenauer could remain in power until 1963 demonstrates once more his skills as a political actor, as well as the reverence given to him by large sections of the public, despite increasing calls for his resignation.

13

Adenauer, the GDR and the Berlin Wall

The rhetoric of Adenauer's policy towards the GDR in many cases did not match the reality on the ground. The language of power politics reached its limit whenever the East took concrete steps and measures; the only two exceptions to this rule were the Western, mainly American-led, airlift during the Berlin Blockade in 1948/49 and in the aftermath of the Khrushchev Ultimatum of 1958. In the most notorious cases of the uprising on 17 June 1953 and the building of the Berlin Wall on 13 August 1961, the realities were such that all Adenauer could offer were empty phrases. When German reunification eventually happened in 1989/90, it was not through any Western power politics. During the two decades prior to the fall of the Berlin Wall in 1989, all leading Western politicians had accepted German partition and had changed to a policy of *Wandel durch Annäherung*, change through rapprochement.

In his first speech to the Bundestag on governmental policy (see Doc 84), the Chancellor had made it clear that only the Federal Republic and its government could speak for the German people. This claim implied that any attempt to unify the country could only happen under the conditions posed by the FRG and the West and with little regard of Eastern and in particular Soviet considerations. It has been argued by some historians and political scientists that particularly in the early years of the German division Adenauer rejected any proposal for unification because such a move would have prompted all-German elections. During the Weimar Republic, the Social Democrats had had their political heartland in the area that now was the GDR, so there was a good chance that Adenauer's CDU could have lost those elections. For this reason alone – while there were plenty of other motives not to do so – proposals for German unification had to be unsuccessful, regardless of who had made them. When proposals came from the West and the FRG, they

271

came with so many preconditions attached that they were simply unacceptable to the East; when proposals came from the East and the GDR, they were rejected or kicked into the long grass by the Bonn government with little real consideration for the seriousness of the offer. A good example for this is the letter by the GDR Minister President to the government in Bonn from 30 November 1950 and the latter's reaction to it.

Doc 136 Grotewohl letter, 1950

To the Government of the Federal Republic of Germany
F/A/O Chancellor Dr Adenauer
The division of Germany caused a national emergency which was intensified by the remilitarisation and inclusion of West Germany into the plans for war preparations. The German people are deeply worried by the threat to its national interest posed by the imperialist powers.

Faced with this situation, maintaining peace, the signing of a peace treaty as well as the reestablishment of German unity will be especially dependent on the agreement of the German people. We believe that such agreement is possible since the entire German people want a peaceful settlement. It would conform to the wishes of all peace-loving Germans if an all-German Constituent Council comprising an equal number of representatives of East and West Germany were to be set up; the task of which would be to prepare the establishment of an all-German sovereign, democratic and peace-loving provisional government and which would pass on to the governments of the USSR, USA, Great Britain and France the relevant proposals for approval. At the same time, this Council would consult the above governments on the drafting of a peace treaty until the establishment of an all-German government. This proposal can, under certain conditions, be put to the German people in a plebiscite. We believe that the all-German Constituent Council could take over the preparations of the conditions for the implementations of free all-German elections for a national assembly. In this way, the establishment of an all-German Constituent Council could create the conditions for the immediate commencement of discussions for the signing of a peace treaty; while at the same time the Council could make the preparations to establish a government.

The Government of the German Democratic Republic, in the spirit of honest understanding and agreement, is prepared to negotiate on all questions that are connected to the establishment and tasks of an all-German Constituent Council.

Large sections of the population in East and West Germany are of the opinion that the next step towards solving our nation's vital issues would be to put forward a shared German plan to the four occupying powers ... We propose that each government appoints six representatives for this purpose. Agreement on the time and the venue could be reached between the state secretaries to the respective minister presidents.
Government of the German Democratic Republic
O. Grotewohl, Minister President

Trans. from: *Die Bemühungen der Bundesrepublik um die Wiederher-stellung der Einheit Deutschlands durch gesamtdeutsche Wahlen*, Bonn 1952 (2nd edn).

In this case it was not difficult for the West German government to reject the GDR proposal. They only had to point out that it had been Grotewohl who had signed a treaty between the GDR and Poland that recognised the Oder-Neisse line as Poland's official western border. In so doing, he had given up any claims of the Eastern terri-tories of the former Reich, a move that was totally unacceptable to West Germany's mainstream parties. The tone in Adenauer's reply to Grotewohl made this very clear.

Doc 137 West German response to the Grotewohl letter

Statement by the Federal Government, 15.1.1951

I.
Since the establishment of the Federal Republic all the efforts of the Federal government were directed towards the reestablishment of German unity in freedom and peace. The Federal Government was the first one to declare itself for German unity in freedom and had pointed out concrete ways to achieve this aim. To name just one of these impor-tant steps, we recall the statement by the Federal Government of 22 March 1950 concerning the implementation of all-German elections. The statement read:
'Since its establishment, the German Federal Government does not know a more obligatory task than the reestablishment of German unity. It is aware that the state order that has to encompass all Germany that is being striven for has to arise out of the free decision of the whole people. Out of the responsibility which arises for it from the preamble

and the final article of the Basic Law, the Federal Government makes an appeal to all Germans, all occupying powers and beyond that to the entire world public, to assist the German people in their reunification in peace and freedom.'

The essential point of the statement of 22 March 1950 says:

'After the passing of an election law by the four occupation powers, all-German elections for a constituent assembly are to be called.'

The preconditions for such elections were laid out in the statement as follows:

'1. Freedom to operate [*Betätigungsfreiheit*] for all parties in the whole of Germany and the abandonment of all occupying powers of their attempts to influence the establishment and work of political parties.

2. The personal security and protection against economic discrimination of any person working for political parties has to be guaranteed by all occupation powers and all German authorities before and after the elections.

3. Licensing and freedom of distribution for all newspapers in the whole of Germany.

4. Freedom of all personal travel within Germany and the discontinuation of the interzonal pass.'

...

II.

When the authorities in the Soviet zone declare in their written communication of 30 November 1950 their intention to strive for Germany's reunification, it has to be said that those who renounced the German territory east of the Oder and the Neiße in the Warsaw Agreement do not appear legitimised to talk about Germany's reunification ...

IV.

Concerning the assertion made in the introduction of the note of 30 November that 'the remilitarisation and inclusion of West Germany into the plans for war preparations has deepened the division of Germany', the Federal Government emphatically stresses that: 'The disastrous split of Germany is due to the system of government that has been introduced in the Soviet zone, which is contrary to German tradition and German character; and which denies the population of the zone any means of freely structuring their political, economic and social life and cuts them off from free movement with their brothers in the West. In this way Germany's growing together on a liberal basis has been prevented by force. This division was increased by the establishment of a strong People's Police force, which is ... part of the extraordinary military expansion of the Soviet occupying force. In contrast to this, the Federal Government has so far refrained from taking any military measure –

something which cannot have gone unnoticed by the authorities of the Soviet zone.

Trans. from: *Die Bemühungen der Bundesrepublik um die Wiederherstellung der Einheit Deutschlands durch gesamtdeutsche Wahlen*, Bonn 1952 (2nd edn).

The next and perhaps most serious proposal for unification was the 1952 Stalin Note (see Doc 69). One year later events took a more dramatic turn that showed the limits of power politics. In June 1953 the GDR government had raised the labour norms for all sections of the economy, in particular in the construction sector. Faced with severe supply shortages for goods required for daily life, workers in East Berlin downed tools on 16 June and took to the streets in protest. The following day there were mass demonstrations all over the country. What had started out as a protest against the regime's economic policy quickly turned into anti-communist rallies, with calls for free elections and unification with the FRG. On the afternoon of 17 June, Soviet tanks began to crush what the Federal Republic would soon refer to as the '17th June Uprising'. The reaction of Adenauer and his government was to quickly condemn Eastern repression, but other than verbal assurances to the GDR population, they took no further action. *Realpolitik* forbade them every other option; any active interference would have made matters worse, but this exposed the government's usual rhetoric simply as a series of clichés. Adenauer's own statement on the uprising demonstrates his real helplessness and marks out his otherwise tough talk as pure political theatre.

Doc 138 Adenauer on the 17th June uprising

The events in Berlin have found strong resonance in the German public and elsewhere in the world. The Federal Government has the following statement to these events:
Regardless of how the beginnings of the East Berliner workers' demonstrations will be judged, they have turned into a major expression of the German people's will for freedom in the Soviet zone and in Berlin. The Federal Government sympathises with the men and women who today in Berlin demand liberation from suppression and distress. We assure

them that we stand in total inner solidarity with them. We hope that they will not be provoked into rash actions that could endanger their lives and their liberty. A real change in the life of Germans in the Soviet zone and Berlin can be achieved only through the reestablishment of German unity in freedom. The way to achieve this, as the Bundestag confirmed in its meeting on 10 June, is

1. The holding of free elections across the whole of Germany;
2. The establishment of a free government for the whole of Germany;
3. The signing of a peace treaty that is freely negotiated with this government;
4. The settlement in this peace treaty of all pending unresolved territorial issues;
5. Securing the freedom of action for an all-German Parliament and all-German Government within the framework of the United Nations' basic principles and aims.

...

The Federal Government will be following the development of events as closely as possible and is in constant close contact with representatives of the Western powers. In this significant hour, regardless of our political views, we all stand together in support of our large common goal.

Trans. from: *Bulletin der Bundesregierung* no. 112 (1953).

Adenauer's inflexibility on matters concerning the GDR appeared even more amazing if one keeps in mind that he was probably the most shrewd and flexible political operator in twentieth-century German politics. The reason for this inflexible approach had to do with the pessimistic opinion he held about the political understanding of his fellow Germans. He believed that he had to reject all advances from the East and the easiest way was to reject them out of hand. In his heart Adenauer thought *Westintegration* more important than unification. Following the Four Power summit on the German question that took place in Geneva in July 1955, Adenauer began to fear a more flexible Western position. His ambassador in London told the British Permanent Undersecretary at the Foreign Office what he thought of more flexibility and the political reliability of his fellow Germans.

Doc 139 Adenauer on the political reliability of ordinary German

German unity

1) The German Ambassador told me yesterday that he wished to make a particularly confidential communication to me on this subject. I would recollect that I had told him on my return from Geneva that I had come to the conclusion that we might eventually have to be more elastic than the Americans are prepared to be and that we might have to move to a position in which we declare that provided that Germany was unified by means of free elections, and provided the unified German government had freedom in domestic and foreign affairs, we would sign any reasonable security treaty with the Russians.

2) The Ambassador told me that he had discussed this probability very confidentially with the Chancellor. Dr Adenauer wished me to know that he would deprecate reaching this position. The bald reason was that Dr Adenauer had no confidence in the German people. He was terrified that when he disappeared from the scene a future German government might do a deal with Russia at the German expense. Consequently he felt that the integration of Western Germany with the West was more important than the unification of Germany. He wished us to know that he would bend all his energies towards achieving this in the time which was left to him, and he hoped that we would do all in our power to sustain him in this task.

3) In making this communication to me the Ambassador naturally emphasised that the Chancellor wished me to know his mind, but that it would of course be quite disastrous to his political position if the views which he had expressed to me with such frankness ever became know in Germany.

I. Kirkpatrick
December 16, 1955

From: NA PRO, FO 371 109277.

It has to be assumed that the statement made by the German ambassador was to a degree an attempt 'to play to the audience' and part of Adenauer's usual scare tactics, but the statement nevertheless points towards the Chancellor's real motives.

It is said that Adenauer, the conservative Catholic mayor of the Rhineland's first city of Cologne, never liked Berlin, the symbol of Protestant Prussia and a beacon of modernity in inter-war Germany.

There were sarcastic rumours that, whenever he had to travel to Berlin during his time as president of the Prussian State Council during the Weimar years, he pulled down the blinds of his rail carriage once the train had crossed the river Elbe since Adenauer regarded the territory east of the Elbe as 'part of Siberia'. The personal dislike for central Germany could easily have strengthened his resolve not to meddle with the post-war political and geographic status quo.

Throughout the 1950s, the situation of the three Western zones of Berlin, in particular its economy, had slowly improved and they developed into a unique and invaluable asset for the West in the Cold War conflict. West Berlin had an island position deep within the Soviet controlled territory that was exploited by the Americans for intelligence gathering. From West Berlin radio stations anti-communist propaganda was broadcasted into most of the GDR. Worse for the GDR was the fact that its citizens from all over the country could go to East Berlin and then simply cross over into the Western sectors, turning West Berlin into the escape route of some three million people between 1949 and 1961. Most of these refugees were young and highly educated; thus their fleeing meant a significant brain drain for the GDR. It has been estimated that because of this influx of highly trained human resources the Federal Republic saved some DM 3 billion on education and training costs during the period.

By 1960 it had become clear that the continuation of such a drain of human capital would soon lead to the collapse of the GDR, and rumours were rife how the East German regime would react. Just a couple of days prior to the erection of the Wall on 13 August 1961, the Communist leader Walter Ulbricht made a public statement denying that any plans for the creation of a wall existed. Then, on 12 August, the GDR Council of Ministers made the following declaration on travel restrictions for GDR citizens.

Doc 140 GDR travel restrictions

On the basis of the declaration of the Warsaw *Pact* member states and the *Volkskammer* resolution, the Council of Ministers of the GDR has resolved:
In the interest of peace, the actions of West German revanchists and militarists need to be stopped and, by means of a German peace treaty, the way must be paved for peace and the rebirth of Germany as a peace-loving, anti-imperialist, neutral state. The standpoint of the government

in Bonn – that the Second World War has not yet ended – is tantamount to a call for a licence for militaristic provocation and civil war measures. Such imperialistic policy disguised as anti-communism represents a continuation of the aggressive goals of fascist German imperialism at the time of the Third Reich. The defeat of Hitlerian Germany in the Second World War has led the Bonn government to give the criminal politics of German monopoly capitalism and its Hitler generals another try by renouncing the policy of a German nation-state and transforming West Germany into a NATO state, a satellite of the United States.

...

Revanchism has intensified in West Germany, with increasing territorial claims against the GDR and neighbouring states. This sentiment is closely tied to accelerated rearmament and acquisition of nuclear weaponry by the West German army. The Adenauer administration is making systematic preparations for civil war against the GDR ... West German militarists wish to use all kinds of deceptive manoeuvres such as 'free elections' in order to expand their military basis first as far as the Oder River and then begin the great war.

West German revanchists and militarists are abusing the peaceful policies of the USSR and Warsaw Pact states in regard to the German question. Their intentions are to use hostile agitation, solicitation, and diversionary manoeuvres to harm not only the GDR but other socialist states as well.

For all these reasons, the Council of Ministers of the GDR in accordance with the resolution by the Political Advisory Committee of the states of the Warsaw Pact, is instituting the following measures to secure peace in Europe and protect the GDR, and in the interest of ensuring the security of states in the socialist camp:

To stop hostile activities by revanchist and militaristic forces in West Germany and West Berlin, a border control will be introduced at the borders to the GDR, including the border with western sectors of Greater Berlin, as is common on the borders of sovereign states. Borders to West Berlin will be sufficiently guarded and effectively controlled in order to prevent subversive activities from the West. Citizens of the GDR will require a special permit to cross these borders. Until West Berlin is transformed into a demilitarized, neutral free city, residents of the capital of the GDR will require a special certificate to cross the border into West Berlin. Peaceful citizens of West Berlin are permitted to visit the capital of the GDR (democratic Berlin) upon presentation of a West Berlin identity card. Revanchist politicians and agents of West German militarism are not permitted to enter the Capital of the GDR (democratic Berlin). For citizens of the West German Federal Republic wishing to visit the democratic Berlin, previous control regulations remain in effect.

Entry by citizens of other states to the capital of the GDR will not be affected by these regulations.

...

From: US Department of State (ed.), *Documents on Germany, 1944–61.*

The following morning East German police and paramilitary units sealed off any access to West Berlin from the eastern part of the city with barbed wire and the construction of the Wall began. The shock in the West was deep and for two days no proper official political reaction followed. On the evening of 13 August, Adenauer, who was campaigning for the upcoming federal elections, only managed to give a statement full of platitudes but continued his electioneering.

Doc 141 Adenauer's press statement on the building of the Wall

This evening, those in power in the Soviet zone began to cut off West Berlin from its surroundings, in open violation of the Four-Power Agreement. This measure is being taken because the regime forced upon the people of central Germany by a foreign power can no longer overcome the internal problems in its sphere of power. The other East Bloc states demanded from the Zone government that it eliminate this condition of weakness and insecurity. Every day, mass flight from the Zone showed the world the pressure under which its citizens lived, as well as the fact that they were denied the right of self-determination recognized throughout the world.

Through the despotism of the Pankow regime, a serious situation has developed. Necessary countermeasures will he taken along with our allies. The Federal Government asks all Germans to have confidence in these measures; we are called upon now to meet the challenge from the East firmly but calmly, and not to do anything which could only worsen the situation rather than improv[ing] it.

We continue to feel close ties to Germans in the Soviet zone and East Berlin; they are, and remain, our German brothers and sisters. The Federal Government holds unswervingly to the goal of German unity in freedom. Given the significance of the action, I have asked the Foreign Minister to inform foreign governments through the German embassies.

Reprinted in: Konrad Jarausch (ed.), *Uniting Germany. Documents and Debates 1944–93*, Oxford 1994.

On 16 August the headlines of the tabloid newspaper *Bild*, the Federal Republic's most influential print medium, read: 'The East acts – what does the West do? The West does nothing! President Kennedy is silent ... Macmillan goes hunting ... and Adenauer scolds Willy Brandt'.

Doc 142 *Bild* front page

As a matter of fact, the newspaper was not totally correct. On the day before the headline, the Allies had indeed reacted and sent a note of feeble protest to the Soviet Commandant of East Berlin.

Doc 143 Allied letter of protest to the Soviet Commandant

During the night of August 12–13 the East German authorities put into effect illegal measures designed to turn the boundaries between the West sectors of Berlin and the Soviet sector into an arbitrary barrier to movement of German citizens resident in East Berlin and East Germany.

Not since the imposition of the Berlin blockade has there been such a flagrant violation of the four-power agreements concerning Berlin. The agreement of June 20, 1949, in which the U.S.S.R. pledged itself to facilitate freedom of movement within Berlin and between Berlin and the rest of Germany, has also been violated.

In disregard of these arrangements and of the wishes of the population of this city, for the welfare of which the four powers are jointly responsible, freedom of circulation throughout Berlin has been severely curtailed. Traffic between the east sector and the western sectors of Berlin has been disrupted by the cutting of S-Bahn and U-bahn service, the tearing up of streets, the erection of road blocks, and the stringing of barbed wire. In carrying out these illegal actions, military and paramilitary units, which were formed in violation of four-power agreements and whose very presence in East Berlin is illegal, turned the Soviet sector of Berlin into an armed camp.

Moreover, the East German authorities have now prohibited the many inhabitants of East Berlin and East Germany who were employed in West Berlin from continuing to pursue their occupations in West Berlin. They have thus denied to the working population under their control the elementary right of free choice of place of employment.

It is obvious that the East German authorities have taken these repressive measures because the people under their control, deeply perturbed by the threats on Berlin recently launched by Communist leaders, were fleeing in large numbers to the West.

We must protest against the illegal measures introduced on August 13 and hold you responsible for the carrying out of the relevant agreements.

From: US State Department (ed.), *Documents on Germany, 1944–1961.*

Without a doubt there was not much more the West could have done without risking the outbreak of a Third World War. However, as long as their position in the Western sectors of the city was not directly threatened they had no reason to start any conflict. What had enraged people in West Germany and West Berlin even more than Allied passivity was Adenauer's reaction. In contrast to his political challenger for the chancellorship, West Berlin's mayor Willi Brandt – who immediately interrupted his election campaign in the Federal Republic and returned to Berlin – Adenauer remained on the election trail. Only after the most ferocious public outcry did he return to Bonn to address a special session of the Bundestag where he gave the following statement.

Doc 144 Adenauer's Bundestag statement, 18.8.1961

Since the early morning of 13 August, the rulers in the Soviet-occupied zone of Germany have brought traffic between the Soviet sector and the three Western sectors of Berlin to an almost complete standstill. Along the sector border barbed wire entanglements have been put up; large units of the People's Police and Border Police have taken up position on the sector border in order to block all traffic between East and West Berlin. At the same time troops of the National People's Army have been installed in East Berlin.

...

The Federal Government notes with deep regret that this reckless act has been carried out with the consent of the Government of the USSR as the leading power in the Warsaw Pact. In giving its consent the Soviet Government has contradicted its own constant assertions about wanting to solve the problem of Germany and Berlin by means of negotiations. While the American President at his last press conference on 10 August expressed anew the readiness of the United States Government to negotiate on the problem of Germany and Berlin, the rulers of the Soviet-occupied zone of Germany have reacted to the West's desire for peace and negotiation by taking military measures. This reaction demonstrates more strikingly than any words possibly could, to the whole world, that the present crisis has been touched off alone by the German and Berlin policy pursued by the Soviets ...

The Federal Government wants, however, to state emphatically that by this illegal action the rulers of the Soviet-occupied zone of Germany have shown to the whole world once and for all in which part of Germany militarism and aggression are practised.

...

In such a situation, grave enough in itself, the rulers of the Soviet-occupied zone through military preparations are playing dangerously with fire ...

It is both macabre and grotesque when the spokesmen of the Ulbricht regime stand up and declare that the Germans in the Soviet-occupied zone have already exercised their right of self-determination. The permanent flow of refugees in recent weeks tells a different story ...

It is with deep emotion that the Federal Government is mindful of the personal fates of the many millions who have fallen victim to those inhuman measures. Nearly three and a half million people have in recent years fled the Soviet-occupied zone of Germany and the Eastern sector of Berlin because no other possibility of living a life in freedom was left to them. Relinquishing their occupations and leaving behind their property, they also broke off personal ties with their families, relatives, and friends. Now the door has been slammed in the face of countless people intending to take the same road. The Federal Government expresses the hope and, indeed, the conviction, that at the beginning of the negotiations, which it, too, desires, those measures will be revoked.

...

Let us finally say a few words to the inhabitants of the Eastern sector of Berlin and the Soviet zone of Germany. Your sorrow and suffering are our sorrow and suffering. In your particularly difficult situation you were able at least to derive some comfort from the thought that, if your lot should become quite unbearable, you could mend it by fleeing. Now it looks as if you had been deprived of this comfort, too. I request you with all my heart: do not abandon all hope of a better future for yourselves and your children. We are convinced that the Free World, and particularly we here, shall some day be successful in our efforts to obtain freedom for you. The right to Self-determination will continue its victorious march throughout the world and will not halt at the boundary of the Soviet zone. Believe me, the day will come when you will be united with us in freedom. We do not stand alone in the world; justice is on our side, and so are all the nations who love freedom.

From: *Verhandlungen des Deutschen Bundestages, 3. Wahlperiode,* translated in: US State Department (ed.) *Documents on Germany 1944–1961.*

The speech was again full of platitudes and could not disguise the fact that Adenauer was helpless; nor could it disguise the fact that his power politics had failed. Many people would also have been upset that he had given the impression that he did not care about

Berlin. His public image was further damaged when President Kennedy sent Vice-President Johnson and former Military Governor Clay to Berlin to boost morale. The Americans refused Adenauer permission to fly to Berlin on the Vice-President's plane. They justified this by claiming that doing otherwise would intervene in the ongoing German election campaign, but it demonstrated to the German public that Adenauer's standing with the Americans was on the wane as well.

In late August, the next step of the GDR regime was to issue a decree about the access of West Berliners and West Germans to East Berlin, and began to take control of the transit routes to Berlin, all in breach of Four-Power agreements. Once again, the only Western reaction came in a statement issued by the US Embassy in Bonn.

Doc 145 US Embassy in Bonn rejecting pretension by GDR officials, 3.9.61

On August 30, East German officials issued a decree entitled 'Decree on Entry into the Capital of the German Democratic Republic (Democratic Berlin) by Citizens of the Federal Republic of Germany', and also published a 'Declaration Against Misuse of West Berlin and Revanche Agitation'. Thereafter certain citizens of the Federal Republic have been prevented from travelling by road and rail between the Federal Republic and the city of Berlin.

The Government of the United States of America wishes to reject emphatically the pretension that East German officials are competent to issue decrees applying to Greater Berlin, which city, as is well known, retains its quadripartite status resulting from the unconditional surrender of Germany in 1945. The decree is thus objectionable in its inaccurate designation of the Soviet sector of the city as the 'capital' of the so-called 'German Democratic Republic'. This false claim of sovereignty over a portion of Berlin is used as a basis for the illegal imposition of fresh restrictions on free circulation within the city.

East German interference with access to and from Berlin by road and rail is also illegal; in particular it constitutes a flagrant violation both of the New York Four- Power agreement of May 4, 1949 and the Paris decision of the Council of Foreign Ministers of June 20, 1949, in which the normal functioning and utilization of rail, water and road transport were secured.

In their declaration East German officials stated inter alia that air corridors between the Federal Republic and Berlin were set up only to provide for troops of the Western Powers stationed in West Berlin. The three Allied Powers are bound to point out that the air corridors were established by the quadripartite decision of the Allied Control Council on November 30, 1945 and they are no concern whatever of the East Zone authorities. The Allied Control Council approved creation of the three presently existing corridors in use by aircraft of the powers occupying Berlin. There has been no subsequent change in the status of the corridors. The three Allied Powers acknowledge no restrictions on the use of the Berlin air corridors by their aircraft.

From: US State Department (ed.), *Documents on Germany, 1944–61.*

The same month the writer Michael Mansfeld published an essay in which he summarised the failure of Adenauer's GDR policy and the hypocrisy that lay behind it. Not without some justification, he argued that the disaster could have been avoided if a more realistic approach had been taken. Now after the East had created facts, Mansfeld criticised, the only thing Bonn did was playing the blame game.

Doc 146 M. Mansfeld on the hypocrisy of the FRG Foreign policy

What happened on 13 August in Berlin – the sealing off of the GDR from the West – could have happened on any day in any year – it was foreseeable. The surprise is feigned. The outrage about the Ulbricht regime is also false: for years we have known about the methods with which the man governs. The outrage about the Soviets is hypocritical: they have always announced in advance what they subsequently carried out. Years ago they said that the Federal Republic's entry into a Western military alliance system would mean the end of reunification and that two German states would automatically emerge – well, they kept their word. Who is upset that the other German state is closing its borders?

The sympathy with the 'brothers and sisters' in the GDR is also hypocritical. What has been done in the last years to redeem them from their situation? Nothing. Not even an alibi has been arranged: not once was any attempt made to remove the Zone from the Eastern Block through negotiations. And what alternative was there anyway? None. Or war? Nobody wants that. So it is pure hypocrisy to feel sorry today for people who believed in promises nobody was prepared to keep. If only there had been one serious attempt: the failed attempt itself would have been a signal for a further five or eight million people in the GDR to set out and move to the West. Their lives, their freedom would have been saved. Well, negotiations were not wanted. That, too, is a standpoint. Then there was the possibility to tell the people over there: 'Come here ye who labour and are heavily laden, if you love freedom – move.' Instead they were told to hold out. Some weeks ago this was the advice from the relevant Minister for All-German Clichés.

The Federal Government's policy could not lead to reunification. Every child with any political knowledge knew that. It is hypocritical today to pin the blame on the Soviets. Or maybe one day the Americans? The Western Powers? Their rights in Berlin are unaffected.

In the recent weeks the strange practice of blaming all unpopular measures on the Americans was introduced in Bonn. Is there talk of sacrifices – the Americans want them, is there talk about lengthening the period of military service – the Americans want it. Will the all-German failure that has just become apparent one day be blamed on the Americans as well? That would be the height of all hypocrisy. Eventually the day had to come when all mistakes and omissions, false promises and broken oaths became obvious to all. This day of reckoning has come closer with the 13 August 1961 ...

Trans. from: Kurt P. Tudyka (ed.) *Das geteilte Deutschland: Eine Dokumentation der Meinungen.*

14

'Mein Gott, was soll aus Deutschland werden ...': the Presidency, the Spiegel affair and the successor question

Already in 1954 Adenauer, in his typical 'modest' manner, had uttered the infamous words '*My God, what will become of Germany once I'm no longer Chancellor*'. Prior to his eventual resignation in 1963, during his last four years in office, he tried to cling on to power and got embroiled in one of the Republic's greatest scandals, the so-called Spiegel Affair. Even before his misjudgement of the Berlin Wall crisis, he had been involved in, and more likely even initiated, an embarrassing discussion about the succession of Theodor Heuss, the Federal President. After the 1961 election and the CDU's loss of the absolute majority, coalition negotiations with the Liberal party, the FDP, turned out to be more difficult than expected. They became somewhat humiliating for Adenauer since right from the start the Liberals demanded that he step down early as Chancellor. Many of the problems and affairs Adenauer faced were due to him clinging on to power, partly for the sake of power, partly because he believed his successor apparent, Ludwig Erhard, to be the most unsuitable candidate possible. This sentiment arose out of the belief that Erhard was not a real politician but an economics theorist who in particular lacked foreign-policy experience. There was certainly some vanity involved on Adenauer's part, since Erhard surpassed him in popularity. By the late 1950s, scandals or political blunders were becoming almost annual affairs. They damaged Adenauer immensely but he did not seem to realise this. Eventually his retirement was greeted with relief by most Germans.

In 1959 Theodor Heuss's second term as Federal President came to an end and, since the Basic Law prevented a further re-election, the question of his succession became acute. Konrad Adenauer's first reaction had been to nominate Ludwig Erhard for the office so that he would not become chancellor. Initially, Erhard liked the idea but when he realised Adenauer's intentions he withdrew his candidacy. Then Adenauer nominated himself as successor to Heuss. He had been inspired to this idea by the example he had seen across the border in France, where General de Gaulle had set up the Fifth Republic with himself as a strong president at the top. Once he realised that the Basic Law would not allow him anything more than representative functions, Adenauer, too, withdrew his candidacy. In the end the CDU had to announce what can only be described as a second-rate candidate, Agriculture Minister Heinrich Lübke, who was then duly elected. By this time Adenauer had smashed so much political porcelain that even the tolerant and mild-mannered inaugural holder of the office, Theodor Heuss, was annoyed with the Chancellor, as he made clear in a letter.

Doc 147 Heuss letter to Adenauer on presidency

9 April 1959
Dear Herr Adenauer!

I am by nature, or at least I believe I am, benevolent enough not to spoil someone's holidays by using disgruntled or disgruntling words. But a measure of self-esteem and the appreciation of my office's work over the last ten years *force* me to say something in response to the comments you gave to the candidates' committee. Quite simply, I find them *totally unreasonable* ...

Following Erhard's undiplomatic stance and furthermore: following the flogging to death of honourable men which was so bad for the office, your candidacy appeared to be the best and most impressive solution from a party-political perspective.

We both know that although we have a harmonious personal relationship, we are still very different in nature: I won't say that you need 'the noise', you have your idyllic sides as well; I can do without scenery and action [*Idylle und Krach*] (the election meetings being a good example) but there is a particular point beyond which I will not tolerate what is happening. In this case it concerns the impression – based on what I hear and feel – that only your candidacy will be capable of eventually giving the Federal President the political standing that Heuss – who talked about art, opened museums, wrote books and talked to students – apparently never appreciated ...

[I]t was Krone, I believe, who announced that you wanted to update the political day-to-day remit of the Federal President by participating in, and chairing Cabinet meetings, respectively. This I can understand because it is your life elixir and you got used to regarding many of your colleagues [*Mitarbeiter*] as worthless [*nonvaleurs*]. The Basic Law does not 'prohibit' this – as careful interpretation of the text shows. But may I remind you of the following: when in late 1949, September or October, I expressed the wish to 'occasionally participate in Cabinet meetings if the issue at hand was something fundamental' – this wish was not new but adhered to official state practice in France – you declined this wish categorically and unequivocally on the grounds that the Constitution made no provision for such a request, nor was it compatible with the Cabinet's standing orders. I abandoned my wish – what other choice did I have in the face of the power and legal situation. Nevertheless, I remained – please excuse my arrogance – deeply convinced that in all the agreements over the basic directions of government policy, my advice on personnel decisions would have prevented a lot of stupidity – I opposed right from the beginning your procedure to move the selection process of foreign envoys [*Auslandsvertreter*] to the parliamentary groups [*Fraktionsabstimmungen*] … I also believe that I could have prevented the factual mis-formulations of Hallstein, a man you so overrated …

Please excuse my writing to you in such a detailed and personal manner. It is not so much that I feel offended by the psychological debasement of the present political Federal President – I know that you will write to me stating that this is a misunderstanding – but rather that I am concerned for the State [*staatliche Sorge*]. De Gaulle's position impresses you – recently I told you that you believe a similar approach would suit you. But it is not appropriate for Germany.

Against my sober-ironic nature I will now become emotional: I have never aspired to the office that I administered for ten years. I received it, in a manner of speaking, out of your hands after you had realised how much more 'power' (which I personally was never interested in) the Federal Chancellor had in contrast to the Federal President. But I am defending myself out of plain masculine self-respect against the impression you have created with your 'constitutional comments'.

Wishing you a speedy recovery, hoping that you recover from this angry letter as well,

Your Theodor Heuss

Trans. from: R. Morsey and H.P. Schwarz (eds), *Adenauer Rhöndorfer Ausgabe: Heuss – Adenauer Unserem Vaterland zugute. Der Briefwechsel 1948–1963.*

How angry Heuss was is obvious from the address he uses in the letter, which is difficult to translate into English. Instead of the normally used phrase '*Sehr verehrter Herr Bundeskanzler*', on this occasion Heuss only wrote '*Verehrter Herr Dr. Adenauer*' to demonstrate his exasperation.

Just over a year after Adenauer had shown himself to be weak during the building of the Berlin Wall, NATO staged a major military exercise in the Federal Republic, code-named 'Fallex 62'. The analysis of the manoeuvre revealed severe weakness and shortcomings of the Bundeswehr which were published in several newspapers, including the weekly news magazine *Der Spiegel*, whose proprietor Rudolf Augstein had established a reputation for himself as an opponent of Adenauer and even more so of Defence Minister Franz Josef Strauß. The rising star of the Bavarian CSU, Strauß had been tipped by many as the most likely alternative to Erhard to succeed Adenauer in the top job. These political ambitions were threatened on 10 October when, under the title 'Only partially suitable for defence' (*Bedingt abwehrbereit*), *Der Spiegel* published its lengthy article summarising the disastrous results the NATO exercise meant for the German army.

Doc 148 '*Bedingt abwehrbereit*'

… The purpose of 'Fallex 62' was to test the military readiness of NATO and the operational capability of commands and in particular to practise the emergency planning for the population. For this reason, numerous civilian authorities – the federal and state interior ministries, the chairmen of regional councils [*Regierungspräsidenten*], the district councils as well as the federal ministries for post and transport – participated in the exercise.

It became very obvious that the Federal Government's preparations for a case of defence [*Verteidigungsfall*] were totally inadequate, with the lack of emergency laws being only one of many evils. The medical services were the first to collapse. There was a lack of doctors, auxiliary hospitals and medicine. Not much better were food supplies and the maintenance of essential services or the whole transportation network. Air-raid protection proved totally inadequate. Directing the stream of refugees was impossible. The telecommunication network, too, was out of action within no time. The civil servants and spectators participating in the exercise … as well as representatives of the Federation of German Industry were shocked by how the manoeuvre was going …

The shortcomings in the Bundeswehr had already become obvious during the 'tension period' – that is, before the attack commenced.

American army units on the western European semi-continent were combat-ready with 85 per cent of their full strength within two hours. By contrast, the Bundeswehr's nine mobile divisions that are already under NATO command were not fully manned; furthermore, weapons and equipment were lacking. Only one-quarter of medical officers' posts were filled. For the hundreds of thousands of Bundeswehr reservists who had their active duty behind them and who – according to the war gamers' assumptions – registered at the defence co-ordination agencies [*Wehrleitstellen*] there were no officers and NCO cadres and certainly no weapons. Territorial defence units with their few heavy engineering units could barely fulfil their task. The territorial defence had no troops at all to combat tanks that had broken through. NATO headquarters qualified allied forces in four stages:
– fully suitable for attack;
– partially suitable for attack;
– fully suitable for defence;
– partially suitable for defence.
The Bundeswehr has today – after nearly seven years of German rearmament and after six years in office of its commander-in-chief, Strauß – still only achieved the lowest of these NATO categories: partially suitable for defence.

Trans. from: *Der Spiegel*, No. 41/1962.

Although *Der Spiegel*'s editor-in-chief Conrad Ahlers had checked and cleared the story with the military and even with the Federal Intelligence Service so as to avoid publishing any secrets, on the evening of Friday 26 October the publishing house of *Der Spiegel* was raided and several journalists arrested on suspicion of high treason. Augstein himself surrendered to the police the following week. It then transpired that Defence Minister Strauß had organised the illegal arrest and rendition back to Germany of Ahlers, who had been holidaying in Spain at the time of the raid. The arrests and the occupation of the publishing house caused a public outcry not seen in the Federal Republic before or since. More and more of Strauß's illegal procedures became public. Although even today not all questions concerning the affair are answered there are indicators that Adenauer's involvement behind the scenes was considerably larger than initially thought. At the time he did not publicly question any of his minister's claims and actions. On 7 November, he even defended Strauß's methods in Parliament as a means to prevent 'high treason'.

Doc 149 'An abyss of high treason ...'

Dr Adenauer, Federal Chancellor: Herr President! Ladies and Gentlemen! The declaration by Herr Deputy Ritzel includes the following closing sentence which Herr Ritzel did not read out:

(*Shouts from the SPD*: He's already read it!)

'The protection against high treason is supposed to protect our people against a foreign power and foreign despotism. This also implies that a citizen is protected against arbitrariness in his own country.'

(*Lively applause from the SPD and isolated individuals in the FDP. – Deputy Seuffert*: Do you disagree? – *Further shouts from the SPD*).

He then said the following in his speech: 'The worries about the methods which had been applied here,

(*Lively shouts from the SPD*: Very true! – *Deputy Seuffert*: Because of that you had a crisis in government! *Deputy Dr. Schäfer*: Why did you have a crisis in government?)

led us to this question.'

(*Deputy Dr. Schäfer*: Just ask Herr Güde! – *Deputy Seuffert*: Ask the Justice Minister!)

Ladies and Gentlemen, the declaration Herr Ritzel has just read out,

(*Continuing shouts from the SPD*) or in what he has added, the following is contained: first the high treason, but on the other side, the protection of the citizen from mistakes by ministers, state secretaries and –

(*Agreement by CDU/CSU. Lively shouts from the SPD*)

And then, ladies and gentlemen, he has just now declared: The worries about the methods which had been applied here –

(*Lively shouts from the SPD*: Very true! – *Deputy Seuffert*: Do you have no worries? Has the Justice Minister no worries? – *Shouts from the SPD*: Why did the Justice Minster want to resign? – *Deputy Hermsdorf*: He's lost it! He's really lost it!)

Now, ladies and gentlemen, (*Continuing shouts from the SPD*) we have (*ongoing shouts from the SPD*) an abyss of high treason in our country

(*Deputy Seuffert*: Who says so?)

I say so. (*Loud shouts from the SPD*: Aha! So? – *Deputy Seuffert*: Is this an ongoing investigation or is it not?)

Because, ladies and gentlemen (*shout from Deputy Seuffert*)

If a magazine that is published with a print-run of 500,000 copies systematically, to make money, commits high treason –

(*Infuriated shouts from the SPD*: Tut tut! Boo! – *Whistling and continuing shouts from the SPD among others by Deputies Seuffert and Hermsdorf*).

President Dr Gerstenmaier: Ladies and gentlemen, I ask you to keep order, as is necessary to continue the discussion. It is futile – Herr Hermsdorf! – Herr Hermsdorf, calm down!

(*Continuing infuriated shouts from the SPD*)
Dr Adenauer, Federal Chancellor: I am very surprised. You didn't really want to protect *Der Spiegel* at all.
(*Applause from CDU/CSU. – Continuing infuriated shouts from the SPD*)
You really want to protect the methods by which the high treason has been uncovered – That is what you don't like, you have just said so.
(*Continuing disorder*)
Ladies and gentlemen, I repeat again: I regard myself bound by my conscience to state that the officers of the Federal Court, the Federal Prosecutor's Office, the CID [*Kriminalpolizei*], the Cabinet deserve our fullest confidence and the gratitude of the German people.
(*Applause by the CDU/CSU. – Deputy Seuffert:* Why, then, did you sack the state secretary? – *Continued infuriated shouts from the SPD*).

Trans. from: *Verhandlungen des Deutschen Bundestages, 4. Wahlperiode.*

At a time when half the Republic was up in arms for the defence of the freedom of the press, and when analogies to the Nazi seizure of power were made even by moderate commentators, the Chancellor's biased and judgemental comments on an ongoing investigation were seen as outrageous and damaged him considerably. Eventually all charges against Augstein and his journalists had to be dropped and the FDP threatened to leave the government if Strauß was not sacked. The Spiegel Affair did cost the Defence Minister his job but its real significance lay in the fact that it brought an end to Adenauer's style of government that more critical contemporaries had dubbed a '*Demokratur*' by mixing the German words 'Democracy' and 'Dictatorship'. As such, the Spiegel Affair was highly significant as it symbolised the coming of age of a democratic society in West Germany.

Even *Bild*, a newspaper which was usually on Adenauer's side unreservedly, had to admit the government's mistakes. However, they dismissed outright as scaremongering the earlier 'Just like Weimar' calls made by some commentators who feared for the FRG's democracy. Instead and not without reason *Bild* praised the Republic's new democratic spirit. However, the paper remained true to its political colour by suggesting that the squabbling should be stopped and the country should come together to fight the FRG's real enemy.

Doc 150 *Bild* on the Spiegel affair

Dear *Bild* Reader,
The Federal Government has disgraced itself. It is the disgrace of the weakest Cabinet we have had since 1949.
The Justice Minister has failed.
The Defence Minister has withheld the full truth.
The Chancellor has, under pressure from the FDP, 'put down' two State Secretaries of outstanding merit.
The Bavarian SPD deputies who said 'Put your trousers down, even if there is dirt' were listened to too late.
The opposition has taken a tough stance [*scharf zugegriffen*] in Parliament and continued to ask questions until the truth came to light. They nearly came to blows [*fast die Köpfe eingeschlagen*] in the Bundestag and the intellectuals who have already buried the freedom of the press two weeks ago now mourn democracy. They, who are so readily pessimistic, uttered the mortal phrase: 'It's just like Weimar.' But what came after Weimar? Hitler! Should this happen again? No! For that reason *Bild* calls upon the politicians: Control yourselves! Come to your senses!

We need freedom but we also need the State. Don't destroy the tender confidence of the people, which is growing very slowly. Even if German ministers behave more foolishly and naively [*närrischer und einfältiger*] than over the last few days: our freedom is not in danger. The Supreme Court and Constitutional Court deserve our trust. There are independent judges, elected for life, who neither imprison for fun nor to do somebody a favour. Herr Strauß can have as many phone calls to Spain as he wishes, he cannot imprison people without the order of a judge.

Our Basic Law is exemplary. There are no strong men who threaten our personal freedom, and the supposedly strong man has just cut a poor figure. Our Parliament has proven – even if noble composure does not always work – that it can detect scandals without *Der Spiegel*. And the Press has shown that it is free and will remain free. One day we will even catch the traitors in the ministries. And if we shout loudly and clearly enough then the listeners-in to our telephone calls will disappear.

Fellow Germans! [*Landsleute*] Don't let pessimists, moaners, hysterics and semi-communists run down your young state. This liberal state is better than its reputation and also better than its ministers.

Fellow Germans! Quarrel among each other if it is necessary – and in those weeks it was necessary. But also join together again because this is necessary as long as the Wall stands, as long as 17 million fellow Germans are subjugated, as long as we are threatened by Communism. Fellow Germans, see the little enemies, fight them, but by doing so don't forget the big one, the red danger. Remember our national anthem. Live it – don't just sing it. '*Deutschland, Deutschland über alles*' the first verse

everybody knew – right until the bitter end. The third verse we still have to learn: '*Einigkeit und Recht und Freiheit für das deutsche Vaterland. Danach lasst uns alle streben, brüderlich mit Herz und Hand*' [Unity and justice and freedom for the German fatherland. Let us all aspire to this, brotherly with heart and hand].
Yours
Peter Boenisch, Editor in Chief, *Bild*.

Trans. from: *Bild*, 12.11.1962.

The Spiegel Affair was the death knell for Adenauer's chancellorship. Following the 1961 election his coalition was weak, not in terms of parliamentary seats but because the FDP had made it a precondition for their support that he would not serve a full term. Now the FDP ministers resigned from the government under the pretence that they 'could not sit in the same Cabinet with a man like Strauß'. In reality their move was as much directed against Adenauer as it was against Strauß. Obviously the Chancellor had to abandon Strauß but he also had to go so far as to threaten the possibility of a great coalition of the CDU with the Social Democrats to bring the Liberals back to the Cabinet table.

How difficult the situation must have been already during the 1961 coalition negotiations becomes clear in a letter to the Chancellor from Heinrich von Brentano, the Foreign Minister, who was one of Adenauer's greatest admirers and most loyal subordinates.

Doc 151 Brentano on coalition negotiations

My Dear Honoured Herr Chancellor,
I will not say anymore about yesterday's meeting of the federal party board. All in all, the outcome was more shameful than pleasant ...

For the upcoming coalition negotiations you have an argument at your disposal which you should use both in private talks and in the public debate: the international situation. It would be disastrous for Germany's position if, in the moment of the highest tension, the Federal Republic did not have a government ready to act. I believe that all personal considerations have to be subordinated to this claim ...

I can imagine that Herr Erhard's consternation will disappear if you tell him before such a meeting that his involvement would mean you involving him right from the start in the responsibility of forming the new Government – and in so doing, declaring your intentions and ensure a smooth hand-over of power.

Furthermore, I believe that this arrangement will convince the FDP that the CDU and CSU are not prepared to talk about another Chancellor. I have not the slightest doubt that a large part of the FDP will revise yesterday's decision of the parliamentary group [*Fraktion*] ...

We cannot change the election results of 17 September. But we have to do all we can to take a handful of sensible people out of the FDP, if necessary. I believe informal contacts by third parties could contribute to this end. I consider the great influence Herr Pferdmenges has and I don't doubt that he will be prepared to get involved and will speak privately to some new FDP members. I also believe that Herr Berg and Herr Stein could conduct such talks via the Federation of Industry. As soon as we can be sure that your election is assured in the first ballot, then although the main problem of forming the government has not been solved, the main difficulty will have been overcome. However, we also must have the courage to wait, if necessary, for the third ballot in which you most certainly would be elected with the votes of our parliamentary group. This path would not be pretty but perhaps it would allow parts of the FDP to accept the consequences of the fait accompli and join a coalition government.

If you think that I can be of any help to you in any way please say so. I have nothing to add to what I said last Monday. I am still prepared to accept any consequence if that should be necessary.

In loyal conviction and admiration

your always faithful

von Brentano

Trans. from: Arnulf Baring (ed.), *Sehr verehrter Herr Bundeskanzler: Heinrich von Brentano im Briefwechsel mit Konrad Adenauer, 1949–1964.*

Brentano did indeed lose his post as foreign minister and became once again chairman of the CDU parliamentary group, a post he had held between 1949 and 1955. Adenauer's position within his coalition and even within his own party was considerably weakened as a result of the election and the forming of the coalition. The Spiegel Affair ended the hopes of Franz Josef Strauß to succeed Adenauer as Chancellor; and it damaged Adenauer to such an extent that it was only a matter of time before he had to tender his resignation. In April 1963 the CDU declared Erhard officially their candidate for the chancellorship although he, too, had not performed well during the crisis. In the end, on 15 October 1963, Adenauer resigned as Chancellor. To mark the occasion, Parliament President Gerstenmaier called a special session in which he gave the following speech to the House.

Doc 152 Gerstenmaier's farewell speech for Adenauer, 15.10.1963

Dear Herr Chancellor, both this House and you are aware that it is not unusual in a parliamentary democracy for a head of government to leave his office and return to his place as deputy ... But this House in its entirety is so struck by the extraordinariness and significance of this moment that there was nobody who spoke out against this session ...

Under your presidency the Fathers of the Basic Law drew very practical consequences from the lessons of the Weimar past ... Certainly, you profited not only from the strong position the Basic Law provides the chancellor with, but also from the protection of the constructive vote of no-confidence ...

For years the Federal Republic has stood as an equal member in the alliance of the free world; ... The rubble heaps are gone, the economy prospers, social security is still on the increase.

We experienced an unforgettable reconciliation with France: this is one of the events in which you personally played a great part (*lively applause from the government parties and the SPD*) ... The great idea of European unification, for which you gave your best, has taken the first steps towards its realisation and although there will be heavy struggles to achieve its completion, the idea has given Europe a new face and questioned the orthodox methods, aims and values of the old nation-states' sovereignty policy so that we no longer have to fear its return.

All of this, Herr Chancellor, has to be taken into account and it has to be seen against the miserable scenery of May 1945 and even of 15 September 1949. If this is done, then it becomes clear why we speak of gratitude in this hour ...

On 15 September 1949 you rose from your seat as deputy to take the position of Chancellor of the Federal Republic. Today you are leaving it with a historic achievement, unbowed and with honour. Back then you stood up and stepped before this House. Today the German Bundestag is standing up before you, Herr Chancellor (*all the deputies rise to their feet*) to say on behalf of the German people: Konrad Adenauer has rendered great service for this fatherland (*long-lasting, lively applause from the whole House*).

'Mein Gott, was soll aus Deutschland werden ...?'

Trans. from: *Verhandlungen des Deutschen Bundestages, 4. Wahl-periode.*

Without a doubt, Adenauer deserved praise for what he had achieved. But despite the 'economic miracle', the integration of the refugees, the return to (qualified) sovereignty and NATO member-ship and *Westintegration*, by the mid-1960s more and more people looked back on the Adenauer era and were glad that it was over. Not everyone would have put it as drastically and in such a biased way as a young and talented left-wing journalist by the name of Ulrike Meinhof did in 1964, but she had raised a series of lasting concerns.

Doc 153 Ulrike Meinhof on the Adenauer era, 1964

Actually, everything has been said before: that the city of Bonn is the darkest tourist province on the Rhine; that Adenauer was already bloody old when he took office; that his policy of West integration [*Westorien-tierung*] could be achieved only for the price of German reunification; that there are far too many old Nazis in the army, the legal system, the police and in the teaching professions, in short: in exalted positions; that the best thing about the Federal Republic is its Basic Law which typically enough while it was created without him came before his era. The unspoken arguments of the other side are not unknown: that a solid and quick rearmament without the backing of a couple of trained, experienced Nazi officers would have been impossible; that they, in turn had to prevent the revelation of the role German militarism played in the Kaiserreich, in Weimar and in the NS state if they wanted to build an army with some degree of tradition and self-confidence – a usable army – without contributing to its own subversion; that the glorious rise of the Federal Republic – admired at home and abroad – with a near-seamless incorporation into the Western military alliance and its superstructure would not have been possible with only that little fric-tion without using experienced, tested and loyal civil servants and other specialists who would not have been so highly qualified if they hadn't worn, uncontested, a certain party emblem and with it the brown state as well ...

Fourteen years of Adenauer have turned 55 million Germans, writer and readers, politicians and commentators, viewers and producers on TV and on the silver screen into a people of semi-informers and half-informed, of which some only say half of what they know and the others only discover half of what they need to know; burdened with prejudice, surrounded by taboos, wrapped in illusions so that they can no longer recognise their own advantages and are no longer aware of their own interests ...

The people of the Federal Republic are passing by their own lives and their history, uninformed, unenlightened, disoriented, unable to decide between Pril and Sunil, in the know about Alete baby food and kitchen appliances but oblivious to non-aggression treaties and nuclear weapon-free zones ...

In the face of hydrogen bombs that could destroy the earth several times over, it is old-fashioned to put one's fortune into French atomic-weapons policy; old-fashioned to crawl into air-raid shelters against atomic bombs ...; it is old-fashioned in the face of hunger, homelessness and illiteracy in the world to make the fight against communism one's main objective; old-fashioned to flirt with the Spanish doctrine of divine right [*Gottesgnadentum*] and with Salazar's authoritarian clericalism; old-fashioned to threaten potentially unruly employees [*Arbeitnehmer*] with emergency legislation; old-fashioned in the face of overcrowded universities and a coinciding lack of new academic blood to try to keep students away from universities ...

Provincial diffidence and parochialism is displayed when ministers, presidents and chancellors are nominated according to proportional representation determined by religious denominations; when a candidate's bid for the chancellorship is marred by his illegitimate background; when students' oppositional spirit is labelled as the foolish exuberance [*Narrenfreiheit*] of youth; when opposition writers are suspected of setting up a secret 'Reichs Chamber of Literature' [*Reichsschrifttums-kammer*]; when a priest is denied the right to stage a sit-in in the street in protest against the authorities; when professors who participate in politics are called unworldly; when a member of the Bundestag is rebuked because there is a debate in his magazine about the existence or non-existence of hellfire; when a secular government refuses to tolerate criticism of a dead pope; when, with the Hallstein Doctrine, the existence of a state of 17 million people, Europe's fifth-largest industrial producer, is being denied; ...

The Adenauer era was a bleak time. To cope with it and to overcome it means to describe, to analyse and see through it and then make everything totally different to how HE had thought, different to what HE had done, and different to what HE would have wanted.

Trans. from source in: *Die Ära Adenauer: Einsichten und Ausblicke*, reprinted in: Bührer (ed.), *Die Adenauer Ära.*

Meinhof's criticism of the social stagnation and backwardness of the Adenauer years is not without justification. Her scathing analysis of how the Nazi past had been handled in the FRG and her frustration about it would be one of the reasons why, in 1969, Meinhof would become one of the founding members of West Germany's terrorist Baader-Meinhof gang.

The day after Adenauer's resignation Ludwig Erhard was elected Chancellor. The former Economics Minister was still popular with the voters and in the 1965 general election he increased the CDU's share of the vote. In his first statement on government policy after the election he borrowed his political style from the US presidents Kennedy and Johnson who had spoken about a 'New Frontier' and the 'Great Society'. Erhard, a great admirer of Johnson, now announced the creation in the Federal Republic of a 'Formed Society'.

Doc 154 Erhard's 'Formed society'

... the German society has lost the character of a class society. It has been replaced by an achievement-oriented society [*Leistungsgesellschaft*]. But we should not deny that it can still be threatened from within by too many attempts to create a predominance of partial interests. If we want to remain on the path of our current success, progress, political and social peace, the German society will have to take further steps towards that modern order that we call a 'formed society'. It is not created by a single action but develops out of a process. It is not ordered like a corporative state; but rests on the conviction that human beings are prepared to do what is good for them not only because of laws but because of their understanding of its values.

The 'formed society' is anything but a philanthropic vision. It does not start from an unworldly idealistic picture of human kind. This modern, achievement-oriented society is certainly not free of opposing interests. But they are no longer elements causing its unity to collapse, but will instead increasingly become the motor of a permanent balance of interests looked at from the perspective of the common good.

This new order is a socio-political consequence of the social market economy. Using the social market economy as an example, it can be demonstrated that the 'formed society' is no utopia. In 1948 and in the years following, concerns were raised with apparently good reason that the total liberalisation of the German post-war economy would be to the detriment of weaker members of society. Fears were voiced that the social changes resulting from the economic reforms and techno-logical developments would cause irreversible damage to the nation or that the limited production would be insufficient to absorb the level of purchasing power. By now, all levels and groups of society have experi-enced that the representation of their own interests does not necessarily lead to conflict with others but that striking a balance between them is a good way to conduct democratic politics.

A 'formed society' shaped in this way demands an informed society. The citizen can only make the right decision if comprehensive infor-mation is available to him. He has to be informed quickly, correctly and comprehensively about the State's actions and intentions. Since the State also needs information to flow in the opposite direction, the use of the latest technological possibilities and speedy application of scientific knowledge is also necessary ...

The 'formed society' is in its nature a peaceful society based on the dynamic powers of the balance of interests of domestic and foreign policy. This also means that our State's portrayal of itself abroad becomes a significant tool, perhaps even the prerequisite of our foreign policy ...

Trans. from: *Verhandlungen des Deutschen Bundestages, 5. Wahl-periode.*

As this example shows, Adenauer had been right with his predic-tion that Erhard was not good in selling politics. Although contrary to its intention the term 'formed society' reminded many people of National Socialism, and the idea remained unclear and never took off. Then, at the end of 1965 the economy began to slow down and by mid-1966, there were 600,000 people out of work, at the time a staggeringly high figure. Although the economic downturn of 1965/66 is now regarded as a small blip in economic performance, at the time it caused panic and a revival of the extreme right-wing party, the NPD, who were elected into several Land parliaments not least because of the economic situation. With no real political power base of his own and, as Adenauer had predicted, with a chaotic foreign policy and little leadership in the Cabinet, Erhard's strongest asset, his economic competence, was suddenly called into question as well. On 27 October 1966 the FDP ministers left the government and as a result, on 1 December, Erhard's own CDU forced him to resign. With the subsequent establishment of a grand coalition of CDU and SPD, the Adenauer era had come to its political end as well.

15

The Nazi past

Ulrike Meinhof's comments on the Adenauer era and its lack of any considerable dealing with the Nazi past were certainly true. *Vergangenheitsbewältigung*, the coming to terms with the past, a phrase often used by Federal President Heuss, did not really take place. Here, with one notable exception, the (re)construction of West Germany had a significant deficit that was in part sanctioned by Adenauer and how he handled the personnel policy of the ministerial bureaucracy. Not dealing with the crimes of Nazism was a significant judicial and, even more, moral shortfall of the Bonn Republic, but one that can easily be explained – though not justified – by a closer look at the contemporary circumstances. First of all, Adenauer saw an imperative need to integrate former active Nazis and fellow travellers into the social structure of the Bonn Republic and at the same time use their essential administrative skills and expertise for the (re)construction process. Former Nazis were prevalent in the civil service and the judiciary and there was a genuine fear that prosecuting them would only alienate them from the new state. The experience of the Weimar Republic, when many judges and civil servants were never truly loyal to the state would have certainly been on people's minds. Secondly, most Germans, including former Nazis, regarded themselves as victims of the war as well, so they would have found it hard and unfair if they had been prosecuted by their own government. Thirdly, the Cold War made it inconvenient for all Western governments to dig up German crimes and mass murder. In 1950, neither the full scale of German war crimes nor that of the Holocaust were known. If more information about them had become available, it would have been impossible for the Germans to point to the atrocities committed by the Soviet Union during their advance into East Germany in 1945 and their suppressive regime afterwards; this strategy of 'offsetting' one atrocity against another was applied by many Germans to deflect from German crimes. Many Germans just wanted to be 'nice' again; to enjoy the economic miracle and not being reminded of mistakes and crimes of the past. Those few who tried to keep the memories awake were regarded as *Nestbeschmutzer* (persons who soil their own nest). The resulting 'out of sight, out of mind' mentality created its own scandals which shook the governments once the CVs of some of their leading members were made public. The most infamous case was that of Hans Globke, Adenauer's Secretary of State and right-hand man in the chancellery. Although Globke was never a Nazi party member, he had drafted several anti-Jewish laws and, most notoriously, had written the commentary for the 1935 Nuremberg race laws. Globke's close proximity to Adenauer caused outrage, as did the fact that Adenauer stood by him. This was in part because Globke was 'only an obedient civil servant doing his work', but not a convinced Nazi.

That was different in the case of Theodor Oberländer, who was Minister for Refugees from 1953 to 1960. Oberländer had already participated in Hitler's 1923 Beer Hall putsch and during the 1930s and 1940s had contributed to the theoretical basis of the ethnic cleansings the Nazis had anticipated in Poland and the Soviet Union. It was only in 1960 that the pressure on him had increased so much that he had to step down, but when he did so he rejected all accusations of wrongdoing.

The attitudes of the wider public towards Nazi crimes only began to change as a result of the Ulm *Einsatzgruppen* trial in 1958, and then more markedly after the Frankfurt Auschwitz trials (1963–65) in which the public was confronted with the systematic mass murder of the extermination camps for the first time. However, the trials 'confirmed' to the public that the crimes had been committed by a small group of SS and SD men. They confirmed the myth that the regular army and ordinary people had done nothing wrong and were not at all involved in the crimes in any way. It was only during the 1990s that this view began to change.

There was a stark contrast between how Adenauer approached the domestic and the foreign-policy aspects of the Nazi legacy. At home, there was the public's unwillingness to question their own involvement in the Nazi state and the government's deliberate lack of interest in dealing with the judicial and the moral matters that had been caused by the legacy of the Nazi past. On the international scene, there was Adenauer's desire for recognition of the crimes against the Jews and a genuine wish to offer compensation. This led to the 1952 compensation agreement with Israel. There is little doubt that Adenauer had a sincere wish to make a moral gesture towards Israel and the Jews; however no such gesture was made towards any Eastern European nation that had suffered during the war, or any other individual group persecuted by the Nazis. This leads to the conclusion that political calculation also played a part in Adenauer's motives.

While the Allies' early attempts of political denazification had originally been welcomed by many Germans, the cumbersome and bureaucratic way it was carried out soon put off even those who had initially approved of the measure (see Docs 7, 8). An early American effort to confront ordinary Germans with the crimes committed in the camps was a documentary film *The Mills of Death* which in early 1946 was shown in all cinemas. The film consisted of the newsreel footage taken when concentration camps were liberated. In 1946 Erich Kästner – a writer who had opposed the Nazis and whose books had been burned in 1933 – worked for *Neue Zeitung*, a newspaper set up by the Americans. He wrote down his thoughts and observations after having seen the film.

Doc 155 Erich Kästner, 'Value and degradation of a human being'

(Wert und Unwert des Menschen)

It is night. I am supposed to write about the film *The Mills of Death* [*Die Todesmühlen*] which has been put together from American filming when they occupied 300 German concentration camps – last April and May. When a couple of hundred hollow-cheeked, madly smiling surviving skeletons stumbled towards them. As bent, charcoaled bodies still hung on the electric fences. When there were still storage halls, trucks and freight trains full of stacked skin and bone corpses. When in the meadows, long stiff rows of people 'finished off' by a shot in the neck could be viewed in a horizontal parade. When in front of the gas chambers, the pitiful clothes of the last killing series still hung on the laundry lines. When in the loading channels that lead out of the crematoria like slides, the last hundredweight of human bones piled up ...

It is night. The film was shown for a week in all Bavarian cinemas. Fortunately all children were banned from watching it. Now the copies are being shown in the western part of the American zone. The cinemas are full of people. What do they say when they come out?

Most are silent. They go home in silence. Others step out pale, look up to the sky and say 'Look, it's snowing again'. Some others mumble 'Propaganda! American propaganda! Propaganda before, propaganda now!' What do they mean by this? They hardly can mean that it is a propaganda *lie*. What they saw has after all been photographed. They can't seriously believe that American troops have shipped several convoys of corpses across the ocean in order to film them in German concentration camps? So do they mean: propaganda based on true facts? But if they mean that, why does their voice sound so reproachful when they say 'propaganda'? Should the truth *not* have been shown to them? Did they *not* want to know the truth? Would they have preferred to turn their heads away, as some men did at Nuremberg when they were shown the films? And some say: 'The film should have been shown months ago.' They are right. But is it not better to show and see the truth belatedly than not at all?

Trans. from: Erich Kästner, 'Wert und Unwert des Menschen', in: *Gesammelte Schriften vol. 5, Vermischte Beiträge.*

Kästner's observation of people's reaction is telling. Other than the shock about the images screened, there seems to be shame about the crimes committed in the name of Germany. It can be argued that out of this shame grew suppression of those crimes and a desire to forget about them. The material gains and emerging consumer society of the 1950s provided enough distractions for this voluntary amnesia. It is interesting to note that there were not many people, not even among those who had been persecuted by the Nazis themselves, who tried to keep the memories alive and investigate the crimes.

For political reasons, Adenauer applied this form of selective amnesia in his domestic policy, too. He was more interested in getting former Nazi party members integrated into the new society and the state than in digging up dirt on anyone who was not directly involved in the killings. In foreign-policy terms, however, his agenda was quite different and he was quick to act in this way. In his usual manner of outlining his policies by giving press interviews, in late November 1949 he told a German Jewish weekly newspaper about his plans to provide financial aid to Israel in recognition of the damage inflicted on Jewish citizens.

Doc 156 Adenauer interview with Jewish newspaper, 1949

Q.: Certain circles express the hypothesis that stressing the CDU's Christian character contains anti-Jewish tendencies. Would you, Herr Chancellor, make a statement on the matter?

A.: In my first statement to the Bundestag on government policy, I declared in the name of the government and the political forces that are behind it that our work will be carried by the spirit of Christian Western [*abendländische*] culture and the respect for the rights and dignity of man ... In the spirit of this tolerance we regard our Jewish compatriots as equal citizens. It is our wish that they participate with the same rights and duties in the spiritual, political and social construction of our country. We cannot, and neither do we want to do without their co-operation. In this context, this is where we see the meaning of the term 'Christian'.

Q.: Do you believe, Herr Chancellor, that the measures taken against the Germans after the war, for example the expulsion from the eastern territories, can compensate for the injustice that was committed in the name of the German people up to 1945? This view is widely held.

A.: Injustice and suffering that has been brought upon people can never be compensated for by injustice or suffering that is inflicted on others. The German people have the will to atone as far as possible for the injustice that had been committed in their name against the Jews by a criminal regime after millions of lives have been irretrievably destroyed. We regard this atonement as our duty. Far too little has happened since 1945 to achieve this atonement. The Federal Government is determined to take the necessary measures.

Q.: For us the compensation is not only an economic issue but also a moral one. What are the Federal Government's intentions in order to encourage this atonement?

A.: The moral atonement is part of our state's [*rechtsstaatliche*] reestablishment of law and order ... The Federal Government will focus its attention in particular on the compensation of economic damage inflicted on Jewish citizens. Here the existing laws need several improvements and amendments. The state of Israel is the outwardly visible expression of the union of Jews of all nationalities. The Federal Government intents to provide goods to the state of Israel to the value of DM 10 million, as an initial and immediate sign that the injustice committed by Germans against Jews all over the world has to be recompensed ...

Trans. from: *Allgemeine Wochenzeitung der Juden in Deutschland*, 25.11.1949, reprinted in: Bührer (ed.), *Die Adenauer Ära*.

Although he did not explicitly acknowledge any moral responsibility for the past, Adenauer made it clear that atonement and compensation towards the Jews was nevertheless a moral obligation. It is also significant to consider the date of the interview, which took place just ten weeks after he had been elected Chancellor. This, too, demonstrates that in the face of all the problems the young state was confronted with, compensation was high on Adenauer's agenda.

After Adenauer had acknowledged German foreign dept in early 1951, and had accepted a conference to settle that issue, Jewish organisations had approached the Americans to demand compensation from Germany. The US High Commissioner, John McCloy, told Adenauer that he would not press for such payments; however, he made it also clear that Western public opinion – not least because of the ongoing *Westintegration* – would turn against the FRG if no compensation agreement could be reached. Thus, on 27 September 1951, the Federal Government declared its willingness to pay compensation to Israel as the state representing the Jews, and two days later Adenauer made the following statement to the Bundestag.

Doc 157 Adenauer's Bundestag statement on compensation for Israel

Recently global public opinion has looked into the Federal Republic's attitude towards the Jews. Here and there the question has been raised whether the new state is guided in this significant question by principles that bear in mind the horrible crimes of the past period and put the relationship between Jews and the German people on a new basis. The Federal Republic's attitude towards its Jewish citizens is stated unambiguously in the Basic Law ...

In the same spirit, the Federal Government has signed the human-rights convention drafted by the European Council and bound itself to the obligations of the legal principles laid down therein ...

So that the work of educating [the people] will not be disturbed, and to keep the inner peace within the Federal Republic, the Federal Government has decided to fight those circles that still stir up anti-Semitic hatred by initiating uncompromising criminal proceedings against them. The Bundestag has received proposals for the amendment of the penal code in which, among other things, racist propaganda will receive severe punishment ... The Federal Government, and with it the large majority of the German people, are aware of the immeasurable suffering that was brought upon the Jews in Germany and the occupied areas during the time of National Socialism. The German people have detested the crimes committed against the Jews in an overwhelming majority and have not participated in them ...

However, unspeakable crimes have been committed in the name of the German people which demand moral and material compensation, both in regard to the individual damage Jews have suffered, as well as compensation for Jewish property for which proof of personal entitlements no longer exists. In this regard, initial steps have been taken but a huge amount remains to be done ... Further restitution will follow. Concerning the amount of compensation – in view of the atrocious destruction of Jewish values by the National Socialists a very significant problem – the limits of German ability that arise from the bitter necessity to provide for the many war victims and from the care for refugees and expellees have to be considered. The Federal Government is prepared to co-operate with Jewish representatives and the state of Israel – which has accepted so many homeless Jewish refugees – to bring about a solution to the problem of material compensation, so that the path to spiritual [*seelischen*] and emotional healing of such immeasurable suffering may be made easier.

Trans. from: *Verhandlungen des Deutschen Bundestages, 1. Wahlperiode.*

This speech was written very much for the German audience. It pointed out that international opinion would turn against Germany if no compensation agreement could be reached. It emphasised the claim that the vast majority of Germans had not participated in the crimes against Jews but had actually detested them; and, most importantly, Adenauer stressed that compensation would be limited by the Federal Republic's ability to afford the payments. The latter part of the statement was directed towards the refugees and those Germans who, like those who had been bombed out, had suffered material losses and were still waiting for compensation of their own.

The talks on a compensation agreement began on 20 March 1952 in the Netherlands, parallel to the negotiations on the London debt agreement. Despite their difficult and delicate nature, and despite at one point being close to a breakdown, the negotiations were concluded five months before the talks in London. Even a parcel-bomb plot against Adenauer that had been carried out by a radical Jewish organisation who wanted to sabotage any Israeli-German negotiations could not stop the agreement. The plot was swept under the carpet and covered up by the German authorities so that a deal could be reached. Finally, on 10 September 1952, the agreement was signed in Luxemburg.

Doc 158 German–Israeli compensation agreement

In consideration of the fact that unspeakable crimes have been committed against the Jewish people during the National Socialist terror regime
And that
The Government of the Federal Republic of Germany in its Bundestag statement of 27 September 1951 has expressed its willingness to compensate for the material damage of these deeds within the limits of German capacity
And that
The state of Israel has taken on the heavy burden of resettling so many uprooted and destitute Jewish refugees from Germany and the formerly German-occupied territories, and thus has made a claim against the Federal Republic of Germany for the global reimbursement of the resulting integration costs
The State of Israel and the Federal Republic of Germany have reached the following agreement:

Article 1
a) In view of the aforementioned considerations the Federal Republic of Germany will pay to the State of Israel the sum of DM 3,000 million.
b) Beyond this, the Federal Republic of Germany will pay – in accordance with the obligation of Article 1 of the agreement signed today between the Government of the Federal Republic and the 'Conference on Jewish Material Claims against Germany ... – to Israel for the benefit of the said Conference the sum of DM 450 million ...
c) The following regulations will be applied to the resulting total amount of DM 3,450 million ...

Article 2
The Federal Republic of Germany will provide the amount specified in Article 1 paragraph c) according to Articles 6, 7 and 8 and for the purchase of such goods and services as will support the expansion of resettlements and reintegration options for Jewish refugees into Israel. In order to make the purchase of these goods and the acquisition of these services easier, the Federal Republic of Germany will take measures and grant concessions in as far as determined in Articles 5, 6 and 8.

Article 3

a) The financial obligations undertaken in Article 1 of this agreement ... will be paid in annual payments as follows:

i) From the coming into force of this agreement until 31 March 1954 in a sum of DM 200 million for every budget year. The first budget year runs from the coming into force of this agreement until 31 March 1953; thereafter the budget year will run from 1 April of every year until 31 March of the following year.

ii) From 1 April 1954 onwards in nine annual payments of DM 310 million each, and a tenth annual payment of DM 260 million ...

iii) If the Government of the Federal Republic of Germany is of the opinion that it cannot fulfil the obligations of the above sub-paragraph (ii), then it will notify the Israeli Mission mentioned in Article 12 in writing, three months before the start of the next budget year about the reduction of the annual payments according to sub-paragraph ii), with the condition that under no circumstances must an annual payment be less than DM 250 million ...

Article 6

a) Goods and services to be acquired by the Israeli Mission will be itemised in goods lists.

b) In the drawing up of these goods lists, investment goods are to be given particular consideration.

c) Goods delivered according to the regulations of this agreement can be of non-German origin.

...

Completed in Luxemburg on the tenth day of September 1952 in two original copies in English, of which one copy each is destined for the Government of each contracting party.

For the Federal Republic of Germany   For the State of Israel
Signed Adenauer   Signed M. Sharett

Trans. from German version in: *Bundesgesetzblatt 1953 II*, 20.3.1953.

For the young state of Israel, which faced major economic problems at the time, the agreement meant an economic lifeline; for the Federal Republic it meant increased international prestige and some increased moral respectability, not least because there were further big payments on the horizon deriving from the London negotiations, and because the GDR refused any payments. At a time when the West

German reconstruction process was far from over, the compensation payments would cause criticism at home. Indeed, when the treaty was voted on in the Bundestag the following March, many government MPs abstained or even voted against the bill and it was passed only with the support of the opposition SPD. Ernst Majonica, the CDU's youngest MP, documented the events in his diary.

Doc 159 Majonica on the Bundestag vote on the compensation agreement

Wednesday 18.3.1953. Discussion with a school class from Hagen. Plenary session. Disgusting discussion about the Refugee Bill. Israel treaty accepted. A part of the parliamentary group voted against, a large part (especially from the CSU) abstained. Beforehand Dr Gerstenmaier [the Parliament President] had said that this was about Germany's honour!!! I am ashamed. This now is a Christian parliamentary group. Even if the agreement came about in a botched way. This was meant to be a grand gesture to alleviate the unspeakable crimes against the Jews. A part of the parliamentary group shares my outrage. Afterwards sat together for a long time with Theo Blank, Muckermann, Lemmer and some journalists. They too are outraged. This is not the way. Theo is a good man. Drunk a bit because of fury.

Trans. from: ACDP, 01-349-023/1 (Transkript).

Majonica's frustration was not without reason. While there may have been some MPs who did not like the idea of large sums of money being given to other countries when there was still considerable need at home, most of those who voted against it would have done so because they could or would not take the moral responsibility for the crimes that had been done in the name of Germany. Those attitudes would not change overnight. Individual survivors of the Holocaust who tried to receive life-insurance pay-outs for killed relatives or to gain access to their relatives' bank accounts, were often refused their claims on legal technicalities.

In 1957 a trial began in the provincial city of Ulm that would have a long-term impact on the process of West Germany coming to terms with the crimes committed by the Nazis. The former police chief of Memel and member of *Einsatzgruppe A* – one of the infamous killing squads which executed Jews behind the advancing Wehrmacht in the Soviet Union – together with nine other members of the *Einsatzgruppe*, were put on trial. The trial lasted more than a year. On 29 August 1958 all accused were sentenced to imprisonment for between 3 and 15 years. The judgement passed on one of the main culprits highlights some of the issues at the time.

Doc 160 Judgement of the Ulm Einsatzgruppen trial

In the name of the people:
Criminal matter against:
1) the businessman Bernd Fischer-Schweder, born 12.1.1904 in Berlin-Spandau, last residence Ulm/Danube,
...
sentenced are:
The accused Fischer-Schweder because of the crime committed of being a common accessory to murder in 526 cases is sentenced to 10 years imprisonment [*Zuchthaus*]; he will lose his civil rights for a period of seven years ...
B. Personal Particulars:
... after the war he lived under a forged identity – that of 'Bernd Fischer, born 13.2.1902 in Berlin' – and in his denazification questionnaire hid his former membership of the NSDAP or its affiliated groups. As a result, he managed to become classified as 'not affected' by the Bad Neustadt/Saale tribunal ... By hiding his former NSDAP membership he managed to become employed as director of the Ulm-Wilhelmsburg refugee camp. After his political past had partly become known to the district government North Württemberg, he terminated his contract with effect of 31.1.1955, but challenged his termination later on ... It was his application to be reinstated in the CID in the district of South Baden which provoked an investigation which then led to the start of criminal proceedings.

Reasons for the Sentence:
...
To the disadvantage of the accused, the following has to be considered: besides his great desire for recognition, he has also a very presumptuous manner which he displayed during the trial – at least in the beginning. Out of his desire for recognition he also got involved with the executions and used a police detachment [*Schutzpolizeikommando*] as a firing squad with no authorisation to do so. By doing so he implicated the accused Schmidt-Hammer and the members of the police detachment

into the terrible event and made them participate in the crime of cleansing [*Säuberungsverbrechen*].

As a SA Oberführer (Colonel) he held the highest rank of all those present during the executions for which he was under investigation; he made use of this fact – without justification since the accused Böhme had been in command – by giving orders and making critical remarks and – again out of his desire for recognition – even took command during the executions at Garsden and personally carried out follow-up shots. He has so far shown no remorse or regret ...

Trans. from: C.F. Rüter (ed.), *Justiz und NS Verbrechen. Sammlungen deutscher Strafurteile gegen nationalsozialistische Tötungsverbrechen 1945–1966*, vol. 15.

The trial at Ulm showed the German public for the first time what kind of crimes had been committed in the East, and would have caused some shock and upset. However, the language used in the judgement portrayed an individual who was desirous of recognition at all cost, a true, lying Nazi who had shown no remorse for his crimes; in other words a deranged monster who had nothing in common with the public at large. Thus the mass murder could once more be blamed on only a few individuals.

Nevertheless, the way the trial had come about and the way evidence had to be gathered made it clear that there were totally insufficient structures in place (or none at all) to systematically investigate war crimes. As a consequence, a central body was set up at Ludwigsburg near Stuttgart, tasked with recording and examining all reported war crimes and with trying to find the culprits and bring them to justice. In the wake of this development, the biggest trial in post-war German history, soon to be known as the Frankfurt Auschwitz trial, began on 20 December 1963. It would last until 20 August 1965. This time the German public was not only confronted with horrendous description given by survivors of life in the most notorious of all camps, but also with the fact that the defendants had integrated themselves well into the post-war German society. They had appeared as the 'nice man next door' and no longer as deranged brutes. Perhaps this helps to explain why large parts of the public were opposed to the trial, because other than showing the enormity of the mass killings committed in the name of the German people, it proved that the perpetrators were not beasts but 'ordinary men'.

A problem in both the *Einsatzgruppen* trial and the Auschwitz trial was the legal definition of murder in the German penal code, which explains the relatively lenient sentences. To achieve a full murder conviction the prosecutors had to prove that the accused killed their victims individually and that the killings were premeditated; otherwise they could only be sentenced for 'communal murder' (*gemeinschaftlichem Mord*) which carried no life sentence. Furthermore, there was a limitation by statute for murder and manslaughter of 20 years in the penal code, which would have prevented the prosecution after 8 May 1965 of any perpetrator. Not least under the impression of the Auschwitz trial, in November 1964 the Federal Government appealed to all relevant countries in Eastern Europe (with the exception of the GDR) to send them all available documents on war crimes so that trials could begin before the limitation by statute could take effect. It soon showed that a reasonable sifting of the material in the remaining time was not possible, and a public debate about the limitation by statute began. Led by the CDU MP Ernst Benda, later to become President of the Constitutional Court, a bill was proposed that would extend or even abolish the statute of limitation for murder. Only one month before the old statute would have taken effect and prevented further prosecutions, a compromise was reached which allowed prosecutions until 1969, 20 years after the foundation of the FRG. Ernst Benda's passionate plea in the Bundestag before the vote took place gives testimony of some of the underlying political motives at the time.

Doc 161 Benda on the end of statute of limitation

From various, very respectable sides we were requested to discuss this question dispassionately. I agree. I am of the opinion that on this issue a form of emotion – if it would obscure clear thought about what is necessary – would be harmful ...

Yesterday the petitioners decided to amend the original motion. The original draft ... intended to increase the statutory criminal prosecution for crimes punished by life imprisonment [*Zuchthausstrafe*] under Article 67 of the criminal code from 20 to 30 years. According to our current proposal, Article 67 should be amended such that there be no limitation to criminal prosecution of crimes threatened with life mprisonment (*Applause from CDU/CSU members and the SPD*) ...

The German Bundestag on many occasions, and in agreement of the

315

whole House, has expressed its disgust at the crimes of the National Socialists and its willingness for compensation and a rejection of any nationalism or neo-Nazism in our people in such an unambiguous way that I believe: this Parliament represents the German people – and it represents the whole of the German people – including those on the other side of the zone border as well – a people that has overcome the false doctrine of National Socialism. (*Applause from CDU/CSU*)
...

For the petitioners, above all kinds of legal consideration, stands simply the consideration that the people's sense of justice would be corrupted in an unbearable way if murder were to remain unpunished although it could be punished. I have here among many letters I've received, the letter of a man totally unknown to me, a social worker [*Sozialinspektor*] from Hamburg who works with juveniles who are in danger of becoming criminals. He writes of the young boys who committed acts of stupidity and now are in a youth prison – they don't deny what they have done, they say that they are quite rightly in a youth prison because they have done something stupid. However, they do ask him about the kind of justice that exists in a state in which someone goes to prison for a juvenile prank [*Jugendstreich*] while people who have committed murder walk free. (*Objections from the right and from CDU/ CSU members*) ...

I come to a final point, but to me it is a very important one. In connection with our topic, there is an increasing tendency to ask about the crimes of others. Ladies and gentlemen, I know and we all know that regarding the issue of expulsion, in connection with events of the final years of the war, crimes were committed not only by Germans but also against Germans. Who of us doesn't know that?! And we should address this here. I don't reject [*wehre mich nicht*] the understandable opinion of the expellees in this matter, which says: 'We want justice to be done here as well'. I am prepared to say this, too. But I reject a political calculation that says that where such a sentiment exists, votes could perhaps be won. (*Lively applause from the SPD and from CDU/CSU deputies*) ...

Ladies and gentlemen, I will conclude with an ambitious word from a colleague whose opinion on this matter is in total contrast to my own. He told me that for the sake of the nation's honour there has to be an end to the trials. Ladies and gentlemen, the nation's honour – this is for me one of the last reasons why I believe we have to extend or abolish the statutory limitations [for murder]. (*Applause from the SPD and the CDU/CSU*)
...

For me it is part of the national honour that the admittedly insufficient but honest attempt is made to do what is necessary so that we can say: we have done everything possible. – I know there are legal constraints within this difficult topic, that today we cannot do anything like the kind of things that perhaps could have been done in the past – but at least we tried. And finally there is a saying that I want to include here at the end of my speech, this saying, written on a memorial in Jerusalem for the six million murdered Jews, in a very impressive form in a very plain hall, is a quote which is not from our century, but from a Jewish mystic in the early eighteenth century – I'll say it in German – it is written there in Hebrew and English: 'Trying to forget extends the exile, and the secret of redemption is remembrance.' (*Lively continuing applause from SPD and from CDU/CSU*)

Trans. from: *Verhandlungen des Deutschen Bundestages, 4. Wahlperiode.*

Of course, Benda's speech only managed to postpone the problem for four years, but in 1969 a coalition government of CDU and SPD was in place and on 26 June 1969 the Bundestag abolished the statute of limitation for genocide and murder.

The *Einsatzgruppen* trial and even more the Auschwitz trial, as well as the debate about the statute of limitation, did raise the question of why the West Germans were so hesitant during the 1950s and 1960s – and often beyond – to confront the Nazi past. One explanation is given by the psychoanalyst couple Alexander and Margarethe Mitscherlich in their groundbreaking 1967 book *Die Unfähigkeit zu trauern – Grundlagen kollektiven Verhaltens* (The Inability to Mourn – The Basis of Collective Behaviour).

Doc 162 A. and M. Mitscherlich, *The Inability to Mourn*, 1967

2. It was all the Führer's fault

... The repulsion [*Abwehr*] of guilt, shame and mourning about the losses that the collective post-war Germany population performs is, although it is the same infantile self-protection, not the infantile experience of guilt, but real guilt on a grander scale. The application of infantile exoneration techniques on the consequences of failed massive conquests and programmes of extermination, which could not have begun without the enthusiastic action [*Einsatz*] of this collective and even less held out 'up to the thirteenth hour' without it, is scary. The attempts to master the past in this way appear grotesque to the distant onlooker ...

One of the means of denying guilt is the since then widely expressed opinion that the descent of a dictatorship is a natural phenomenon that takes shape independently of individuals and sweeps over them, so to speak. On closer inspection, this is an imprecise, and therefore only a half-true statement. It is, however, very difficult to depict the connection between individual patterns of behaviour, established reactions and the dictator's political success ... We very much agreed with a leadership that was able to once again combine typically German ideals with our self-esteem: there was a chance to display our self-worth in uniform. Clearly structured hierarchies of authority suddenly emerged before the eyes of national comrades [*Volksgenossen*], so disappointed by the political infighting. The precision of our obedience was duly tested and the almost boundless will to show ourselves worthy of the Führer's hopes was allowed to run riot. Assuming this Führer had been satisfied with minor annexations and been moderate in his Jewish policy up to that limit of infamy to which large groups in the other Christian states had been willing to follow with tacit approval, the end of the Thousand-Year Reich would most likely still not been foreseeable today ... This is the success of the reversal of conscience. The Führer personifies a new conscience. Only his failure, not the old conscience, helps the feelings of guilt to break through ... By aligning oneself with these victors, by recognising them as the new overlords, in particular as the creators of the new state form, the pre-fascist conscience was reinstated in its old function. There were no more reasons for massively overrated self-assessments and no more admiring spectators. Even if the economic progress, the export surplus, provided pleasant comfort, a dream had come to an end, a dream to belong to a master race, not bound to the limits of conscience if that conscience stood in the way of their 'ideals' ...

We now can summarise: The inability to mourn for the suffered loss of the Führer is the result of an intensive denial [*Abwehr*] of guilt, shame and fear; it succeeds through the retreat of previously strong libidinal occupation. The Nazi past is de-realised. Not only the death of Adolf Hitler as a real person causes mourning – but in particular his coming to an end [*Erlöschen*] as the representative of the collective I-ideal. He was an object one could lean on, to whom responsibility deferred, and an inner object. As such, he represented and invigorated anew the ideas of omnipotence we harbour from early childhood; his death and his debasement by the victors meant also the loss of a narcissistic object and thus an impoverishment and self-devaluation of the self ...

The mechanisms we are concerned with here are emergency reactions, processes that are very close to biological survival, perhaps even its psychological correlation. It is therefore useless to construct an accusation from these reactions immediately after the collapse [of Germany]. The one aspect that does become problematic is the fact that – because of the de-realisation of the Nazi period – even later on, there was no mourning [*Trauerarbeit*] for the fellow human beings that were killed in masses because of our actions …

Trans. from: Alexander and Margarete Mitscherlich, *Die Unfähigkeit zu trauern: Grundlagen kollektiven Verhaltens*, 1967 (Piper).

The Adenauer era: a summary

The often conjured claim of a German 'Zero Hour' in 1945 has to be rejected even more firmly than the claim that the Adenauer era was a period of complete restoration of the old system in regards to the political, economic and social elites. Although Germany was liberated from Nazism – a view on which the majority of Germans could agree only from the 1980s onward, after the older generation of contemporaries had died – it was simply impossible to build a new Germany without any connections to the past. That the reconstruction could proceed with such a speed has to be understood in the context of the Cold War, which turned the Federal Republic from a defeated enemy first into a potential and then into a factual ally of the Western Allies. While Adenauer's policy towards the West made this possible, it was the rapid economic recovery that ingrained itself in people's memories. The 'economic miracle' became the founding myth of the FRG. This myth suited the German people, who after the Nazi atrocities could claim to be decent and hard-working again, as well as the Western powers. They could point to the fact that their policies had transformed a previously expansionist, militarised country into a role model for non-aggression and good neighbourliness, admired for its economic success all over the world. It is quite ironic that the man hailed as the 'father of the economic miracle', Ludwig Erhard, was one of the most vehement opponents of the term. To him, the recovery was due to his economic policies, a claim that can be challenged in view of the negative impact some of Erhard's reforms had in the early years and of the structural shortcomings which came to light during the Korean crisis. Instead the origins of the economic recovery have to be seen in the booming world economy and the improved industrial assets which had survived the war.

The most amazing feats West German society achieved during the

1950s are far too often overlooked. In material terms this was, first, the construction of six million dwellings between 1949 and 1961 which, secondly, contributed to the successful integration of millions of refugees into West German society and thus prevented political radicalisation. In terms of mentality the big achievement was the creation of a stable democratic state and system which allowed the integration of former Nazis (both nominal and real Nazis) into the new republic. In sharp contrast to circumstances in the Weimar Republic, right-wing extremism never materialised as a political force in post-war Germany. The price for this may well have been that few Nazi war criminals and collaborators were ever prosecuted in any significant way by the German judiciary. To not actively prosecute those involved in Nazi crimes was clearly a moral shortcoming of the Adenauer government. Many critics at home and abroad were outraged by the fact that many civil servants, people from the business community or the judiciary who had been deeply involved with the regime could continue their careers in the post-war years more or less uninterrupted. It is therefore not surprising that Adenauer has been accused of facilitating the restoration of the old order. But since the continuity in personnel did not mean a continuity of the previous anti-democratic attitudes, this claim has to be qualified. In social life there was undoubtedly a very strong emphasis on old-fashioned family values and traditional gender roles which went even beyond some of the Nazi policies in this field. However, it has to be kept in mind that a similar trend appeared in most Western countries as well.

One of the biggest and most lasting successes the politician Adenauer achieved was undoubtedly the integration of West Germany into the Western camp and with it the eventual reconciliation with France. His overall conduct of policy can be called Machiavellian – in the negative as well as in the positive meaning of the word – and was criticised as authoritarian even at the time. The German historian Sontheimer has argued that this (still democratically legitimised) authoritarianism provided the strong hand many Germans seemed to have wanted. If one looks at Adenauer and 'his' era in this way and considers it within the overall long-term trend of twentieth-century German history, then one can interpret this era as the bridge between the pre-war German authoritarianism and 'proper' German democracy. Looked at it in this way, despite their shortcomings Adenauer and the era which is named after him have to be seen as an unparalleled success.

Selected reading

This reading list is far from complete. It is an attempt to list some of the most important books and articles available in English and entice readers to find out more about post-war German history. The list should therefore be understood as an introduction to further reading.

Overviews and biographies

Adenauer, Konrad, *Memoirs*, vol. 1, London 1966.

Alter, Peter, *The German Question and Europe: A History*, London 2000.

Bark, Dennis and Gress, David, *A History of West Germany*, 2 vols, Oxford 1989 (esp. vol. 1).

Berghahn, Volker, *Modern Germany: Society, Economy and Politics in the 20th Century*, 2nd edn, Cambridge 1987.

Edinger, Lewis J., *Kurt Schumacher: A Study in Personality and Political Behavior*, Stanford and London 1965.

Katzenstein, P.J., *Policy and Politics in West Germany: The Growth of a Semi-Sovereign State*, Philadelphia 1987.

Kettenacker, Lothar, *Germany since 1945*, Oxford 1997.

Mierzejewski, Alfred C., *Ludwig Erhard: A Biography*, Chapel Hill 2004.

Moeller, Robert G. (ed.), *West Germany under Construction: Politics, Society, and Culture in the Adenauer Era*, Ann Arbor 1997.

Schwarz, Hans-Peter, *Konrad Adenauer*, vols 1 and 2, Oxford 1995.

Williamson, David G., *Germany since 1815: A Nation Forged and Renewed*, Basingstoke 2005.

Allied occupation and the emerging Cold War, 1945–49

Clay, Lucius D., *Decision in Germany*, Westport, CT 1970.

Deighton, Anne, *The Impossible Peace: Britain, the Division of Germany and the Origins of the Cold War*, Oxford 1990.

Selected reading

Diefendorf, Jeffrey, Frohn, A. and Rupieper H.J. (eds), *American Policy and the Reconstruction of West Germany*, Washington, DC 1993.

Gimbel, John, *The American Occupation of Germany: Politics and the Military 1945–49*, Stanford 1968.

Loth, Wilfried, *The Division of the World 1941–55*, London 1988.

Marshall, Barbara, *The Origin of Post-War German Politics*, London 1988.

Merkl, Peter, *The Origins of the West German Republic*, New York 1963.

Turner, Ian (ed.), *Reconstruction in Post-War Germany: British Occupation Policy and the Western Zones*, Oxford 1989.

Willett, Ralph, *The Americanization of Germany 1945–49*, London 1989.

Economic policy, reconstruction and the 'economic miracle'

Berghahn, Volker, *The Americanisation of West German Industry 1945–73*, Leamington Spa 1986.

Grünbacher, Armin, *Reconstruction and Cold War in Germany: The Kreditanstalt für Wiederaufbau 1948–1961*, Aldershot 2004.

Hughes, Michael L., *Shouldering the Burden of Defeat: West Germany and the Reconstruction of Social Justice*, Chapel Hill 1999.

Maier, Charles, Bischof, Günther (eds), *The Marshall Plan and Germany: West German Development within the Framework of the European Recovery Program*, New York 1991.

Milward, Alan, *The Reconstruction of Western Europe, 1945–51*, London 1984.

Milward, Alan, *The European Rescue of the Nation State*, London 1992.

Nicholls, Anthony, *Freedom with Responsibility: The Social Market Economy in Germany 1918–1963*, Oxford 1994.

Van Hook, James C., *Rebuilding Germany: The Creation of the Social Market Economy 1945–1957*, Cambridge 2004.

Warner, Isabel, *Steel and Sovereignty: The De-concentration of the West German Steel Industry, 1949–1954*, Mainz 1996.

Domestic policy, Berlin and the GDR

Bunn, Ronald, *German Politics and the Spiegel Affair: A Case Study of the Bonn System*, Baton Rouge 1968.

Glees, Anthony, *Reinventing Germany: German Political Development since 1945*, Oxford 1996.

Grünbacher, Armin, 'Sustaining the island: Western aid to 1950s West Berlin', in: *Cold War History*, vol. 3, no. 3 (April 2003).

Nicholls, Anthony, *The Bonn Republic*, London 1997.

Selected reading

Padgett, Stephen and Burkett, Tony, *Political Parties and Elections in West Germany*, London 1986.

Schwartz, Thomas, *America's Germany: John McCloy and the Federal Republic of Germany*, Cambridge, MA, 1991.

Steininger, Rolf, *The German Question: The Stalin Note of 1952 and the Problem of Reunification*, New York 1990.

Wettig, Gerhard, 'Stalin and German Reunification', in: *Historical Journal* vol. 37, no. 2 (April 1994)

Foreign policy

Becker, Josef and Knipping, Franz (eds) *Power in Europe? Great Britain, France, Italy and Germany in the Post-War World 1945–50*, Berlin 1986.

Di Nolfo, Ennio (ed.), *Power in Europe? II. Great Britain, France, Germany and Italy and the Origins of the EEC 1952–57*, Berlin 1992.

Dockrill, Saki, *Britain's Policy for West German Rearmament 1950–1955*, Cambridge 1991.

Large, David Clay, *The Germans to the Front. West German rearmament in the Adenauer Era*, Chapel Hill 1996.

McGeehan, Robert, *The German Rearmament Question: American Diplomacy and European Defence after World War II*, Urbana, IL 1971.

Arts, culture, gender and consumption

Brockmann, Stephen, *German Literary Culture at the Zero Hour*, Columbia, SC 2004.

Burges, Gordon J.A., *The Life and Works of Wolfgang Borchert*, Rochester, NY 2003.

Carter, Erica, *How German is She? Post War West German Reconstruction and the Consuming Woman*, Ann Arbor 1997.

Höhn, Maria, *GIs and Fräuleins: The German American Encounter in 1950s West Germany*, Chapel Hill 2002.

Poiger, Uta, *Jazz, Rock and Rebels: Cold War Politics and American Culture in a Divided Germany*, Berkley 2000.

Pommerin, Reiner (ed.), *Culture in the Federal Republic of Germany*, Oxford, 1996.

Pommerin, Reiner, *The American Impact on Post-War Germany*, Providence, RI 1997.

Roseman, Mark, *Generations in Conflict: Youth Revolt and Generation Formation in Germany*, Cambridge 1995.

Selected reading

Sandford, John (ed.), *Encyclopedia of Contemporary German Culture*, London 1999.

Schissler, Hanna (ed.) *The Miracle Years: A Cultural History of West Germany, 1949–68*, Princeton 2001.

The Nazi past

Benton, Wilbourne, Grimm, Georg (eds), *Nuremberg: German Views on the War Trials* (no place) 1955.

Fulbrook, Mary, *German National Identity after the Holocaust*, Cambridge 1999.

Herf, Jeffrey, *Divided Memory: The Nazi Past in the Two Germanys*, Cambridge, MA 1997.

Moeller, Robert, *War Stories. The Search for a Usable Past in the Federal Republic of Germany*, Berkley 2001.

Monson, Robert A., 'The West German Statute of Limitations on Murder', *American Journal of Comparative Law*, vol. 30, no. 4 (Autumn 1982).

Niven, Bill (ed.), *Germans as Victims: Remembering the Past in Contemporary Germany*, Basingstoke 2006.

Wittmann, Rebeca, *Beyond Justice: The Auschwitz Trial*, London 2005.

Index

Page numbers in italics refer to mentions within sources

327

Index

Index